A History of Drinking

To my friend Tony Black
and in memory of the late Jim Robertson

A History of Drinking

The Scottish Pub since 1700

Anthony Cooke

EDINBURGH
University Press

© Anthony Cooke, 2015

Edinburgh University Press Ltd
The Tun – Holyrood Road
12 (2f) Jackson's Entry
Edinburgh EH8 8PJ
www.euppublishing.com

Typeset in 10.5/13pt Sabon by
Servis Filmsetting Ltd, Stockport, Cheshire
printed and bound in Great Britain by
CPI Group (UK) Ltd, Croydon CR0 4YY

A CIP record for this book is available from the British Library

ISBN 978 1 4744 0012 1 (hardback)
ISBN 978 1 4744 0762 5 (paperback)
ISBN 978 1 4744 0013 8 (webready PDF)
ISBN 978 1 4744 0736 6 (epub)

Contents

Tables

Figures

Abbreviations

CAMRA – Campaign for Real Ale
CC – Commissary Court
CS – Court of Session
DCA – Dundee City Archives, City Square, Dundee
GUA – Glasgow University Archives
ML – Mitchell Library, Glasgow
NLS – National Library of Scotland, Edinburgh
NMRS – National Monuments Record of Scotland, Edinburgh
NRS – National Records of Scotland, Edinburgh
NSA – New Statistical Account of Scotland
OSA – (Old) Statistical Account of Scotland
PKA – Perth and Kinross Archives, A. K. Bell Library, Perth
PP – Parliamentary Papers
RCAHMS – Royal Commission on the Ancient and Historical
    Monuments of Scotland
SBA – Scottish Brewing Archive, Glasgow University Archives
SC – Sheriff Court
SLTA – Scottish Licensed Trade Association

Acknowledgements

A NYONE WHO ENGAGES IN historical research owes a great debt to other people. I have made heavy use of libraries and archives across Scotland and would like to thank the dedicated and knowledgeable staff in these places. It is always a pleasure to work at the National Records of Scotland, the National Library of Scotland and the National Monuments Record of Scotland in Edinburgh, and the Mitchell Library in Glasgow. I have used the City Libraries in Aberdeen, Dundee, Edinburgh, Perth and Stirling, Glasgow University Archives and the City and County Archives in Dundee and Perth, and have appreciated their knowledgeable and helpful staff, particularly Steven Connolly of Perth and Kinross Archives, Ian Flett of Dundee City Archives and the staff of the Local History Collection in Dundee. I have also made heavy use of the University Libraries in Dundee and St Andrews.

I have received a good deal of support, information and help from members of the licensed trade in Scotland. Jonathan Stewart, of Dundee, encouraged the project from the start and introduced me to the Scottish Licensed Trade Association. I should like to thank members of the SLTA and others for agreeing to be interviewed for the book and for speaking so frankly about their lives and working experiences. They include: Marshall Bain of Queen Charlotte Rooms, Leith; Jim Clancy of the Lauriston Bar, Glasgow; Alistair Don of the Doublet Bar, Glasgow; Willie Mutch of the Windsor Bar, Dundee and the Central Bar, Arbroath; Jonathan Stewart of the Speedwell Bar, Dundee and the Royal Arch, Broughty Ferry; Paul Waterson of the Golden Lion Hotel, Stirling (Chief Executive, SLTA); Petra Wetzel of West, Glasgow; and Colin Wilkinson, Edinburgh (Secretary, SLTA). I should also like to thank customers and staff of the various pubs I have visited across Scotland, who have shown genuine interest in the project and been most helpful in answering my questions, particularly Lee McQueen of the Globe Inn, Dumfries, who opened up the private rooms in the building and was a mine of information about the place, and the landlord of Poosie Nansie's Inn in Mauchline, Ayrshire.

Ian Donnachie of the Open University was a pioneer in this field, publishing *A History of the Brewing Industry in Scotland* in 1979 and early articles on 'Drink and Society in Scotland' and 'World War One and the Drink Question'. Ian has encouraged the project from the start and has lent me some of his considerable collection of books on public houses and the history of drinking. Caroline McCracken-Flesher of the University of Wyoming worked on the Pae family papers in our house. Her subsequent book, *The Doctor Dissected* (Oxford, 2012) is a re-examination of the Burke and Hare story and a stimulating contribution to the cultural history of Scotland, which has informed this book. My friend and drinking companion, Tony Black, of Dundee University, has discussed the project at length with me and has suggested some of the approaches I have adopted. The late Jim Robertson of Dundee University introduced me to many fine pubs across Scotland, including those in his native Dumfries, and I regret he is no longer around to see the book published. Brian Dempsey and Richard Dunphy, both of Dundee University, have been most helpful in suggesting reading material for the section in Chapter 5 on 'Below the Radar – Gay Pubs in Scotland'. I should like to thank the two anonymous referees who recommended publication of the typescript by Edinburgh University Press.

Within Edinburgh University Press, my Editor, John Watson, has been a tower of strength, responding to my emails with sometimes alarming speed. I should also like to thank Ellie Bush, Assistant Commissioning Editor, James Dale and other staff at EUP (and my copy-editor, Neil Curtis). Thanks are also due to staff in Leisure and Culture, Dundee; Edinburgh Public Libraries; the Mitchell Library, Glasgow and the Royal Commission on the Ancient and Historical Manuscripts of Scotland who have helped me track down and copy illustrations. My son Alistair, daughter-in-law Louise, and my friend Stephen Hole have also supplied photographs. My wife Judith has travelled round with me to obscure places and pubs and has helped in photographing them and editing the photographs afterwards.

My family has been most supportive, as usual. I have spent quality time in Glasgow pubs with my sons Alistair and Michael and have enjoyed their hospitality and that of their wives Louise and Gill, as well as the company of my boisterous grandsons, Ralph and George. My wife Judith's family papers have proved invaluable, as her great grandfather, David Pae, founding editor of the *People's Friend*, was an evangelical Christian, self-improver and teetotaller, who wrote sensationalist novels in serial form about urban life in Victorian Scotland, such as

Lucy the Factory Girl, or the Secrets of the Tontine Close (1858) and *Mary Paterson, or the Fatal Error* (1864).

I should like to thank the group of friends that meets on Wednesday nights at various pubs in Dundee for providing argumentative and stimulating conversation over the years – Tony Black, Graeme Fraser, Neil Gray, Stephen Hole, Dave Johnston and Jack Searle. Thanks are also due to another group that meets on Friday mornings for coffee, lunch and concerts – Jim Angus, Tony Black, John Brush, John Cheyne, Les MacKay and Roy Partington. Other friends and relatives who have shown interest in the book and made useful suggestions or asked difficult questions include Ian Duncan of Glamis; Judith and Eric Grant of Tarradale House on the Black Isle; Russell and Susan Meek of Dundee; David and Ross Morrison of Monikie; Rosemary and Peter Moss of Muswell Hill, London; Finlay McKichan of Aberdeen and Doreen Pae of Christchurch, New Zealand. Finally, I have discussed the themes of the book with well-informed people in some unlikely locations, including the Garfagnana in northern Tuscany.

1

Introduction
A History of Drinking: The Scottish Pub since 1700

> If fewer instances of intemperance, impurity and prodigality appear in the country than in the town in proportion to the number in each, it is perhaps chiefly, because simplicity of manners is less liable to corruption in the former than the latter, from a multiplicity of low ale houses, these seminaries of impiety and dissipation (*Old Statistical Account*, Forfar, 1792)

THE SCOTS HAVE LONG had a problematic relationship with alcohol. The quotation above from the Reverend John Bruce, minister of Forfar, shows that, even before the rise of the temperance movement in the 1820s, ministers of the Church of Scotland were critical of the role played by ale houses, dram shops and tippling huts in the lives of their parishioners. The *(Old) Statistical Accounts*, published in the 1790s on a parish-by-parish basis, are full of criticisms by Presbyterian ministers of rising levels of crime, drunkenness, alcoholism and consequent impoverishment of families, as a result of the replacement of beer by whisky as the drink of choice for the masses. Their anxieties were strengthened because this was a period of rapid social and economic change, with large-scale population growth and population movement, growing urbanisation and industrialisation, accompanied by widening social divisions. It was also a period in which existing social and political orthodoxies were being challenged, as the examples of American independence and revolutionary France lent encouragement to republicans, secularists and others who questioned the existing social, religious and political order. Pubs and ale houses were closely involved in these changes, as public spaces, often below the radar of the authorities, where artisans, labourers, craftsmen, farmers, shopkeepers and others could meet to discuss matters including economics, work, religion and politics, as well as local gossip. For example, the Reverend John Scott of Perth, a substantial burgh with a population of 19,800 in 1792, condemned 'the lamentable effects which happen to some persons, from their being too ready to leave their loom, or their workshop, to meet in companies, or in clubs, or in the ale house.'[1]

The centrality of the pub as a meeting place and as the location of choice, together with the church, for the celebration of major life rituals such as births, christenings, marriages and funerals has been played down or ignored by many Scottish historians. In *The Making of the English Working Class*, E. P. Thompson referred to 'the enormous condescension of posterity' when faced with 'the poor stockinger, the Luddite cropper, the "obsolete" hand weaver, the "utopian" artisan, and even the deluded follower of Joanna Southcott'.[2] A similar condescension may explain why many historians have tended to ignore the importance of the ale house, the inn, the tavern, the dram shop, the tippling house, the shebeen and the licensed grocer in the lives of the mass of the Scottish population.[3] An exception must be made for the folklorists, ethnologists and anthropologists, associated with the School of Scottish Studies in Edinburgh, who have consistently adopted a different and more inclusive approach.[4]

Academic historians, however, have recently begun to focus on studying the everyday in Scottish life, as exemplified by the four-volume series *A History of Everyday Life in Scotland*, published by Edinburgh University Press, which is based on the premise that Scots 'made sense of their everyday lives . . . through ritual and belief, by their interactions with others and by self-reflection'.[5] This has been the approach in this book, where I argue that the public house and its numerous variations were, in the words of the Scottish writer Ian Rankin, 'a place of rules and rituals'.[6] Everyday life has more commonly been studied in other European countries and in North America than it has in Scotland. The Annaliste historians in France, for example, have concentrated on material culture and on 'microhistories' of an individual, village or particular incident to understand the *mentalité* of the particular society they were drawn from.[7]

HISTORIOGRAPHY

There is no Scottish equivalent of Peter Clark's *The English Alehouse. A Social History, 1200–1830* (1983), or of Brian Harrison's detailed examinations of nineteenth-century English pubs and the temperance movement.[8] Many Scottish historians have exercised a kind of self-censorship and remained largely silent about the functions and impact of public houses, taverns, ale houses, shebeens, dram shops and licensed grocers. For example, a book on Victorian Dundee[9] where, in the 1840s, there was one pub for every twenty-four families,[10] has only two ref-erences to drunkenness in the index, one to whisky but none at all to ale, dram shops, shebeens, licensed grocers or public houses. Similarly, Martin Mitchell's otherwise excellent book on *The Irish in the West of Scotland, 1797–1848*[11] contains no references at all to public houses, dram shops, shebeens or even whisky in the index, despite the fact that keeping a pub or a shebeen was a well-recognised route out of poverty for first- or second-generation Irish immigrants, or that pubs, together with churches, functioned as places where recently arrived migrants went to look for work and lodgings and to seek the company of their fellow countrymen. Finally, a recent photographic record of Scotland includes many photographs on popular and obscurer sports in its section on 'Leisure and Recreation' but not a single one of a pub interior or exterior, despite the centrality of the Scottish pub in the development and support of sports such as horse racing, football, boxing, rugby or curling. It does include, however, some illustrations of breweries and distilleries.[12]

Certainly, the Scottish temperance movement made no such mistake in underestimating the importance of drink and the public house in Scottish society. In his *Artificial and Compulsory Drinking Usages of the United Kingdom*, published in 1839, the prominent Scottish temperance reformer, John Dunlop, displayed a detailed and well-researched knowl-edge of the numerous functions of public houses in early nineteenth-century Scotland. They included the use of drink in life rituals such as marriage, baptism and funerals, the payment of wages in public houses, and their function as a location for other workplace rituals, such as those associated with apprenticeship rites of passage, the 'treating' of foremen by workers, and 'pay-off' celebrations.[13]

There are, however, honourable exceptions among historians to this relative neglect of the history of the public house. Interestingly, given the male-dominated ethos of many Scottish pubs, some of the earliest work on the topic was written by women. Marie Stuart's book on *Old Edinburgh Taverns* (1952) may be somewhat antiquarian in tone but is nonetheless generally well informed, particularly on the many literary associations of Edinburgh pubs.[14] Some thirty years later, two female museum curators published well-researched booklets on drink-related topics – one on the temperance movement in Scotland, the other on Dundee drinking places. Elspeth King's excellent study of the Scottish temperance movement dates from 1979 while Veronica Hartwich's *Ale an' A'Thing*, a pioneering study of the licensed trade in Dundee, was published a year later.[15]

Among male historians, the pioneer in this, as in many other subjects, was Laurence Saunders in his remarkable *Scottish Democracy, 1815–1840*, published in 1950, which included a section on the temperance movement and drinking practices in Scotland.[16] In 1979, Ian Donnachie produced a major study of the Scottish brewing industry and, in the same year, an article on 'Drink and Society'.[17] Another pioneer was T. C. Smout whose *Century of the Scottish People, 1830–1950*, published in 1986, contained a masterly chapter on 'Drink, Temperance and Recreation'.[18] Two years later, Chris Whatley, in a chapter on the 'Experience of Work', explored the ways in which 'alcohol continued to be an integral part of the working lives of Scots well into the nineteenth century', a theme continued in a later work, *Scottish Society, 1707–1830*.[19] Bill Knox discussed similar themes in his *Workplace Nation, 1800 to the Present*.[20]

The recent *The Scottish Town in the Age of the Enlightenment* claims that, in the eighteenth century, 'Inns and taverns remained the principal sites of sociability among lower-class males, weavers and other artisans', where 'artisan clubs and societies met' and were 'very much part of the fabric of normal urban living for working males'.[21]

APPROACHES

The ideas for this book emerged partly as a result of research for two previous publications. While researching *From Popular Enlightenment to Lifelong Learning*, I discovered that Scottish pubs had been the meeting place for numerous self-improvement groups for working men until the rise of the temperance movement in the 1820s and 1830s.[22] Similarly, research for *The Rise and Fall of the Scottish Cotton Industry, 1778–1914*, revealed that urban pubs were the meeting places of choice for trades unions, strike committees and radical political groups until the 1850s and, as such, fell under the scrutiny and suspicion of the authorities and their network of informers.[23] In this way, they functioned as a more 'democratic' and less exclusive version of what Jurgen Habermas has characterised as 'the bourgeois public sphere' where the literate urban bourgeois public took on a political role in the discussion and evaluation of contemporary affairs and state policy. Habermas used as an example the clubs, salons and coffee houses of eighteenth-century London which were supported by a growing and increasingly free press to form a 'critical forum', largely independent from the court. In both England and France, coffee houses and salons emerged as 'centres of criticism – literary at first, then also political'. There were, however, striking national differences. In England and Scotland coffee houses and taverns were largely male institutions whereas the French salon was 'essentially shaped by women', and upper-class women at that.[24] In Scotland, urban and rural pubs and taverns functioned at a humbler social level with a wider and less elitist clientele. Their regular clientele in the eighteenth century ranged from the labouring poor to skilled artisans, as well as lawyers, doctors, merchants, farmers and shopkeepers, and they became centres for many kinds of social and political debate – from anti-Unionists and militant Jacobites to the Friends of the People and United Scotsmen.

Anthropology can also offer insights into drinking spaces, drinking practices and behaviour across different cultures. Mary Douglas, in the late 1980s, argued that 'in most cultures, alcohol is a normal adjunct to celebration' and that 'drinking is essentially a social act, performed in a recognised social context'.[25] She claimed that alcohol has three major constructive functions. Firstly, it has a social role in everyday life, often linked to celebration of life events. It can also be linked with informal social networks of friends, work colleagues, and family and community groups. Secondly, it can be seen as a form of ritual. The American anthropologist, Joseph Gusfield, contrasted the roles of coffee and alcohol. He argued that 'coffee cues the shift from playtime to work-time and alcohol cues the transition from work to playtime'.[26] Of course, this is very much a late twentieth-century North American viewpoint, and the divisions between work and leisure were not so clear-cut in eighteenth-century Scotland, though they became more marked in the next century. Finally, Douglas argued that drinking, selling drink and the production of alcohol are significant economic activities and 'entrenches the alternative economy'. The example used in the book is the alcohol (vodka-based) economy in eighteenth-century Poland[27] but it could apply equally well to Scotland where the 'black economy' flourished in the form of unlicensed ale houses and dram shops, illegal whisky stills and, in urban areas, the underground shebeen and the brothel.

In this book, I want to examine what went on in Scottish pubs, their social history and economic importance. I want to explore the differences between Scottish and English pubs, to set the pub in its European context, and discuss the ways in which pubs functioned as public spaces and how this was modified by the temperance movement. I also hope to make a contribution to the history of popular culture in Scotland. Public houses and the drinks they sold were important revenue raisers for local and national government and were licensed, regulated and documented accordingly. They were frequently viewed with suspicion by the authorities as places where the lower classes could gather to discuss unorthodox opinions, largely removed from the scrutiny of their social betters. In this way, pubs could provide space for a subversive or alternative culture and act as a counter to the somewhat stifling hegemony of Presbyterianism, thrift, self-help, temperance and respectability that came to dominate nineteenth-century Scotland from the 1820s onwards. The French philosopher Michel Foucault defined 'the Other Victorians' as those who lived 'below the radar' of convention and challenged, rejected or ignored dominant cultural norms such as thrift, sobriety, self-denial, sexual repression and 'respectable' behaviour. In Foucault's scenario, 'the brothel and the mental institution would be those places of tolerance'.[28] To this duo we can add the pub and its various manifestations, together with the prison.

Because this is a wide-ranging survey over three centuries, the book will not attempt to cover all aspects of the subject but rather those that illustrate continuity and change in the functions of Scottish drinking places, and how they were influenced by changes in society and by practices and habits from other cultures and other countries. Most previous books about Scottish pubs have taken the form of city or regional guides and concentrated on the buildings, their interiors, location, the types of drink served and so on. Because of that, this book will not focus primarily on buildings, interiors and locations, except where they illustrate significant changes taking place in response to social, cultural, economic or political pressures. It will also not concentrate on the Scottish brewing industry or whisky distilling because these have been treated at length elsewhere.

There is a rich literature on Scottish pubs, from the eighteenth-century poets, who spent a good deal of their time drinking and socialising in Edinburgh taverns, to contemporary Scottish novelists, such as Irvine Welsh and Ian Rankin, who write knowledgeably and perceptively about late twentieth-century and present-day pubs. There have been numerous books about pub architecture, buildings and interiors, fixtures and fittings, and the types of drink that were, and are, sold in them. These books, often written from the standpoint of a member of the Campaign for Real Ale (CAMRA) can be at worst a rather tedious list of public houses and the types of beer sold in them. At their best, however, they can represent a real labour of love, with a lifetime of detailed knowledge and research going into them. There has also been a thriving literature on local and regional pubs, particularly those in urban centres, such as Aberdeen, Dundee, Edinburgh, Glasgow and Stirling.[29] In the last decade, the architectural historian David Walker has written on 'Inns, hotels and related buildings' in Scotland, CAMRA has published a book on Scotland's heritage pubs and their interiors, and Historic Scotland has produced a book on historic pubs.[30] The recent *Scottish Life and Society, A Compendium of Scottish Ethnology*, Vol. 5, *The Food of the Scots* also contains valuable insights and information into the Scottish drink trade and Scottish drinking practices.[31] There are numerous books on Scotch whisky making and drinking practices, from Bremner and Barnard's nineteenth-century classics[32] to more recent publications.[33] Brewing has been well served by Barnard's four-volume nineteenth-century study and a modern history by Ian Donnachie.[34] Gourvish and Wilson's book on the *British Brewing Industry* also contains valuable material on Scotland, as does G. B. Wilson's much earlier book *Alcohol and the Nation, 1800–1935*.[35]

DEFINITIONS

There was, and is, a complicated hierarchy of drinking establishments in Scotland with a nomenclature to match – hotels, taverns, inns, public houses, ale houses, brewseats, change houses, dram shops, tippling houses, shebeens and licensed grocers. As early as 1424, the Scots Parliament passed an act for inns to be set up for travellers and their horses, providing food and accommodation for men and animals. Twelve years later, a curfew of 9.00 p.m. was imposed on the consumption of wine, ale or beer in inns by travellers, which suggests that such inns actually existed.[36] In 1480, William Moyses was authorised or licensed to sell red Gascony wine in his Aberdeen tavern at 6d a pint.[37] This shows that state and local regulation of drinking places in Scotland predated the Reformation. In the sixteenth and seventeenth centuries, a range of alcoholic drinks, including ale, wine and spirits, was available for sale, often in private houses, where brewing was frequently carried out by women.

The brewing of beer was heavily gendered, with women dominating the trade in some periods, men in others. One of the earliest references to ale and brewing in Scottish literature is to a female alewife or brewer – *The Ballad of Kind Kittock* – which Maurice Lindsay attributes to William Dunbar (1460?–1520?).[38] Kind Kittock is a Fife alewife or 'Guddame' who dies and goes to heaven but quits in disgust because the ale there is sour, poor-quality stuff. She returns to earth to drink her own good ale, 'for to get hir ane fresche drink, the aill of hevin wes sour . . . than to the ailhouse agane she ran the pycharis to pour, and for to brew and baik'.[39] In the same period, a list of 152 brewsters (brewers), drawn up in 1509 in Aberdeen, revealed that all of them were female, though most were married to free burgesses, who had the right to brew and to bake bread.[40]

Dundee was a stronghold of the reformed faith, being 'honoured with the appellation of a second Geneva'.[41] In January 1558/9 the Bailies and Council of Dundee imposed a curfew after 10.00 p.m., when 'no person (was) to be found walking in the streets or gaits of the burgh, or drinking in any ale house or wine tavern efter ten hours of the nicht, under the pain of forty shillings for the first fault and for the second fault to be banished'. A few years later, they also prohibited 'dancing, drinking, playing or sic vain exercise' after 9.00 p.m., 'under the pain of the breking of the minstrel's instruments'. In October 1564, Dundee Town Council appointed some of their members personally to inspect the quality of ale in the burgh and found that 'the ale brewen be David Spankie's wife was sufficient'.[42]

After the Reformation, the kirk session often took it upon itself to monitor ale houses rather than rely on the secular authorities. For example, in Balmerino in Fife, the kirk session decreed in 1637 that any brewer selling ale on the Sabbath 'after or befoir noon, betwixt the ringing of (the) hindmost bell and the dissolving of the preaching' should pay a fine of 40 shillings 'and make their repentance before the pulpit'.[43] Similarly, in Govan in Lanarkshire, the kirk session summoned Elisabeth Craig, wife of John Watson, in 1651, to question whether 'shoe did detain ane drunken man in her hous and sell aile to him'. She denied this but admitted that 'ane cam (whom shoe knew not) and desired a pynt of aile and so went his way'.[44] This kind of semi-domestic, proto-industrial arrangement involving alewives lasted a long time in Scotland.

English travellers famously gave horrified descriptions of the failings of Scottish lodgings and drinking places, and Scots sometimes agreed with them. In 1598, Fynes Morrison claimed that, in Edinburgh, English-type hostelries were unknown but 'in all places some houses are known, where passengers may have meat and lodging: but they have no bushes or signs hung out, and for the horses, they are commonly set up in stables or in some out-lane, not in the same house where the passenger lyes'.[45] The continuing absence of English-style pub signs in Scotland is confirmed a hundred and fifty years later by a traveller to Aberdeen in 1748 who complained 'when we entered New Aberdeen, it was with difficulty we found a Public House, which they call Change Houses, there being but one Sign in the whole Place to notify such a House, tho' there are many of them in it'.[46] As late as 1774, the English Captain Topham wrote of Edinburgh 'there is no inn that is better than an alehouse, nor any accommodation that is decent, cleanly or fit to receive a gentleman'. In the Pleasance, they were shown to 'the best inn in the metropolis' which was full of 'about twenty Scotch drovers . . . regaling themselves with whisky and potatoes'.[47]

TAVERNS

The dividing line between inns and taverns in Scotland could sometimes be rather blurred. Taverns sold wine, ale, beer, brandy and other spirits and were run by burgesses or guild brethren, or by their wives or widows. The personal name, Taverner, dates back to at least 1361 and, by the mid sixteenth century, women taverners were not uncommon.[48] By the late eighteenth century, a prosperous burgh like Dumfries, a port and an expanding market town of 7,000 in 1792, contained '2 principal inns, a coffee house and several taverns',[49] including the Globe Tavern (now Inn), patronised by Robert Burns. In Perth, another growing market town, textile centre and port of 19,871 in 1796, the Reverend James

Figure 1.1 Interior, The Globe Inn, Dumfries. One of Robert Burns's favourite howffs. © Anthony and Judith Cooke.

Scott described how 'there are great taverns and a coffee room'.[50] As living standards rose in the early nineteenth century, Scottish inns and taverns responded by adding extensions in the latest style, influenced by developments in London, the market leader of fashion. The George IV Tavern in Perth announced in 1830 that it had expanded to include 'a large and commodious TAP ROOM' on the London system, selling Barclay and Perkins's London porter and 'the best Scotch Ales'. Its clientele consisted of 'farmers and others doing business at the weekly markets' and it carried 'newspapers with the latest London prices for corn'.[51] In this way, Scottish inns and taverns were inextricably linked with the development of the market and cash economy across Britain.

INNS

Generally, inns provided some type of accommodation, as well as food and alcoholic drink – beer, wine and spirits – together with stabling for the travellers' horses, though in earlier periods this was often in a separate place. Taverns, particularly those in Edinburgh, often provided basic food as well as drink but were less likely to provide accommodation. Robert Chambers, a Scot, claimed that in the mid eighteenth century the traveller had a poor choice of accommodation in Edinburgh. The only two inns were 'the White Horse, in a close in the Canongate, or the White Hart, a house which now appears like a carrier's inn, in the Grassmarket'.[52] The English traveller, Sir William Burrell, described Edinburgh inns in 1758 as 'indifferent, generally adapted only for the service of beasts, men being obliged to lodge at private houses, the New Inn excepted, which accommodates both extremely well'.[53] Twenty years later, Edinburgh inns were still being described (by a Scot) as 'mean buildings; their apartments dirty and dismal; and if the waiters happen to be out of the way, a stranger will perhaps be shocked by the novelty of being shown into a room by a dirty sun-burnt wench, without shoes or stockings'.[54] Generally, lodgings and stables were kept separate in Edinburgh.

Before the 1750s, 'Glasgow possessed no inns for the accommodation of travellers, except small public houses to which stabling was attached, and the signboard of these petty hostelries generally bore the well-known intimation to wayfarers of "Entertainment for men and horses here".'[55] The first purpose-built inn in Glasgow was the Saracen Head, built in 1755, with stones recycled from the nearby medieval archbishop's palace, on land donated by the Glasgow magistrates to Robert Tennant, a founder member of the famous brewing dynasty. The inn boasted '36 fine rooms, now fit to receive lodgers', with separate bed chambers, and beds 'all very good, clean and free from bugs'. There was a good stable and 'a shade within the said yard for coaches, chaises or other wheeled carriages'. The inn had a large meeting room which could accommodate a hundred people.[56]

The mid eighteenth century saw the construction of a number of new purpose-built inns across Scotland in response to rising living standards and a consequent increase in commercial travel. In 1754, a year before the opening of the Saracen Head in Glasgow, Aberdeen saw the building of the New Inn, a fashionable place with a sizeable meeting room, where the Aberdeen Lodge of Freemasons held their meetings.[57] In Paisley, some thirty years later, the New Inn was erected by the Earl of Abercorn in 1781.[58] The Great Inn at Inveraray, Argyllshire in the West Highlands, was designed for the Duke of Argyll by the architect John Adam in 1750 and built between 1751 and 1756. Similarly, the Earl of Breadalbane built the inn at Kenmore in Perthshire in 1760, and the Menzies family built the Weem Inn, on the other side of the Wade Bridge from Aberfeldy, Perthshire, a few years later.[59]

The Highlands was notorious for the poor quality of its inns. Samuel Johnson and James Boswell stayed in one at Glenelg, Inverness-shire on their tour of the Highlands in 1773. It sounds like the stuff of travellers' nightmares. Boswell complained 'there was no provender for our horses . . . a maid shewed us upstairs into a room damp and dirty, with bare walls, a variety of bad smells, a coarse black greasy fir table . . . and out of a wretched bed started a fellow from his sleep, like Edgar in King Lear'.[60] By the early nineteenth century, these primitive inns were beginning to disappear, as the number of travellers increased and their expectations rose. Elisabeth Grant of Rothiemurchus, writing in 1812, remembered 'we never see such inns now, no carpets on the floors, no cushions on chairs, no curtains on windows'.[61]

ALE HOUSES

The most widespread type of drinking establishment found in eighteenth-century Scotland was the ale house which was present in most, but not all, Scottish parishes, from Orkney in the north where, in Birsay and Harray in 1793, there were 'no settled inns in this parish, but plenty of ale houses, as there are no gaugers' (that is, excise men),[62] to Wigtonshire in the south where, in the rural parish of Kirkmalden, there had been a marked reduction in the number of ale houses because of 'the new regulation of licensing the houses of persons of a fair character'.[63] There were numerous ale houses in ports and industrial settlements where there were large numbers of young people of both sexes with relatively high disposable incomes, often living away from their families. By the late eighteenth century, the term 'ale house' was becoming a misnomer, as the drink of choice in ale houses increasingly became whisky. The port and market town of Dunbar in East Lothian, for example, with a modest population of 3,700 in 1792, had 'no fewer than 46 licensed ale houses (one per 80 of population) where low priced spirits are retailed, and where the execrable custom of dram drinking is practiced [sic] . . . the reproach of man and the disgrace of woman'.[64]

Another East Lothian burgh, the coal mining centre of Tranent, with a population of 2,732 in 1792, had thirty licensed ale houses. It also boasted the largest distillery in Scotland at St Clements Wells, and some 3,000 to 4,000 gallons of whisky were 'annually retailed in the parish'.[65] In the west of Scotland, another expanding industrial parish with a large number of 'ale, or rather whisky houses' was Govan in Lanarkshire with a population of 8,318 in 1792. In this thriving textile manufacturing centre, there were no fewer than twenty-two ale houses and, according to the local excise office, when the cotton industry was in a flourishing state, an astonishing '1,500 gallons of whisky were consumed in the village of Govan, in a single quarter of the year',[66] that is, 6,000 gallons a year. The Reverend Thomas Marton, minister of the thriving textile town of Langholm, in Dumfriesshire, characterised beer as 'the natural and wholesome beverage of the country' and condemned 'unlicensed tipling houses and dram shops' as 'haunts of vice where the young of both sexes are tempted from the straight and narrow'.[67] In both Dunbar and Langholm in the 1790s, women were seen by well-informed observers as regular users of ale houses.

DRAM SHOPS AND TIPLING HOUSES

Dram shops and tipling houses were found all over the country, as far north as Shetland where, in Aithsting and Sansting parish in 1792, there were no inns but 'perhaps 30 or 40 gin and tea shops, to the great ruin of the morals, health and circumstances of the inhabitants'.[68] They were generally unlicensed and sold cheap, often poor-quality whisky and spirits to the poor. Their numbers expanded in the second half of the eighteenth century as the increased duties on malt pushed up the price of beer, and spirits became cheaper with a reduction of the duties on whisky retailers in 1794 to 20 shillings in the Highlands and 40 shillings in the Lowlands.[69] This increase was not uniform throughout the country, however, as, in some areas, the magistrates and Justices of the Peace were active in closing down dram shops.

In the whisky distilling areas of Scotland, the correspondents to the *Statistical Accounts* were often more relaxed and less censorious about whisky drinking, as distilling provided a profitable outlet for barley grown by local farmers and the whisky was generally of better quality. In Duffus parish, in Morayshire, 'A Friend to Statistical Inquiries' reported in 1793 that the suppression of smuggling 'has banished foreign liquors and introduced very generally the use of whisky of our own distillery, which is both wholesome and cheaper'.[70] Similarly, Alexander Simpson, the schoolmaster in the Aberdeenshire parish of King Edward, welcomed the local distilleries as 'in every point (of) view . . . a reciprocal advantage to the farmers, and the country at large'.[71] In Killearnan parish on the Black Isle, the Reverend David Dunoon explained the large number of distilleries (seven) in the parish as being owing to the fact that they were the only way for the farmer to convert 'victual' into 'cash for the payment of rent and servants'.[72] Again, the expansion of distilling here was closely linked to an increasing population, rising living standards, and the growth of a cash economy. Fifty years later, the Reverend Archibald McTavish was very positive about the impact of the six distilleries in Kildalton parish, Islay in 1844, 'the introduction of legal distilleries has been of great advantage in this respect (the reduction of drunkenness) and also is giving employment to many of the population'.[73]

SHEBEENS

The shebeen was a largely urban phenomenon, an unlicensed drinking establishment found mainly in places with large migrant Irish populations, such as Dundee or Glasgow, specialising in whisky, often distilled illegally on or near the premises, with a clientele composed mainly of recent Irish immigrants or their descendants. Their functions sometimes overlapped with those of brothels. In December 1870, the *North British Daily Mail* published a sensationalist exposé of 'The Dark Side of Glasgow' which calculated that, in the old city centre, there were some two hundred brothels and 150 shebeens. The article divided Glasgow shebeens into 'respectable', where only the licensing laws were being broken, disreputable shebeens, which provided a base for criminal activity, such as prostitution, robbery or receiving stolen goods, and the 'wee shebeens' on the stairhead of a tenement, where 'a drunken old hag in a greasy mutch' dispensed a toxic mixture of whisky and methylated spirits to be drunk on the spot.[74]

Many shebeens were run and managed by women, though not neces-
sarily owned by them. In May 1861, four Dundee women were jailed
for six weeks for having a shebeen in their Peter Street home, while
fines were imposed on three couples and a single woman for keeping
shebeens in various parts of central Dundee. Two years later, Isabella
Forbes or Smith was given six months gaol or a £30 fine for keeping a
brothel and a shebeen in Couttie's Wynd, Dundee.[75] The use of the term
'shebeen' was not confined to a few urban strongholds, however, but
was understood in other parts of Scotland as a kind of shorthand for an
illegal and unlicensed drinking place. When the Perthshire Justices met
to discuss the Public Houses Hours of Closing Act (Scotland), 1887, a
Colonel Stirling remarked that closing pubs at 10.00 p.m. 'might lead
to more or less shebeening throughout the county'.[76]

Shebeens had a remarkably long life, prolonged by the local veto
campaign of the early twentieth century which attempted to ban alcohol
sales from designated geographical areas of Scotland, based on local
veto polls. In February 1928, for example, the Glasgow and District
Licensed Trade Defence Association reported that levels of drunkenness were increasing in the Southern Police Division of Glasgow, in the
Hutchesontown, Gorbals and Kingston wards of the city. They believed
this was mostly caused by 'drinking of methylated spirits and also from
Clubs and Shebeens'.[77] Five years later, the President of the Scottish
Licensed Trade Defence Association claimed that Wick in Caithness,
which had voted itself 'dry' by local veto, now consumed more liquor
than when the town was 'wet' and that Wick 'was practically a huge
shebeen in 1933'.[78] Shebeen is an Irish Gaelic word meaning an illicit
liquor shop, and the name and the institution itself have been transposed
to the black townships of present-day South Africa where young, often
single, male workers come to find drink, food, lodgings, women and
work.

LICENSED GROCERS

A distinctive feature of the Scottish (and Irish) drinking scene was the
licensed grocer's shop which sold beer, wine and spirits, often on credit.
Licensed grocers were found in most parts of Scotland, though largely
confined to the towns. In 1886, there was a total of 4,515 licensed
grocers in Scotland, of which 451 (10 per cent) were in Edinburgh,
261 in Glasgow, 249 in Aberdeen and 221 in Dundee.[79] Middle-class
observers became particularly agitated when working-class women were
buying and drinking alcohol, especially spirits, in grocers' shops. The

minister of Stevenston in Ayrshire complained in 1837 that the sale of spirits in grocers' shops had had 'a most pernicious influence, especially on the female part of the community, who, when there is no danger of detection, are tempted to add a dram to the other commodities they purchase'.[80] Some fifty years later, licensed grocers in Dundee were accused of entering liquor in their pass books under the headings of 'goods', 'soap', 'snuff', 'tobacco', 'sugar', 'tea' and other articles required in a family, when they were selling liquor to women, so that the male in the household was often unaware that his wife or 'bidey in' (partner) was buying alcohol on a regular basis. The writer added 'That there is a good deal of forenoon and afternoon drinking amongst women is notorious.' In 1889, there were 453 houses in Dundee licensed for the sale of liquor, including eight hotels, 228 public houses and beer houses, and 217 licensed grocers.[81]

HOTELS

A late arrival at the top of the hierarchy was the hotel, a concept imported from France. William Creech claimed that in 1763 in Edinburgh, 'there was no such thing as a Hotel: the word indeed was not known or was only intelligible to persons acquainted with the French'. Twenty years later, there were 'many public Hotels' in Edinburgh where visitors could stay 'not only comfortably, but elegantly'.[82] The arrival of the hotel on the Scottish scene was another sign of the growth of the market economy, linked to increasing wealth and rising living standards. In a thriving commercial nation, travel was becoming more necessary and was required to be speedy, frequent and reliable.

In 1763, there were two stage coaches from Edinburgh to Leith which ran once an hour and took a full hour to get there. Thirty years later, there were five or six stagecoaches on the same route which ran every half hour and took fifteen minutes. Similarly, in 1763 a stagecoach from Edinburgh to London ran once a month and took twelve to fifteen days. Thirty years later, there were fifteen coaches a week to London, arriving there in about four days. Hotel proprietors instigated, as well as benefited from, these innovations. A hotel owner called Dunn 'who opened the magnificent hotels in the New Town' was the first to offer a coach service to Dalkeith, 6 miles outside Edinburgh.[83] This hotel was praised by Arnot in 1779, though he criticised its cost: 'the charge very extravagant, viz. for a dining room, parlour (or rather closet) and three bed chambers, five guineas a week'.[84] The young French aristocrat, Alexandre de la Rochefoucald, stayed at Dunn's Hotel in St Andrews

Square in 1786 and was much impressed by it, explaining 'At Dunns we had a superb salon, with gilded mirrors and every magnificence.' He added 'It is the custom here, as in London, to stay in these houses, as the inns are very bad and dear.'[85]

Two years earlier, another French visitor was less impressed by Dunn's Hotel which he described as 'a magnificent inn, decorated with columns; but the inside of which, though very clean, did not correspond with the external grandeur of the edifice'. They were overcharged at the hotel, 'at more than double the rate which we had paid at the best and dearest inns on the road'. The hotel bill 'was more than an ell long' and they left 'without saying a word, but we return no more to Dun's hotel, to lodge under columns less heavy than the rapacious hand of the landlord'.[86]

Similar developments were taking place in Glasgow, where the word 'hotel' was never used for an inn or a tavern until the Tontine Hotel was opened in 1782.[87] The Tontine Society in Glasgow raised £5,350 in 1781 by issuing 107 shares of £50 each. The money was used to buy Allan Dreghorn's handsome town hall and convert it into the Tontine coffee room and hotel. The socially undesirable were kept out, as subscribers paid £1.12s a year for the use of the reading room, and accommodation was available upstairs.[88] In Greenock, Renfrewshire, an expanding port, cotton-manufacturing and sugar-refining centre, the Tontine Inn was built in 1801 at a cost of £10,000. The subscription for it, at £25 a share, was oversubscribed in two days.[89]

SOURCES

The sources for a study of public houses in Scotland are often compromised by belonging to one opposing camp or the other – the drink trade or the teetotal movement. Much of the material for the study of the nineteenth- and early twentieth-century public house has to be viewed through the distorting lens of the teetotal movement, and the opposing, drink-trade-related sources are often similarly biased. Many working-class memoirs by popular journalists, radicals, trade unionists, and Liberal and Labour political activists were written from a teetotal standpoint, as more obviously, were those by church leaders or missionaries. Out of 127 teetotal leaders in nineteenth-century Britain whose political allegiance is known, no less than 119 were Liberals.[90] Disproportionate numbers of early twentieth-century Independent Labour Party (ILP), Labour and socialist activists had a temperance background, often based on their own hard life experience of the devastating effects of alcohol abuse on tight household budgets and family life. Out of a sample of seventy-six Scottish Labour leaders active between 1918 and 1939, forty-eight (63 per cent) were known abstainers, only three (4 per cent) were known non-abstainers and the remaining twenty-five (33 per cent) were classified as 'not known'.[91]

With the spread of the temperance movement from the 1820s, an increasing amount of literature in Scotland was written from a temperance standpoint. Female working-class poets, such as Janet Hamilton and Ellen Johnston, both wrote poems on temperance themes: for example, Janet Hamilton's 'The Drunkard's Wife, the Victim of Drink or Burnin' Drink'.[92] William McGonagall, the Edinburgh-born, Dundee-based, weaver poet, advised his readers, 'to abstain from all kinds of intoxicating liquor, because seldom any good emanates from it' and wrote poems such as 'The Demon Drink' and 'The Destroying Angel', an apocalyptic poem which described the street-by-street destruction of Dundee pubs.[93] There was nothing remotely equivalent in Scotland to the novels of Charles Dickens, with their knowledgeable and sympathetic portrayals of English pubs, in works such as the *Pickwick Papers*, *Martin Chuzzlewit* or *Barnaby Rudge*.[94] The prolific nineteenth-century Scottish novelist and newspaper editor, David Pae, for example, whose work was published in serial form in popular newspapers, such as the *People's Journal*, wrote from a moralistic, temperance standpoint, and condemned alcohol abuse, in novels such as *Mary Paterson; or the Fatal Error*, which ascribed the downfall of one of Burke and Hare's female victims largely to her immoral lifestyle and use of strong drink.[95]

Similarly, the publications of the licensed trade in Scotland, such as *The Victualling Trades Review*, which was produced monthly in Glasgow from 1889 to 1908, or *The National Guardian*, published weekly from 1889 to 1975, often defined themselves in opposition to the temperance movement and its attempts to restrict or even ban their trade altogether. For example, under the headline 'Teetotal Delusions', the *Review* complained in 1891 about the licensed trade's lack of organisation at the recent municipal elections in Glasgow, compared to the much better organised teetotal lobby, which meant the trade had lost supporters in the council and the licensing courts.[96] Similarly, Dundee, Lochee and Broughty Ferry Licensed Grocers' Association noted with dismay in 1911 that Parliament was likely to support the Scottish Temperance Bill and that Lloyd George had recently increased the duty on spirits by 3/9d per gallon and had also increased licence duties.[97]

The non-conformist Lloyd George was a favourite target of the licensed trade and, in the middle of World War I, the *National Guardian* criticised the 'great Welsh Crusader' who had described alcoholic drink 'as a worse enemy than Germany and Austria'.[98] This fear of the power and influence of the temperance movement persisted into the second half of the twentieth century. The Sederunt Books of the Trustees of Mrs Lilias Smith, wine and spirit merchant of Greenock, who had kept the James Watt Bar in East Hamilton Street, Greenock, record payments in September 1952 of two guineas each to the Greenock and District Licensed Trade Defence Association and to the Greenock Anti-Prohibition Party.[99]

To analyse the wealth created by the licensed trade and its associated trades of brewing and distilling, I have used wills and probate inventories, particularly from the late nineteenth and early twentieth centuries. These have to be treated with some degree of caution but they can give invaluable details of public houses owned, their stock and fittings and the types of drink they sold. They can also give details of share holdings in breweries, distilleries, railway shares, overseas stocks, and so on, and, sometimes, of substantial holdings of whisky in bond in distilleries in Islay, in Campbeltown or on Speyside. Wills can also provide clues as to religious affiliation and the types of local and national charities supported by the deceased, as well as property owned, such as houses, urban tenement property let, and farms or country estates.

Another source used in the book is oral evidence based on interviews with licensees across Scotland in places such as Angus, Dundee, Edinburgh, Glasgow and Stirling. Here, the Scottish Licensed Trade Association was very helpful in identifying suitable interview candidates, and Jonathan Stewart of Dundee, who has shown interest in the project from the start, was particularly supportive. I interviewed a number of licensees, concentrating on how they got into the trade, what training they had received, what changes they had seen in the trade during their working lives and how they saw the future.

THE ORGANISATION OF THE BOOK

The book is divided chronologically. Chapter 1 examines the period from 1700 to 1790 which saw a shift in alcohol consumption from beer to whisky as the drink of choice for the masses. Though the economic benefits of Union were slow to appear at first, the century saw population growth, movement of population, particularly to the west of Scotland, growing urbanisation and industrialisation. All these changes, and the increase in travel across Scotland, including the Highlands, were reflected in an increase in the number and variety of public houses, inns, taverns and hotels. The Malt Tax Riots of 1725 confirm that beer was the favoured choice of drink for the masses in the Scottish Lowlands in the early part of the century. The period saw a challenge to the monopoly privileges of the burghs in areas such as brewing and the production of malt, as population expanded. Pubs fulfilled an important role in the social, economic and cultural life of the country by providing space for commercial and business transactions, as well as life, community and work rituals, and the numerous clubs, associations and societies that flourished in eighteenth-century Scotland, and played a crucial role in the development of civil society.

Chapter 2 looks at the period from 1790 to 1830 which saw rapid social, economic and political change across Scotland. By the 1790s, Presbyterian ministers in parishes all over Scotland were united in condemning the replacement of beer, which they usually saw as a wholesome drink for the labourer, with cheap whisky, which was considered to be a threat to health, sobriety, industry, and family living standards, not to mention morality. In this chapter, I argue that changes in the consumption of alcohol in this period were largely a symptom of rising living standards and changing tastes. Not only did the consumption of whisky and stronger ale by the lower classes increase but more wine and rum were drunk in middle-class households, hotels, inns and taverns. At the same time, there was an increasing degree of social segregation as landowners, wealthy farmers and urban merchants withdrew from the ale house and entertained more in their homes, increasingly moderated by female codes of politeness and sociability.[100]

Chapter 3 examines the period from 1830 to 1914 which saw increasing urbanisation and concentration of population in the Western Lowlands of Scotland. There was considerable population movement from rural areas of the Lowlands, from Ireland and the Scottish Highlands to the cities and industrial towns. By the end of the century, Scotland was one of the most urbanised countries in Europe. The temperance movement, which was solidly rooted in Scotland, had increasing influence from the 1820s onwards. One of its leading campaigners across Britain was John Dunlop (1789–1868), a Greenock-born lawyer and philanthropist, supported by the Glasgow printer and publisher, William Collins. After the 1832 Reform Act, the Liberal Party, generally favourable to temperance, emerged as the dominant force in Scottish politics, including municipal politics, for most of the century. This meant that licensing courts in cities such as Aberdeen, Dundee, Edinburgh and Glasgow supported restrictions in matters such as opening times, Sunday opening, limiting the number of licences issued in certain areas and so on. Despite this, public houses thrived, particularly in the growing cities which attracted large numbers of young single people, often removed from much adult supervision, except in the workplace. By the end of the century, rising living standards among the working and lower middle classes led to the growth of the 'People's Palaces', opulent urban pubs, which vied with one another with lavish fittings and a wide choice of drinks, including wine, beer and own-blend spirits.

Chapter 4 looks at the two world wars and the interwar period from 1914 to 1945. The Temperance (Scotland) Act of 1913 was the culmination of nearly a century of campaigning but its implementation was delayed by the outbreak of World War I. World War I saw a rise in the political influence of the temperance lobby, with prominent supporters, such as Lloyd George and Phillip Snowden, holding government office. There were also successful attempts to nationalise the licensed trade in certain parts of the country, both north and south of the border, to safeguard the munitions industry. From the 1920s, the Local Veto campaign made it possible to prohibit the public consumption of alcohol altogether in parts of the country that voted for it. Relatively few parts of Scotland chose this option, however, and the campaign declined in importance. During World War II, the licensed trade, like many other parts of the economy, came under increasing state regulation and control, though its importance and consequent lobbying power were strengthened by its major contribution to the war effort through the large amount of tax revenue it contributed to the Exchequer.

Chapter 5 looks at the period from the end of World War II to the present. The second half of the twentieth century saw major social and economic changes, including rising living standards, better health care through the new National Health Service, better levels of state education, high levels of employment and an increasing number of women entering the workforce. This was reflected in changes in the licensed trade, with a greater emphasis on comfort in pub layout and increased spending on pub interiors in an attempt to appeal to newly affluent families and to female customers. The Clayson Report of the early 1970s proposed a liberalisation in Scottish opening hours, and many of its proposals were implemented by the Licensing (Scotland) Act of 1976. Greater challenges came towards the end of the century when a combination of rising taxes on alcohol and supermarket price-cutting led to a situation where the total alcohol spend was split 70 per cent supermarkets and 30 per cent in licensed premises whereas, earlier in the century, the position had been the reverse. Pubs had become expensive places to buy a drink, and other factors were at work, such as the increasing emphasis on the effects of alcohol consumption and smoking on people's health and safety. As early as 1967 there had been Britain-wide legislation to limit alcohol levels for drivers and, in the summer of 2007, a ban on smoking in pubs was implemented in Scotland, the first place in the United Kingdom to do so. This was followed by a major downturn in the domestic and international economies in 2008. As a result of all these changes, considerable numbers of Scottish pubs began to close in the last decade of the twentieth century and the early years of the twenty-first, and there was growing concern for the future of the traditional Scottish pub.

NOTES

1. Sir J. Sinclair (ed.), *The (Old) Statistical Account of Scotland (OSA)*, Vol. XI, *South and East Perthshire, Kinross-shire* (Bradford, 1976), p. 503.
2. E. P. Thompson, *The Making of the English Working Class* (London, 1968), p. 13.
3. Elspeth King makes similar comments on the neglect of popular culture by Scottish historians. See E. King, 'Popular Culture in Glasgow', in R. A. Cage (ed.), *The Working Class in Glasgow, 1750–1914* (London, 1987), p. 142.
4. See M. Bennett, *Scottish Customs from the Cradle to the Grave* (Edinburgh, 1992), A. Fenton, *Scottish Country Life* (Edinburgh, 1976) and A. Fenton (ed.), *Scottish Life and Society. A Compendium of Scottish Ethnology*, Vol. 5, *The Food of the Scots* (Edinburgh, 2007).
5. C. A. Whatley and E. Foyster, 'Series Editors Foreword', in Foyster and Whatley (eds), *A History of Everyday Life in Scotland, 1600 to 1800*, Vol. 2 (Edinburgh, 2010), p. xi.
6. I. Rankin, *Resurrection Men* (London, 2001), pp. 241–2.
7. See the remarkable E. Le Roy Ladurie, *Montaillou: Cathars and Catholics in a French Village, 1294–1324* (London, 1980).
8. P. Clark, *The English Ale House. A Social History, 1200–1830* (London, 1983). See also Clark, *British Clubs and Societies, 1580–1800. The Origins of an Associational World* (Oxford, 2000) and Clark (ed.), *European Towns and Cities, 400–2000* (Oxford, 2009). For Brian Harrison, see his 'Pubs', in H. J. Dyos and M. Wolff (eds), *The Victorian City. Images and Realities*, Vol. I (London, 1973), pp. 161–90, and B. Harrison, *Drink and the Victorians, The Temperance Question in England, 1815–1872* (Keele, 1994) 2nd edition. See also S. Earnshaw, *The Pub in Literature* (Manchester, 2000), which largely focuses on England.
9. L. Miskell, C. A. Whatley and B. Harris (eds), *Victorian Dundee. Image and Realities* (East Linton, 2000).

10. W. H. Fraser, 'Developments in Leisure', in W. H. Fraser and R. J. Morris (eds), *People and Society in Scotland*, Vol. II, *1830–1914* (Edinburgh, 1995), p. 241.

11. M. J. Mitchell, *The Irish in the West of Scotland, 1797–1848* (Edinburgh, 1998).

12. M. Mackinnon and R. Oram, *The Scots. A Photohistory* (London, 2011).

13. J. Dunlop, *Artificial and Compulsory Drinking Usages of the United Kingdom* (London, 7th edition, 1844).

14. M. W. Stuart, *Old Edinburgh Taverns* (London, 1952).

15. E. King, *Scotland Sober and Free. The Temperance Movement, 1829–1979* (Glasgow, 1979) and V. Hartwich, *Ale an' A'Thing, Aspects of the Grocery and Licensed Trades in Dundee, 1800–1950* (Dundee, 1980).

16. L. Saunders, *Scottish Democracy, 1815–1840. The Social and Intellectual Background* (Edinburgh, 1950), pp 230–7.

17. I. Donnachie, *A History of the Brewing Industry in Scotland* (Edinburgh, 1979); Donnachie, 'Drink and Society, 1750–1850: Some Aspects of the Scottish Experience,' *Scottish Journal of Labour History*, Vol. 13 (1979), pp. 5–22; and Donnachie, 'World War One and the Drink Question: State Control of the Drink Trade', *Scottish Journal of Labour History*, Vol. 17 (1982), pp. 19–26.

18. T. C. Smout, *A Century of the Scottish People, 1830–1950* (London, 1986), pp. 133–58.

19. C. A. Whatley, 'The Experience of Work', in T. M. Devine and R. Mitchison (eds), *People and Society in Scotland*, Vol. I, *1760–1830* (Edinburgh, 1988), p. 235; and Whatley, *Scottish Society, 1707–1830* (Manchester, 2000).

20. W. W. Knox, *Workplace Nation. Work, Culture and Society in Scotland, 1800 to the Present* (Edinburgh, 1999).

21. B. Harris and C. McKean, *The Scottish Town in the Age of the Enlightenment, 1740–1820* (Edinburgh, 2014), pp. 401–2.

22. A. J. Cooke, *From Popular Enlightenment to Lifelong Learning. A History of Adult Education in Scotland, 1707–2005* (Leicester, 2006).

23. A. J. Cooke, *The Rise and Fall of the Scottish Cotton Industry, 1778–1914* (Manchester, 2010).

24. J Habermas, *The Structural Transformation of the Public Sphere. An Inquiry into a Category of Bourgeois Society* (Cambridge, MA, 1992), pp. 27 and 32–3; and W. Outhwaite, *Habermas. A Critical Introduction* (Cambridge, 2009), 2nd edition.

25. M. Douglas (ed.), *Constructive Drinking: Perspectives on Drink from Anthropology* (Cambridge, 1987), p. 4.

26. Douglas (ed.), *Constructive Drinking*, p. 8.

27. H. Levine, 'Alcohol monopoly to protect the non-commercial sector of eighteenth-century Poland' in Douglas (ed.), *Constructive Drinking*, pp. 250–69.

28. M. Foucault, *The History of Sexuality*, Vol. I (New York, 1976). Quoted in P. Rabinow (ed.), *The Foucault Reader* (London, 1984), p. 293.
29. A. Hopkins, *The Aberdeen Pub Companion. Guide to the City's Licensed Premises Past and Present* (Aberdeen, 1975); J. Alexander, *Dundee Pubs Past and Present* (Dundee, 1992); T. Bruce-Gardyne and J. Skinner, *Rebus's Favourite. The Deuchars Guide to Edinburgh Pubs* (London, 2007); R. Kenna, *The Glasgow Pub Companion* (Glasgow, 2001); J. Gorevan, *Glasgow Pubs and Publicans* (Stroud, 2002); and E. Burns, *Ale in Stirling. A Celebration* (Stirling, 2004).
30. D Walker, 'Inns, hotels and related buildings', in G. Stell, J. Shaw and S. Storrier (eds), *Scottish Life and Society*, Vol. 3, *Scotland's Buildings* (East Linton, 2003), pp. 127–89; M Slaughter (ed.), *Scotland's True Heritage Pubs: Pub Interiors of Special Historic Interest* (St Albans, 2007); Y. Hillyard, *Raising the Bar: An Introduction to Scotland's Historic Pubs* (Edinburgh, 2012). See also the earlier and excellent R. Kenna and A. Mooney, *People's Palaces: Victorian and Edwardian Pubs of Scotland* (Edinburgh, 1983).
31. Fenton, *The Food of the Scots*.
32. D. Bremner, *The Industries of Scotland. Their Rise, Progress and Present Condition* (1868) (Newton Abbot, reprinted 1969), pp. 444–54; and A. Barnard, *The Whisky Distilleries of the United Kingdom* (1887) (Newton Abbot, reprinted 1969).
33. M. S. Moss and J. R. Hume, *The Making of Scotch Whisky* (Edinburgh, 1981); G. D. Hay and G. P. Stell, *Monuments of Industry. An Illustrated Historical Record* (Edinburgh, 1986), pp. 31–63. See also D. Daiches, *Scotch Whisky: its past and present* (London, 1969).
34. A. Barnard, *Breweries of the United Kingdom* (1889–91), 4 volumes; Donnachie, *History of the Brewing Industry in Scotland* (1979).
35. T. R. Gourvish and R. G. Wilson, *The British Brewing Industry, 1830–1980* (Cambridge, 1994); G. B. Wilson, *Alcohol and the Nation, 1800–1935* (London, 1940).
36. Wilson, *Alcohol and the Nation*, p. 116.
37. Hopkins, *Aberdeen Pub Companion*, pp. 2–3.
38. M. Lindsay (ed.), *A Book of Scottish Verse* (London, 4th edition, 2001), pp. 67–9.
39. T. and W. MacQueen (eds), *A Choice of Scottish Verse, 1470–1570* (London, 1972), pp. 134–5.
40. Fenton, *The Food of the Scots*, p. 82.
41. C. McKean, 'What Kind of Renaissance Town was Dundee?', in C. McKean, B. Harris and C. A. Whatley (eds), *Dundee. Renaissance to Enlightenment* (Dundee, 2009), p. 11.
42. A. Maxwell, *The History of Old Dundee* (Dundee, 1884), pp. 78, 80, and 99.

43. J. Campbell, *Balmerino and its Abbey. A Parish History* (Edinburgh, 1899), p. 362.
44. T. C. F. Brotchie, *The History of Govan* (Govan, 1905), pp. 58–9.
45. Stuart, *Old Edinburgh Taverns*, p. 9; and P. Hume Brown (ed.), *Early Travellers in Scotland* (reprinted Edinburgh, 1973), p. 89.
46. Hopkins, *Aberdeen Pub Companion*, p. 3.
47. E. Topham, *Letters from Edinburgh in 1774 and 1775* (Edinburgh, 2003), p. 8.
48. Fenton, *The Food of the Scots*, p. 90.
49. *OSA*, Vol. IV, *Dumfriesshire* (Bradford, 1978), p. 121.
50. *OSA*, Vol. XI, *South and East Perthshire and Kinross*, p. 502.
51. *Perthshire Courier*, 27 May 1830.
52. R. Chambers, *Traditions of Edinburgh* (Edinburgh, 1825) (1856 edition), pp. 8 and 153.
53. J. G. Dunbar (ed.), *Sir William Burrell's Northern Tour, 1758* (East Linton, 1997), p. 78.
54. H. Arnot, *The History of Edinburgh* (Edinburgh, 1779), p. 352.
55. R. Reid (Senex), *Glasgow Past and Present*, Vol. II (Glasgow, 1884), p. 305.
56. *Glasgow Journal*, 10 November 1755 and Senex, *Glasgow Past and Present*, Vol. II, p. 306.
57. Hopkins, *Aberdeen Pub Companion*, pp. 80–1.
58. Harris and McKean, *The Scottish Town in the Age of the Enlightenment, 1740–1820*, pp. 189–90.
59. Walker, 'Inns, hotels and related buildings', pp. 133 and 135.
60. J. Boswell, *The Journal of a Tour to the Hebrides* (London, 1984), p. 239.
61. E. Grant, *Memoirs of a Highland Lady*, Vol. II (Edinburgh, 1988), p. 208.
62. *OSA*, Vol. XIX, *Orkney and Shetland* (Bradford, 1978), p. 18.
63. *OSA*, Vol. V, *Stewartry of Kirkcudbright and Wigtonshire* (Bradford, 1983), p. 433.
64. *OSA*, Vol. II, *Lothian* (Bradford, 1975), p. 470.
65. *OSA*, Vol. II, *Lothian*, pp. 623 and 633.
66. *OSA*, Vol. VII, *Lanarkshire and Renfrewshire* (Bradford, 1973), p. 370.
67. *OSA*, Vol. IV, *Dumfriesshire* (Bradford, 1978), pp. 366–8.
68. *OSA*, Vol. XIX, *Orkney and Shetland*, p. 382.
69. D. M'Laren, *The Rise and Progress of Whisky Drinking in Scotland and the Working of the Public Houses (Scotland) Act* (Glasgow, 1858), p. 22.
70. *OSA*, Vol. XVI, *Banffshire, Moray and Nairnshire* (Bradford, 1982), p. 501.
71. *OSA*, Vol. XV, *North and East Aberdeenshire* (Bradford, 1982), p. 260.
72. *OSA*, Vol. XVII, *Inverness-shire, Ross and Cromarty* (Bradford, 1981), pp. 427–8.

73. *New Statistical Account of Scotland (NSA), Vol. 7, Argyll* (Edinburgh, 1845), p. 667

74. 'The Dark Side of Glasgow', *North British Daily Mail*, 27 December 1870. See also King, 'Popular Culture in Glasgow', p. 161.

75. M. Archibald, *A Sink of Atrocity. Crime in 19th Century Dundee* (Edinburgh, 2012), pp. 220–1.

76. *Perthshire Courier*, 27 December 1887.

77. Glasgow University Archives, Scottish Brewing Archive, GDL, 1/6/1, Glasgow and District Licensed Trade Defence Association, Directors' Minutes, 15 February 1928.

78. M Simmons, *The Scottish Licensed Trade Association, A Centenary History, 1880–1980* (Edinburgh, 1981), p. 54.

79. Donnachie, *Brewing Industry in Scotland*, p. 211 (Table 74, A and B).

80. *NSA*, Vol. 5, *Ayrshire and Bute* (Edinburgh, 1845), p. 473.

81. D. Barrie, *The City of Dundee Illustrated* (Dundee, 1890), pp. 228 and 234.

82. *OSA*, Vol. II, *Lothian*, p. 42.

83. *OSA*, Vol. II, *Lothian*, pp. 25–6.

84. Arnot, *History of Edinburgh*, p. 353.

85. N. Scarfe (ed.), *To the Highlands in 1786. The Inquisitive Journey of a Young French Aristocrat* (Woodbridge, 2001), p. 107.

86. Baron Faujas de St Fond, *A Journey Through England and Scotland to the Hebrides in 1784* (Glasgow, 1907), Vol. 1, pp. 170 and 195–6.

87. Senex, *Glasgow Past and Present*, Vol. II, p. 302.

88. D. Walker, 'Inns, hotels and related building types', in G. Stell, J. Shaw and S. Stonier (eds), *Scottish Life and Society. A Compendium of Scottish Ethnology*, Vol. 3, *Scotland's Buildings* (East Linton, 2003), p. 142.

89. G. Crawford and G. Robertson, *A General Description of the Shire of Renfrew* (Paisley, 1818), p. 421.

90. Harrison, *Drink and the Victorians*, p. 153.

91. W. W. Knox (ed.), *Scottish Labour Leaders, 1918–1938: A Biographical Dictionary* (Edinburgh, 1984), pp. 23 and 113–21.

92. J Hamilton, *Poems, Essays and Sketches* (Glasgow, 1880), pp. 343–64; and E. Johnston, *Autobiography: Poems and Songs of Ellen Johnston, the 'Factory Girl'* (Glasgow, 1867).

93. See Cooke, *From Popular Enlightenment to Lifelong Learning*, particularly Chapter 3, 'Self Improvement', pp. 70–112; and W. McGonagall, *Poetic Gems, More Poetic Gems and Last Poetic Gems* (Dundee, 1969), pp. 11–12, 17 and 35–8.

94. See C. Tomalin, *Charles Dickens. A Life* (London, 2012); and S. Earnshaw, *The Pub in Literature* (Manchester, 2000), pp. 188–207.

95. D. Pae, *Mary Paterson; or the Fatal Error* (Dundee, 1865). See also W. Donaldson, *Popular Literature in Victorian Scotland* (Aberdeen, 1986), pp. 77–100; and C. McCracken-Flesher, *The Doctor Dissected:*

A Cultural Autopsy of the Burke and Hare Murders (Oxford, 2012), pp. 70–88.

96. *Victualling Trades Review*, 12 December 1891.

97. Dundee Public Library, Lamb Collection, 217 (93), Dundee, Lochee and Broughty Ferry Licensed Grocers' Association, 33rd Annual Report (1911).

98. *The National Guardian and Licensed Trade Journal*, 8 January 1916.

99. Mitchell Library, Glasgow (ML), TD 509/13/8, Sederunt Books of Trustees of Mrs Lilias Smith, wine and spirit merchant of Greenock (died 1898), Vol. VIII, 1945–1955.

100. See M. Berg, *Luxury and Pleasure in Eighteenth-Century Britain* (Oxford, 2007), pp. 232–5.

2

'Bousing at the Nappy':
Scottish Pubs and Changing Drinking
Patterns, 1700–90

While we sit bousing at the nappy*,
And getting fou and unco' happy

Inspiring bold John Barleycorn!
What dangers thou canst make us scorn!
Wi' tipenny+ we fear nae evil:
Wi' usquabae we'll face the devil!

(Robert Burns, *Tam O'Shanter*, 1790)

* 'nappy' = strong ale
+ 'tipenny' = small or weak ale

INTRODUCTION

T HE EIGHTEENTH CENTURY IN Scotland was a time of rapid social, cultural and economic change, with a growing and increasingly mobile population, rising levels of urbanisation and widening social divisions. Population rose from just over a million in the late 1690s to 1.25 million in 1755 and to 1.61 million by the time of the first official census in 1801. The population of the Western Lowlands grew faster than the rest of the country. In 1755, the population of the Western Lowlands was 14.3 per cent of the total Scottish population; by 1801, this had risen to 20.6 per cent.[1]

Between the sixteenth and the late eighteenth centuries, Scotland had one of the most rapid growth rates of urban population in Europe.[2] The proportion of the total Scottish population living in towns rose from 5.3 per cent in 1700 to 9.2 per cent in 1750, to 17.3 per cent in 1800. The 1800 figure was comparable with such heavily urbanised countries as England and the Low Countries.[3] Throughout most of the eighteenth century, however, Scotland was still a largely rural economy, heavily dependent on agriculture. It has been estimated that, in 1750, only about one Scot in eight was a townsman or townswoman.[4]

The eighteenth century in Scotland has been described as a period which 'saw the everyday experience of ordinary Scots transformed from one of basic struggle for survival – marked by famines in the 1690s, when as many as many as a fifth of the population died in some northern areas – to unprecedented plenty in food and clothing by the end of the century'.[5] These rising living standards went hand in hand with increasing alcohol consumption and an increase in the number of pubs, ale houses and other drinking places.

SCOTLAND ON THE EVE OF UNION

Daniel Defoe, an astute observer, who had worked as an English spy around the time of the Act of Union, noted that, at the beginning of the eighteenth century, Scottish trade and commerce were growing and diversifying. For example, the east coast ports of Aberdeen, Dundee and Leith all had important Baltic trading links and, in Glasgow, 'a very fine city', the merchants 'send near fifty sail of ships every year to Virginia, New England and other English colonies in America and every year are increasing'. Defoe praised the urban architecture of Glasgow 'the four principal streets are the fairest for breadth and the finest built that I have ever seen in one city together'. Dundee was 'exceedingly populous, full of stately houses and large handsome streets . . . with a large market place in the middle', while Aberdeen also had 'a great market place, which indeed, is very beautiful and spacious'. As for the capital city, Defoe described it as 'a large, populous, noble, rich and even still, a royal city' with 'the most spacious, the longest and best inhabited street in Europe'. He also remarked on the emergence of the market and cash economy in Scotland, characterising the Aberdonians as 'universal merchants to the world'. Dundee, where the merchants 'appear like gentlemen, as well as men of business', sold linen to England and corn to England and Holland. The West Bow, in Edinburgh, was 'a visible face of trade', full of wholesale traders dealing in iron, pitch, tar, oil, hemp, flax, linseed, and storing them in warehouses in Leith. As well as the Atlantic trade, Glasgow also produced striped muslins which were sent to England and to the British plantations.[6]

As part of this changing urban scene in the late seventeenth and early eighteenth centuries, there were large numbers of small, semi-domestic breweries throughout Scotland, many of them selling ale and beer on the premises. In 1693, the city of Aberdeen boasted 144 brewers, many of them burgesses with other trades, or female domestic brewers, while in the heart of the rich farming area of Morayshire, some eighty licensed brewers were operating in Elgin alone at the end of the seventeenth century.[7] In Fife, 522 brewers signed a Memorial in 1698 protesting about the imposition of excise duties on ale and beer. The Memorial shows the importance of the brewing industry to the public finances and the sensitivity of the authorities to increases in the prices of ale and beer, with its implications for public disorder. The brewers were to be fined £10 Scots for selling ale on which excise had not been paid and the price of beer was to be regulated by the Scots Parliament, with another penalty of £10 Scots for exceeding the prices laid down.[8] In Perth there were fifty-seven brewers in 1718, of whom only eight were female.[9] Edinburgh, the brewing centre of Scotland, had 266 people licensed to sell ale in 1730, of whom twenty-eight (just over 10 per cent) were female.[10]

During the eighteenth century, with the industrialisation of brewing and the increase in the number of commercial breweries, the number of small domestic brew houses selling their products on the premises declined, while the number of vintners and innkeepers catering for the increase in travellers grew. In Cupar, situated in the rich arable farming area of north-east Fife, there was a decline in the number of maltmen and brewers, from seventy-eight in 1700 to twenty-four in 1790, accompanied by an increase in the number of vintners and innkeepers from eleven in 1700 to thirty-four in 1790.[11]

The regulation of ale houses, pubs and taverns by the state, by local authorities and by the Church predates the Reformation in Scotland. After the Reformation, there was particular concern by local authorities and kirk sessions about Sabbath violations by licensed and unlicensed premises. This regulation was aimed primarily at the lower classes, however, and it could backfire spectacularly on those who tried to regulate the drinking behaviour of their social betters. On 24 January 1703, George Young, a shopkeeper on Edinburgh's High Street, was acting as a constable, appointed by the Edinburgh magistrates, to police Sabbath violation by Edinburgh taverns. He entered the house of Marjorie Thom, widow of James Allan, vintner, a little before 10.00 p.m. but had the misfortune to fall foul of Archibald Campbell, eldest son to Lord Neil Campbell and first cousin to the Duke of Argyll, who was drinking there, when he threatened to report him to the magistrates for Sabbath violation. Campbell visited Young's shop the next day and drew his sword but was restrained by bystanders. The Town Guard held Campbell prisoner but he brought an action against Young before the Privy Council in which he claimed he was attacked in the High Street. On 9 March, the Privy Council found Young guilty of a riot and fined him 400 merks (£22) to be paid to Campbell for expenses.[12] Archibald Campbell's connections to the Duke of Argyll and the powerful Clan Campbell made him a dangerous enemy for someone as low down the social scale as an Edinburgh shopkeeper.[13] The incident also reveals that, in this period, the (male) Scottish aristocracy patronised some of Edinburgh's many taverns and the tensions between young aristocratic males and the burgh authorities.

From early in the eighteenth century, there are records of pubs and taverns serving as public spaces for meetings and for work purposes, as well as for essential refreshment, particularly in rural areas. An Englishman who travelled in Scotland in 1704 attended church at Crawfordjohn, a sparsely populated parish in the South Lanarkshire uplands. The service began at nine and continued until noon, when 'the minister goes to the minsh-house [tavern] and so many of them as think fit, and refresh themselves'. The rest of the congregation stayed in the churchyard for half an hour, and the service began again and continued until about four or five o'clock in the afternoon. The reason for this was that most of the rural congregation lived too far from the church to go home for lunch. The English traveller recorded that 'their ale is pale, small and thick, but at the most common minsh-houses they commonly have good French brandy and often French wine, so common are these French liquors in this country'.[14] Later in the century, a similar close relationship between kirk and public house was to be found during Robert Burns's years in Lochlea, Ayrshire, where it was accepted practice for men to go with 'friends or lasses to the inn' between sermons.[15]

There was a fine line between Sabbath breaking and the literal observation of the law. An ale seller in Duddingston on the edge of Edinburgh was prosecuted in 1711 for allowing people to drink on the Sabbath. A witness told of three gentlemen and a lady who been in the tavern but 'at the beginning of sermon before noon they went out and walked until the sermon were over; that they then came back to the house and dined . . . at the ringing of the third bell after noon they went out again and walked till sermons were over, and that after sermon they returned to the house again, paid their reckoning and went away'.[16]

The Reverend Alexander Thomson, minister of the rural parish of Carnock in Fife, admitted that public houses were necessary 'for the convenience of travellers and the accommodation of the people who come from a distance to attend public worship on the Sabbath day'.[17] Some ministers were hostile to pubs being situated too close to their churches. The Reverend Lachlan M'Lachlan, of the Argyllshire parish of Craignish, complained in 1791 that the only public house in the parish

Figure 2.1 Sheep Heid Inn, Duddingston, Edinburgh. Old village pub on the edge of Edinburgh with a rare surviving skittles alley. © Anthony and Judith Cooke.

was situated much too close to the church, 'these tabernacles of iniquity should not be placed too close to the house of God'.[18] Others took a more proactive role. There were thirteen ale houses and three inns in the linen manufacturing parish of Fordyce, Banffshire, and the amount of Sunday drinking was said to be very great 'originating from the Sunday market'. The previous minister used to allow a certain time after public worship, then to ring 'the Drunken Bell; after which he visited the ale houses and dismissed any who remained in them'. By the 1780s, the Reverend James Lawtie had discontinued this practice but had still 'been obliged to make a step through the village, after dinner, to break up drinking companies'.[19]

THE MALT TAX AND THE ATTACK ON MONOPOLY PRIVILEGES

By the Treaty of Union of 1707 (Article XIV), the duty on malt (6d a bushel in England) was not to be applied to Scotland during the duration of the War of the Spanish Succession.[20] The imposition of the malt tax in 1713 was not widely enforced for some time until an amended Malt Tax bill was approved in March 1725. This caused widespread social unrest,

culminating in riots in Edinburgh and Glasgow. The Glasgow Malt Tax
Riot of 1725 attacked the opulent and newly built Shawfield Mansion
of Daniel Campbell, MP for the Glasgow burghs, who had supported
Walpole's measure. The Glasgow riot was well organised, with women
taking a prominent role, 'about three in the afternoon, drums were beat
about the street by women, or men in women's cloathes, as a signal to
assemble the mob'.[21] The city authorities appeared to sympathise with
the rioters and were reluctant to take action against them. Eventually,
the army had to step in to restore law and order.[22] This meant that any
change in the supply or price of malt, with its knock-on effect on the
price of ale, beer and spirits and the consequent threat to public order,
was likely to be treated with extreme caution by the authorities.

At this time, brewing in Glasgow was a small-scale affair, with citizens brewing their own ale and beer at home, though they had to buy the
malt from members of the Incorporation of Maltmen. The Incorporation
of Maltmen was a substantial and wealthy trade, one of fourteen affili-.
ated to the Glasgow Trades House. They provided six deputies out of a
total of fifty-six who made up the governing body of the Trades House
and paid the largest sum into the communal funds – £20.13.4d (13 per
cent) out of a total Trades House income of £150.15.6d. The burgh of
Glasgow had a monopoly on grinding malt, and beer had to be made
from malt 'as is grinded at the towns milns',[23] though this was beginning
to be challenged by the late 1730s. There were, however, small commercial ale houses in suburbs such as the Gorbals where, in 1711, it was
decreed that 'prudent, zealous and blameless men' were to be appointed
to inspect 'change houses and oyr places qr they can find those yt haunts
ale houses untimely'.[24] In 1736, there was only one small public brewery
in Glasgow, on the Molendinar Burn. It belonged to Robert Lakie, a
goldsmith, who was Treasurer to the City of Glasgow in 1730.[25] Similar
changes were noted in Aberdeen where 'the people who kept public
houses brewed all the beer and ale which they sold', and private families
also brewed a good deal of ale for their own use. This began to change
with the opening of the first public brewery, the Devanha, by William
Black and Co. in 1768.[26]

As the population of Scotland grew in the eighteenth century, greater
pressure was placed on supplies of food and drink, on drinking water
and on the natural resources of wind and water power to drive grain
mills and mills for grinding malt for beer and spirits. It was a period
when traditional municipal and state regulation of food and drink supplies and prices was beginning to break down under the pressures of a
growing population and an expanding economy. These pressures were

found both in the towns and in rural areas where landowners and estates traditionally controlled grain mills and the supply of grain to change houses or public houses. On the Isle of Jura in the 1760s there were four change houses – at Knocknafeolaman, Lag, Taychorran, and Feolin Ferry opposite Islay. Each paid a modest 'silver rent' to the Campbell of Jura estate and excise duty. The most lucrative part of the traditional estate privileges, however, was the right to sell grain to the tacksmen who ran the change houses on the estate. In 1764, this brought in £10.13.4d for '16 Bolls of Barley' at the Taychorran change house and £20 at the Lag change house for 30 bolls [boll = a measure of capacity for grain amounting in Scotland to 6 imperial bushels 8 gallons per bushel) (Chambers Dictionary, 1999 edition)] of barley 'supplied by farmers of Ardferrat'.[27] At Snizort on Skye, the brewseats' or ale houses' privilege 'of brewing, malting, vending and Distilling all sorts of legal spirits and liquers therein' was the precursor for the inns that opened across the region later in the century.[28]

The growing challenges to the monopoly privileges of the burghs are reflected in a letter from the Maltmen Incorporation of Dundee to a lawyer, James Smyth, Writer to the Signet, dated 1744. It concerned a dispute between the Maltmen and Baxters (Bakers) of Dundee, and the magistrates and town council of the burgh, regarding the latter's monopoly of the Town Mills where the maltmen were obliged to take their malt to be ground. They complained there were only three mills for grinding malt in Dundee, 'all belonging to this Town'. Two were in the town and there was one on the Dighty Burn on the rural edge of the burgh. Of the two in the town, one was a windmill 'the use whereof must be precarious as it depends on the Wind'; the other 'is called a Sea Miln & goes on a Dam gathered in our Towns Meadow and very frequently has no Water, especially since bringing in the Lady Well by Lead Pipes'. In other words, the pressure to supply more drinking water for the growing town was disrupting the traditional water supply to one of the town mills.[29]

Other changes were at work, including a shift in urban tastes from oatmeal to wheat bread, a sign of rising living standards. The Dundee maltmen complained that the 'crook'd Miln' on the Dighty on the edge of the burgh used to grind oats, and was also used to grind malt, 'but now that Miln is entirely converted into a Miln for grinding Wheat'. Two 'Steel Milns' belonging to the town used to grind malt but 'they are now worn out and not fit for Use'. That very week, 'the Wind Miln wanted Wind, the Sea Miln wanted Water . . . and the Malt miln on Dighty wants a Damn by Reason that the Damn Dyke has been broken down for near these three Months past'. Changes in use had also taken place at the 'three Milns of the Mains of easter strathdighty' on the edge of Dundee. Here, one mill continued to grind malt but one had been bought by the 'Laird of Craigy', the other by 'the Walker Trade of this Burgh' and converted into a waulk mill for cloth. The maltmen argued that, if the town council could not supply them with good facilities for grinding malt, then they must be allowed to 'Grind our Malt where or how we find best either at other Milns or by Steel Milns of our own'.[30]

In Glasgow, there were similar challenges to the monopoly privileges of the craft guilds and town council. Robert Tennant was a Burgess and a Guild Brother of Glasgow and the son of a Burgess. He kept a 'publick house' in the town where he had 'been in use of bakeing the bread, butchering the meat, making the malt and brewing the Ale consumed in his own house'. This meant he could sell cheaper and better quality food and drink because it was made on the premises. In February 1749, an action in the Court of Session was brought against him by the Maltmen of Glasgow, complaining that Tennant was refusing to pay the appropriate dues to them on the ale and spirits he was producing. Tennant dismissed the campaign against him as 'spirited up it is believed by others who looked upon the Respondents Success with an envious eye' and blamed 'the Innkeepers within the city of Glasgow'.[31]

PUBS AS SPACES FOR COMMERCIAL AND BUSINESS TRANSACTIONS

In overcrowded urban areas, pubs and taverns were commonly used by merchants and professional groups, such as doctors and lawyers, to conduct their business. In Edinburgh 'hardly any sort of business was transacted but in a tavern. No lawyer received a brief anywhere else. Each had his own apartment, in his particular tavern, where his clients attended him, as in his consulting room.'[32] In some parts of Scotland, this practice continued well into the second half of the twentieth century. A Dundee licensee remembered that, in the 1970s, when he ran the Ladywell Tavern at the foot of the Hilltown, a Dundee solicitor was to be found there every week night from 5.00 to 7.00 p.m., where he conducted much of his business.[33]

In Glasgow 'it was the custom of suburban [linen] manufacturers to transact all their business in some little public house over a gill and a "farl" of oaten cake. It is said that the Anderston "corks" [small linen manufacturers] met in Pinkertons opposite the Tron Steeple.' This was combined with a widespread system of mutual support by the linen trade to provide for family members. If a well-known family fell on hard times, either by the death of the male head of household or bad trade, 'some member of the family, generally the eldest daughter, was set up in a little half-door'd shoppie in a quiet court. A few casks were provided, filled with Stein or Haig of the Brigend's, which as it only paid about one penny per gallon of duty, could be sold by them at about three shillings, with a fair profit.' The shop was provided with 'a row of shining pewter measures ... something like two egg cups wanting the stalk stuck together, bottom to bottom, and each cup fashioned to hold its appropriate mouthful, the whole called a tass or tassie'.[34] This shows the survival of systems of mutual support for the sick, unemployed and bereaved in certain trades and occupations in the Scottish burghs well into the eighteenth century, in line with older traditions associated with the urban craft guilds. By the late eighteenth century, as a result of urban growth, a shifting, more diverse and less settled population and larger units in the workplace, these traditions were coming under pressure from newer ideologies such as laissez-faire, competition, the cash economy, and market forces.

Inns and taverns in urban areas also acted as meeting places for the local political and business elite down to the end of the eighteenth century. In 1716, three Edinburgh men were accused of using the office of City Treasurer to fund city work projects and manipulate funds for their own interests. One of the largest items in the city's finances was tavern bills, though one of the men claimed to have reduced expenses 'particularly in the article of tavern bills and public entertainments'.[35] In Glasgow in the 1750s, it was the custom 'for persons of all ranks and conditions to meet regularly in "change houses" as they were then called, and there to transact business, and hold their different clubs'. Business was done in the mornings and the drink of choice was sherry 'presented in mutchkin stoups'.[36] Dundee town councillors met in inns, such as Morrens on the High Street, where they 'liked to transact their public business over their knives and forks'. Members of Masonic Societies and the 'Trades' met in taverns, as did merchants and farmers on market day.[37] In Aberdeen, the New Inn was built in 1754, a fashionable place where the Aberdeen Lodge of Freemasons held their meetings.[38]

Alcohol played an important role in the eighteenth-century workplace. Water was often dangerous to drink because it transmitted waterborne diseases, such as cholera and typhus, and ale provided a significant amount of the labourer's or artisan's daily carbohydrate intake. The Duke of Gordon's servants at Gordon Castle in 1739 received 62 per cent of their nutrition from bread and meal, 19 per cent from ale; those at Lady Grisell Baillie's Mellerstain House in 1743 received 73 per cent of their nutrition from bread and meal, 12 per cent from ale. The average of eight known diets in Scotland between 1639 and 1743 reveals a daily mean head of 19.7 ounces (558 grams) of meal and 2.1 imperial pints (1.2 litres) of ale.[39]

The growing practice of paying wages in cash coexisted with earlier practices of paying workers partly in cash, partly in kind, including food and drink. When the Smeaton Bridge was built over the Tay in Perth, James Bisset in Bridgend supplied the workmen with 'Liquors and Bread' between 1 August and 26 September 1767, including 42 'gills of whiskie', 515 bottles of ale, 4 Choppins and two Mutchkins of whisky and a bottle of aquavitie at a total cost of £3.14.1d. On 9 October 1767, the 'Boat men' were allowed sixteen bottles of ale at a cost of 1/4d.[40] Later in the century, a 'Flour Mill' was fitted out on Horse Water Wynd in Dundee, and was later used as a flax spinning mill. The accounts for May to August 1793 reveal that masons were paid 10 shillings a week, smiths and wrights 7/6d a week. On 15 June 1793, the accounts register a payment of £1/5s for 'Drink at beginning of work', 17/3d for 'Rolls and ale' and 2/6d for 'Drink money to sundries'.[41]

LIFE, COMMUNITY AND WORKPLACE RITUALS

The pub, together with the church, were often the only places in many parts of Scotland to provide public space for life rituals such as birth, christenings, courtship, marriage and death, and, for many workplace rituals, such as hiring, completion of an apprenticeship, pay nights or the 'pay off' when somebody left the workplace. Births and christenings were generally marked by heavy alcohol consumption. In *Guy Mannering*, Walter Scott describes an Edinburgh birth around 1746, when the 'groaning malt' and the 'ken-no' were drunk in honour of the new mother. This female-only ritual involved ale and cheese, made by the female members of the household, and offered to the female 'gossips' or attendants at the birth.[42]

Thomas Pennant, who toured Scotland in 1769 and again in 1772, described another female-only ritual in Moulin in Highland Perthshire involving the 'kirking' of mothers after they had given birth. The Church of Scotland held no ceremony for this but 'the woman, attended by some of her neighbours, goes into the church, sometimes in service time, but oftener when it is empty; goes out again, surrounds it, refreshes herself at some public house, and then returns home'. Before the ceremony 'she is looked on as unclean, never is permitted to eat with the family; nor will anyone eat of the victuals she has dressed'.[43] Pennant also described a Highland courtship ritual where the man first obtained the private consent of the woman he wished to marry then approached her father for his consent. The would-be groom and his friends assembled on a hill in the parish and invited the father and his friends to 'partake of a whisky cask, which is never forgotten'.[44] In Sandwick and Stromness parish on Orkney, there had been a big shift over the century from ale being the drink of choice at christenings in 1700 to wine in 1794.[45]

Another custom described by Pennant took place at Michaelmas on the Roman Catholic island of Canna, when

> every man on the island mounts his horse unfurnished with saddle, and takes behind him either some young girl, or his neighbour's wife, and then rides backwards and forwards from the village to a certain cross, without being able to give any reason for the origins of this custom. After the procession is over, they alight at some public house, where, strange to say, the females treat the companions of their ride.

They then returned to their houses, where they prepared a cake called 'struan Michaeil' or 'St Michael's cake', made from meal with milk and eggs poured over it and cooked on the fire.[46]

Funerals in the Scottish Lowlands in the eighteenth century were often long, drawn-out, drunken affairs. In the period between death and interment, houses in Perthshire kept open house, when 'bread, cheese, ale and spirits' were served to all visitors. Drinking usually continued at the funeral ceremony itself.[47] The Reverend James Robertson, of Gargunnock in Stirlingshire, condemned the volume of alcohol consumed at funerals, adding that 'the conversation is often very unsuitable to the occasion'. He wished to see these practices reformed but added 'old customs are not easily abolished'.[48]

In more isolated parts of Scotland ale houses and pubs featured prominently in customary rituals and ceremonies connected with the agricultural year and systems of traditional agriculture. In the village of Crawford in the uplands of south Lanarkshire, for example, the traditional runrig system of agriculture survived until the late 1770s. Each householder had:

> 4 or 5 acres of croft land, parcelled out in all the different parts of the town, with a privilege of keeping a certain number of sheep, cows and horses on the hill or common pastures. The little republic was governed by a birley court, in which every proprietor of a freedom had a vote ... From the court that was held weekly, the members adjourned to an ale house. The bills at the ale

house were not cleared above once or twice in the year, namely, when some
sheep or a cow had been sold, and payment received.

The local minister, the Reverend James Maconochie, born in Banffshire
and imbued with fashionable ideas of enlightenment and improvement,
had little sympathy or identification with this traditional and long-
established custom, commenting, 'It is necessary that Gothic manners,
or the indolent habit of all barbarians, be banished, and a spirit of
ambition and enterprise be introduced.'[49]

RISING LIVING STANDARDS AND CHANGING TASTES

Living standards in Scotland were slow to rise in the early years of the
century but began to increase noticeably in the last two decades. This led
to major changes in what the mass of the population wore, what they
ate and what they drank. The lowering of the price of cotton goods led
to better clothing for the masses. Tea and tobacco became staples of the
household budget and, as the consumption of two-penny ale declined,
that of spirits, particularly whisky, increased. A characteristic of the
late eighteenth century in Scotland was a shift in consumer taste from
beer, generally seen as a wholesome drink, to cheaper and often poor
quality whisky, to the detriment of people's health. This increase in
spirit drinking was part of a British and, indeed, European trend, with
the consumption of gin, whisky and rum rising rapidly across Europe,
which 'made distilling of all sorts one of the leading growth industries
of the long eighteenth century'.[50] Again, market specialisation became a
feature of the distilling industry across Europe from the late seventeenth
century, with London specialising in gin, Cracow in Poland in vodka
which was exported to Bohemia and the Ottoman Empire.[51]

   In Edinburgh, the brewing capital of Scotland, there was a steep decline
in the production of weak two-penny ale in the late eighteenth century
in favour of wine and spirits and stronger ale such as porter. In 1708,
288,336 barrels of 2d ale were brewed and paid duty in Edinburgh, rising
to 520,478 barrels in 1720 before plummeting to 97,577 in 1784.[52] By
contrast, the revenue from distilling in Scotland increased from £4,739
in 1763 to £192,000 in 1793, representing 600,000 gallons (2,730,000
litres) of spirits.[53] The number of licensed outlets for whisky sales also
increased exponentially. In 1743, there were only 828 spirit retailers in
Scotland. By 1780, this had increased to 1,358, and in 1794, when the
duties on whisky retailers were dropped to 20 shillings in the Highlands
and 40 shillings in the Lowlands, numbers rocketed to 4,397, as well as

1,304 general licences.[54] Towards the end of the century, the consumption of rum and wine also increased. Increased consumption of alcohol was a sign of rising living standards, brought about by higher earnings for men, women and children in commerce, manufacturing and mining, which had a knock-on effect on agricultural wages.

From the early eighteenth century, urban Scottish tastes in food and drink were becoming more influenced by London fashions, and this trend intensified as the century progressed. In an example of increasing market specialisation, London porter, a strong dark beer, was supplied to Glasgow by the London brewers, from 1706 to 1762, via the east coast port of Leith.[55] This began to change in 1762 when a large brewery was built in Anderston, an industrial suburb of Glasgow, which exported large quantities of ale and porter to Ireland and America.[56] This was the Glasgow brewery described by Thomas Pennant in 1769 as 'a great porter brewery, which supplies some part of unindustrious Ireland'.[57] Nathaniel Chivers, who had been trained in London as a porter brewer, arrived in Glasgow from Dublin in October 1775 to teach the art of brewing porter and was paid the substantial sum of 100 guineas, plus expenses,[58] which suggests that brewing was a highly profitable business. By the early 1770s, 2,916 firkins (119,556 litres) of strong ale were being exported from Glasgow, the bulk of it to Ireland [1,980 firkins (81,180 litres) or 68 per cent] but some also to the American colonies and the West Indies.[59]

Certainly, taxes on beer and ale were an important part of the municipal revenues. In Edinburgh, a duty of two pence Scots on a pint of ale and beer was extended in 1723 to the parish of St Cuthberts, the Canongate and Leith. This brought in an income of £7,939 in 1724 but steadily declined over the next half century as the favoured drink of the masses changed from weak two-penny ale to tea and spirits. By 1776 the tax raised only £2,197 a year.[60] The annual revenue of the city of Glasgow in 1781 was £4,499, of which £1,402 (31 per cent) consisted of an impost on ale and beer brewed in Glasgow and its vicinities, 'called the two penny in the pint'.[61] This major source of municipal income dated back to 1693, when an Act of Parliament allowed Glasgow to levy two pence on every pint of beer or ale to pay off the burgh debts which had accumulated owing to municipal corruption and incompetence. The impost was continued by successive Acts until 1837.[62]

Not only were the labouring poor drinking more and stronger alcohol, the middle classes were increasingly indulging in fine wining and dining as a result of increasing wealth and changing expectations. Alexander Carlyle recalled how, in 1756, a group of his fellow clergymen and other

friends met in the Carrier's Inn in the West Bow during the General
Assembly of the Church of Scotland, having taken care to lay in a good
stock of claret beforehand.[63] By the late 1770s, claret was the drink of
choice in Edinburgh 'as hardly any other liquor is called for after dinner
in taverns' and it was popular in private houses 'where the entertainment is tolerably genteel'. The duty paid on wine imported into Leith
rose from £12,871 a year in 1773–4 to £22,706 in 1777–8.[64] Imports
to Glasgow in the early 1770s included some 39,000 gallons (177,450
litres) of wine, mostly Portuguese. This was dwarfed by the massive
figures for rum imports, however, which reached 179,544 gallons
(816,925 litres) in 1771–2.[65] At dinner, Glasgow colonial merchants
drank 'delicious old West India Madeira' followed by rum punch made
'in the china', a decorated porcelain bowl.[66]

Some ambitious claims have been made over the years about the
popularity and unusually heavy consumption of claret in Scotland in this
period. Henry Cockburn claimed that Scotch claret was exempted from
duty until around 1780, which 'made it till then the ordinary beverage'.
When a cargo of claret arrived in Leith, 'the common way of announcing
its arrival was by sending a hogshead [some 636 litres] of it through the
town on a cart, with a horn; and that anybody who wanted a sample or
a drink under the pretence of a sample, had only to go to the cart with a
jug, which without much nicety about its size, was filled for a sixpence'.[67]
While this may have been true in Edinburgh, it does not seem to have
applied to Glasgow where most wine imports were from Portugal, rather
than France, and the consumption of rum dwarfed that of wine.

PUBS AND INNS IN PLANNED VILLAGES

As part of the improvement project adopted by the landed elite in the
eighteenth century, some 164 planned villages were laid out in Scotland
between 1770 and 1799, followed by another 119 in the next two
decades.[68] Sometimes, the site was selected where people already congregated for social or trading purposes. On the Lovat estates in 1755,
the factors reported 'there is a little village called Beauly . . . an extreme
proper place for erecting a village . . . there are several yearly fairs held
in and about the place, a mercat cross in it and a great collection of
poor people, who live in huts and retail ale and spirituous liquors to the
people who resort there'.[69]

Whereas ale houses, dram shops and tipling huts were generally seen
as undesirable by the landed elite, a well-appointed inn was sometimes
the first building to be erected in a planned village. This was the case at

Gatehouse of Fleet in Kirkcudbrightshire, laid out as a planned village in the 1760s, where the first house in the village was built as an inn. By the early 1790s, the village had grown to a population of 1,150 and was served by a mailcoach twice a day. The water-powered cotton mills at Gatehouse employed five hundred people at this time.[70] Laurencekirk, in Kincardineshire, was laid out by Lord Gardenstone in 1765 and was made a burgh of barony in 1779. It was a textile village with 'bleachfields, a printfield, linen workers, stocking knitters, cabinet makers, smiths and other sort of country tradesmen' supporting a population of about five hundred in the early 1790s.[71] As an enlightened proprietor, Gardenstone had 'built and fitted up an elegant inn, with a library of books adjoining to it, chiefly for the amusement of travellers'.[72] Some landowners used their powers over planned villages to change the drinking behaviour of their tenants. Grantown in Inverness-shire was a planned village laid out by the Grant family in the 1770s. When the village was built, a brewery was erected 'on purpose to keep the people from drinking spirituous liquors'.[73]

One of the best-documented examples of paternalism in an eighteenth-century industrial community is at Leadhills, on the Hopetoun estates, in the South Lanarkshire uplands. Leadhills was an isolated mining community where the lead miners received relatively high wages for a short working day of six hours. Here, the Scotch Mines Company appointed the mathematician James Stirling as mine manager in 1734, at the handsome salary of £220 a year, where he remained until his death in 1770. In 1739, there were twenty-one ale houses in the village ministering to the 'odious and abominable vice of drunkenness', and Stirling moved to quash them and establish a strongly paternalistic regime, with a schoolmaster and a surgeon to attend to the health and education of the villagers. As part of this regime, a library for the workers was established in 1741. Control of alcohol consumption was another important feature of the regime though, in 1784, after Stirling's death, the local minister complained that too many workers still spent their time 'sauntering thro' the town, chatting in the smiddies, tippling in the ale houses and kissing the girls'.[74]

By the 1790s, the Leadhills workers were described as 'the best informed and therefore the most reasonable common people I know', and it was claimed that their drinking habits had changed radically,

about 30 years ago, most of the smelters died either madmen or idiots. Now they retain their senses as well as other people. The reason given is: formerly spirits were cheap and the smelters partook liberally of them at their work. For many years past they drink nothing at their work but pure spring water; they now live as long and as rationally as others.[75]

It is hard to know what to make of these claims, as lead miners, smelters and their communities were subject to dangerous levels of lead pollution and poisoning as part of their daily living and working conditions.

FAIRS, MARKETS AND INCREASING SOCIAL SEGREGATION

Another symbol of rising affluence, greater travel and more productive agriculture in Scotland was the growth in importance of fairs, trysts and markets, accompanied by an increasing demand for food, drink and accommodation, met by a growth in the number of pubs and ale houses. Sometimes, these took the form of what nowadays would be called 'pop-up' pubs, as they sprang up briefly for the period when the

Figure 2.2 Hallow Fair, Grassmarket, Edinburgh, 1905. Horse Fair, Beehive Hotel and Black Bull Inn in background. © RCAHMS.

fair or market was being held. At Kells in Kirkcudbrightshire, the village of New Galloway had two inns 'where entertainment may be had for men and horses', seven smaller ale houses in the town and three others in the rest of the sparsely populated parish but, 'as these cannot afford to pay the licence, they sell only professedly in time of fairs'.[76]

Fairs and markets have not attracted sufficient attention from historians.[77] They fulfilled important social and economic functions, provided a place to meet the opposite sex, and reflected the tensions between popular and elite culture in this period. Hallow Fair was held every Halloween in early November in Fountainbridge in Edinburgh. It was marked by heavy eating and drinking, and equally heavy socialising between men and women, as described in Robert Fergusson's 1772 poem, *Hallow Fair*:

> At Hallow-fair, where browsters rare
> Keep gude ale on the gantries
> And dinna scrimp ye o' a skair
> O' kebbucks frae their pantries
> Fu' saut that day[78]

> 'browsters' = ale wives
> 'gantries' = wooden barrel stands
> 'skair' = share
> 'kebbucks' = cheese

Accommodation could become grossly overcrowded during fairs and markets. A French traveller, looking for accommodation in Dumbarton in 1784, 'found a fair going on in the town, which made it difficult to find beds at the inns, as these were full of strangers'.[79] Two years later, another French visitor reported from Stranraer that he and his companions 'could find nowhere to stay, neither for us nor our horses, on account of the May fair', and were forced to travel on another 6 miles to Portpatrick.[80]

THE HIGHLANDS

At the beginning of the eighteenth century, the Scottish Highlands, particularly the Western Highlands and Islands, provided real challenges for travellers, those running inns and others providing food, drink and accommodation. The Highlands were generally sparsely populated, with scattered communities, high levels of poverty, a population whose native language was Gaelic, and a basic transport system. Much of the terrain was mountainous, with limited areas for arable farming, rivers liable to go into sudden spate and, on the west coast, a highly indented coastline. One of the first writers to leave an account of his travels in the Highlands and Islands was Martin Martin, a native of Skye, who travelled in the Western Isles at the end of the seventeenth century. On the fertile island of Tiree, he found no less than three inns, where the ale was preserved by storage in 'large earthen vessels', which held up to 12 English gallons (55 litres). By contrast on Borera, the concept of an inn was a novelty, and travellers relied on traditional hospitality in people's houses, though an inn had just opened on the island.[81]

Captain Edmund Burt was an English military engineer who travelled in the Highlands in the 1720s. He claimed that the only good inn in Inverness was kept by an Englishwoman who, however, had difficulty in procuring decent food for her guests because of the primitive state of the local markets. Like many English visitors before and after him, he remarked on the filthy condition of Scottish inns, both in the Lowlands and in the Highlands. He was also highly critical of Highland ale which was flavoured with 'peat, turf, or furzes' from the fuel used to dry the malt. It was often drunk before it was cold out of 'a cap or "coif" . . . this is a wooden dish, with two ears or handles, about the size of a tea saucer, and as shallow, so that a steady hand is necessary to carry it to the mouth'.[82] A similar drinking vessel, resembling a quaigh ('cuach' = Gaelic for 'cup') was widely used in eighteenth-century Glasgow, some made of silver, some of pewter 'but the most part of them were formed of wooden slaps, neatly girded together, having an ear at each end'.[83]

Captain Burt was part of the military project launched by the Hanoverian government to pacify the Highlands, in the wake of the 1715 Jacobite rebellion, by building roads, barracks and bridges so that troops could be quartered and moved around quickly and the Highland economy encouraged. Indeed, his last letter is headed 'concerning the New Roads etc.' and is probably dated around 1737, with the sub-heading 'relating to the MILITARY WAYS among the mountains, begun in 1726'. As a result of the new roads, Burt claimed that 'huts of turf' had been replaced by 'houses with chimneys, built with stone and lime, and ten or twelve miles distance from one another' for the benefit of travellers, 'who are seldom many at a time in that country.'[84] These were the King's Houses, some of which still survive, though in a greatly altered form. They were built at places such as Letterfinlay and Dalwhinnie, both in Inverness-shire, Moulinearn, Perthshire, and Dalnacardoch, which survives as a country house.[85] In 1746 it was claimed that, 'From Perth to Inverness . . . there is no town or village of any consequence . . . neither is there any Inn or Accommodation for travellers, excepting a few that have been built on the King's Roads made by Marshal Wade'.[86]

Thomas Pennant, who toured Scotland in 1769, praised the inn at Inver, in Perthshire, on the southern bank of the Tay from Dunkeld, where a tame swan followed the ferry boat across the river.[87] The following year, the Inver Inn was offered for sale, after the death of its owner, James Johnstone. The kitchen contained a roasting spit, grid iron, skillet pan, frying pan, girdle, pots of brass, copper and iron. Ale was clearly brewed on the premises, as there was a maskin vat and worts stone, tubs, a copper, a working vat, barrels, bottles and stoups. Meals were served on pewter trenchers and tin plates, with cups, saucers and teaspoons, stoups for alcohol but no glasses. The inn contained a bed with curtains, linen sheets, blankets, a bolster and pillow on a feather bed for the quality, and a chaff bed for the rest. There were three men servants earning from £4 to £5 a year and the two female servants earned less than £2 a year.[88]

In 1773, Samuel Johnson and James Boswell set out together on a tour of the Western Islands, a project which was much influenced by Johnson's early reading of Martin's work. They were viewing the Highlands in a period of great change, in the aftermath of the bloody defeat of the Jacobite army at Culloden and the subsequent transformation of Highland life by means of what has been described as 'punitive civilising' and 'exemplary civilising'.[89] Johnson himself remarked 'we came thither too late to see what we expected, a people of peculiar appearance, and a system of antiquated life'. At Anoch, near Fort Augustus, they stayed at a village inn, where Johnson was surprised to find 'some books on a shelf, among which were a volume of Prideaux's *Connection*'. In the evening 'the soldiers, whom we had passed on the road, came to spend at our inn the little money we had given them'. These were soldiers from the barracks at Fort Augustus, who had been working on the road when Johnson and Boswell passed and gave them some money. At Glenelg, on the west coast facing Skye, Johnson and Boswell found a poverty-stricken inn where there was 'no meat, no milk, no bread, no eggs, no wine', though a local laird produced some rum and sugar for them. When they reached Skye, they found that the concept of an inn was an alien one. Johnson remarked 'in countries so little frequented as the islands, there are no houses where travellers are entertained for money'.[90] A year earlier than this, Thomas Pennant had claimed that the increase in travellers in the Highlands would lead inevitably to the decline of Highland hospitality but that 'good inns will be the consequence of even a partial subversion of the hospitable system'.[91]

The social and economic changes noted by Samuel Johnson were taking place all over the Highlands, including the Southern Highlands, where the extensive Atholl and Breadalbane estates in Perthshire were experiencing sweeping changes, including clearances for sheep, the uniting of farms, and population movement from the area to the Lowlands and further afield.[92] An increase in travel led to new inns and change houses being built to serve the needs of local agriculture and industry. From Ardeonaig, on the south side of Loch Tay on the Breadalbane Estates, John Thomson, the village smith, wrote to the Earl of Breadalbane in 1786 for permission to build a 'Publick House' in the village. Thomson had spoken to Hugh Cameron, the wright at Lawers on the north side of Loch Tay, who had offered to build the inn for £68.14.4d sterling. At present, there were two public houses in Ardeonaig, both on the high road from Kenmore to Killin. The new inn was planned to be built on 'the best Arable ground of the whole Farm' and Thomson was seeking the earl's permission to move the site to 'one of the stances of the above Publick houses', as the cost would be halved if he could reuse the stones from the old pubs, and the new site would also use less good arable land.[93]

Travelling experiences were varied in the Highlands and traditional hospitality was not always forthcoming. A French traveller arrived at ten o'clock at night in September 1784 at the Luss Inn on Loch Lomond in pouring rain. His party was refused entry by the landlady as the inn was housing a judge on circuit. '"The lord Judge", said the hostess, "does me the honour to lodge here when on circuit. He is there; everybody must respect him. He is asleep. His horses are in the stable; so you see there is no room for yours; have the goodness then to go away."' The French travellers were duly turned away and had to ride another 15 miles to the inn at Tarbert, where they arrived at half past three in the morning and were finally offered accommodation for themselves and their horses.[94]

Robert Burns had a similar experience at the Inverary inn, Argyllshire, in the heart of Campbell country. The Inveraray inn was patronised by the landed aristocracy, particularly members of the ubiquitous Clan Campbell. A bill for February 1776 shows the consumption of whisky, taken with sugar, ale and wine by two local lairds – Campbell of Barcaldine and Campbell of Airds, together with Archibald Campbell, the innkeeper.[95] Burns's stay in 1787 produced a sarcastic outburst about his neglect by the innkeeper, in favour of well-connected visitors who were meeting the Duke of Argyll, a common complaint by visitors to the Highlands. It satirises the fawning treatment of the aristocracy by their social inferiors and the almost divine status bestowed on the great landed Highland families, 'The Lord their God – his Grace':

> Whoe'er he be that sojourns here,
> I pity much his case,
> Unless he comes to wait upon
> The Lord their God – his Grace.
>
> There's naething here but Highland pride,
> And Highland scab and hunger:
> If Providence has sent me here,
> 'Twas surely in an anger[96]

An aristocratic French traveller, the Duc de la Rochefoucauld, toured Scotland in 1786. While travelling along Loch Ness, he dined at an inn called the General's Hut, close to Fort Augustus. He was unimpressed by the accommodation or by his hosts,

> nothing would give you more of an idea of poverty, dirt and squalor than this place offers . . . The hearth is in the middle of the room and made with three or four stones without mortar . . . The beds are only rough bits of wood nailed together with straw for warmth. Chairs are tree stumps. The light gets in only through a door which serves as door, chimney and window. The straw roof-thatch is full of holes and used as a hen roost.

The greatest horror was to find that 'the whole family (running the inn) has scabies' so that the travellers could not face the oatcake offered but ate eggs instead. Further west, however, at Portnachroish in Appin, Rochefoucauld was amazed by the range of food on offer at the modest inn. It included not only the usual 'tea, sugar, rum and wine' but also 'fresh eggs, calf's head ragout, boiled chicken and an excellent bullock's tongue, with a potato cake'. At Bonawe, on Loch Etive, the travellers stayed at the local inn, where the landlady had been in Britain only twelve years, and scandalised them with a frank account of her colourful life history, but redeemed herself by, 'an entire pig she served up and the best port wine I've ever drunk'.[97]

By the 1780s, there was even the beginnings of a Highland tourist trade, mainly composed of Scottish and English visitors. Elisabeth Diggle, an unmarried Englishwoman of comfortable means, toured in Scotland from 19 April to 7 August 1788. She stayed in thirty-three inns and hotels and gave them all ratings. The only two she rated as 'excellent' were both in the Lowlands – the New Inn at Stirling and Walker's Hotel in Edinburgh. Of the six she rated as 'very good', however, five were in the Highlands – the New Inn at Lochloing, the Inn at Inveraray, the inns at Kenmore, Blair Atholl and Inver near Dunkeld, plus Campbell's Hotel in Perth. Of the twelve rated as 'good', only one was in the Highlands, at Killin in Perthshire. The inn at Tyndrum was rated as 'tolerable', while the three rated as 'very bad' were all in the Highlands – the inns at Luss, Cairndow and Dalmally. So, of the ten Highland inns she stayed in, six (60 per cent) she rated as 'very good' or 'good'.[98]

MALTSTERS AND VINTNERS – THE SCOTTISH LICENSEE

Outside the larger urban centres, such as Aberdeen, Dundee, Edinburgh and Glasgow, licensees in eighteenth-century Scotland frequently combined keeping an ale house or tavern with another occupation. In 1772, Perth Burgh Licensing Court granted fourteen one-year licences to sell ale, beer and other excisable liquors in the burgh. Of the fourteen licensed, seven were described as 'maltsters' or 'maltmen' and one as the widow of a maltster. The remaining six were categorised as a flesher, a mason (two), a joiner, a merchant and an 'Indweller'. Of the fourteen, thirteen were tenants and only one sold ale in his own house. The only woman granted a licence was the 'relict' or widow of a maltster.[99]

Small-scale brewing and the accompanying trade of innkeeping played an important part in the urban economy in many small Scottish burghs. In Cupar, situated in the fertile arable farming area of north-east Fife, the maltmen and brewers were 'perhaps the dominant group in seventeenth-century Cupar'. The increasing industrialisation and concentration of brewing in the eighteenth century led to a decline in the numbers of maltmen and small brewers and an increase in the numbers of vintners and innkeepers. Innkeepers in Cupar often held another job, such as merchant, manufacturer, carrier, writer, coachmaker, shoemaker or wright.[100]

In the first half of the eighteenth century, Robert Philp, a Cupar innkeeper, left wort buckets, and other brewing utensils, a cart and horses in his 1742 inventory. Others were clearly more substantial businessmen, with a good deal of capital tied up in premises, furnishings and fittings. Bartholomew Cockburn, of the Blue Bell Inn, was an incomer to Cupar who married twice, in both cases to wives from innkeeping families. His inventory of 1795 lists ten rooms and a garret in the inn, with fourteen tables, thirty chairs and eight beds. He possessed eleven candlesticks, five coffee pots, five china and three stoneware punchbowls, forty-two dram glasses and over a hundred plates. He had a card table, a backgammon table and a chaise for hire. His stocks of drink included gin and whisky. Inns provided the setting for the town council's annual election dinner for sixty years, and even meetings of the presbytery were sometimes held in inns. The historian of Cupar concluded 'Innkeepers were central to the development of leisure in towns, and their social status grew as they provided increasingly elaborate travel and entertainment facilities, as well as accommodation.'[101]

John Dove, 'Johnny Pigeon', the innkeeper at the Whitefoord Arms at Mauchline in Ayrshire,[102] was satirised and immortalised by Robert Burns who acknowledged Dove's lack of religious belief which had been replaced by an almost religious faith in alcohol:

> Here lies Johnny Pigeon
> What was his religion?
> Whaever desires to ken,
> To some other warl'
> Maun follow the carl,
> For here Johnny Pigeon had nane.
>
> Strong ale was ablution,
> Small beer persecution,
> A dram was memento mori;
> But a full flowing bowl
> Was the saving his soul,
> And Port was celestial glory.[103]

In urban centres, such as Edinburgh and Glasgow, licensees and landlords of city centre inns and taverns could be men of substance and reputation who owned valuable assets. Peter Williamson set up a coffee house or tavern in the precincts of Parliament House in Edinburgh, patronised by the town magistrates on execution days. The European idea of the coffee house was adopted with enthusiasm in Edinburgh but a Scottish twist was added with alcohol being served as well as coffee. Williamson had lived an eventful life, having been kidnapped at the age of eight in Aberdeen and sold to the colonies, rather like David Balfour, the fictional hero of Robert Louis Stevenson's *Kidnapped*. Williamson was described as 'one of the greatest liars who ever lived' but his narrative belongs in a long tradition of captivity, associated with the world of Empire.[104] He eventually made his way back to Aberdeen in 1759 but was banished from there and moved to Edinburgh. He died in 1799 when he was keeping a tavern in the Lawnmarket.[105]

John Dowie kept a tavern in Libberton's Wynd, near St Giles, running down to the Cowgate. His ale, brewed by Archibald Younger at Croft an Righ, Holyrood, was famous:

> O, Dowie's ale! Thou art the thing
> That gars us crack, that gars us sing[106]

Figure 2.3 John Dowie's Tavern, Edinburgh. © Capital Collections, Edinburgh.

Dowie's Tavern was patronised by some of the leading lights of the Edinburgh Enlightenment, including Henry Raeburn, Robert Fergusson, David Hume and Robert Burns. Burns lodged in Baxters Close in 1786, across the road from Dowie's, and his friends, Willie Nicol and Allan Masterton, were immortalised in the song:

> O Willie brewed a peck o'maut
> And Rab and Allan cam' tae pree[107]

James Graham kept two of the largest and busiest inns in eighteenth-century Glasgow – the Black Bull on Argyll Street and the Saracen Head. He died on 25 September 1771 aged seventy-one, leaving a widow, Jean Leckie. Graham was well connected with the municipal elite of Glasgow. His executors were Duncan Niven, barber, 'late Bailie' (magistrate) of Glasgow, William Ewing, baker, 'late Bailie' of Glasgow, James Leckie, 'Watchmaker in Glasgow' and his widow, Jean Leckie. James Graham was a man of some wealth and, in November 1779, his total estate at death was valued at £1,745.17.6d. The 'Wines and liquors' in his cellars were valued at £182.15.9d, his horses and hay at £360.5.6d, his 'Coaches and chaises' at £169/14s. His household furniture was valued at a substantial £310.9.3d, his silver plate at £160/4s. He owned a farm, Lancefield, on the edge of Glasgow, where his household furniture was valued at £185.4.6d, his cows and swine at £21/5s and the 'growing Corn and Garden Roots' at £16.3.4d. James Graham owned three watches, 'a Gun, Sword and Pistol' and a silver snuff box. He had debts of £307 owed to him by the landed and mercantile elite of Glasgow and West of Scotland society, including the Duke of Argyll, the late Earl of Eglinton (£230), Sir John Cathcart of Carleton, Lord Stonefield, Captain Montgomery of Calsfield, 'Doctor Williamson of the University of Glasgow', 'the Members of the Royal Arch Club', 'the Members of the St Mungo's Lodge', and by Mr Robertson and Mr Lammie, both from Jamaica, presumably connected with the sugar trade.[108]

Both the Saracen Head and the Black Bull Inn were substantial Glasgow business enterprises that had been purpose-built in the mid eighteenth century. The Saracen Head was built in 1755 'as a great inn, all of good hewn stone'. It functioned as a mail inn and, when the mail arrived, 'the idlers of the city' crowded around and it was greeted by two waiters 'with embroidered coats, red plus breeches and powdered hair'. The Saracen Head was used by the judges on circuit and, when they or the Duke of Hamilton were expected, the waiters put on silk stockings.[109] This was the licensed trade as theatre.

The Black Bull had different origins. It was built by the Highland Society of Glasgow in 1760 and the profits were used to 'educate, clothe and put out to trade the children of industrious Highland parents'. The profits came from 'hundreds of pipes of claret, port and sherry, thousands of puncheons of whisky and oceans of Glasgow punch'. It contained a commercial room, a coffee room, a ballroom, nine parlours, twenty-nine bedrooms and stabling for thirty horses.[110] The Glasgow Highland Society had been founded as early as 1727 and was joined in 1780 by a Gaelic Club. It played an important role in providing mutual support and preserving the cultural identity of Highlanders who had settled in Glasgow, and was part of a network of some eighty clubs and societies in the rapidly growing city, many of which met in 'inns, taverns, coffee houses and alehouses', which 'lodged an ever increasing number and variety of clubs and societies'.[111]

'LUCKIES' AND BREWSTER WIVES

In Edinburgh, in the early part of the century, most brewing took place in houses or 'howffs', and traditionally, women did the brewing and ran the tavern. This was in spite of the existence of a law of 1699 which forbade the employment of women in taverns as 'a great Snare to the Youth, and Occasion for Lewdness and Debauchery'.[112] Maggy Johnston was a well-known brewer, a 'Lucky' or guidwife of the house, who ran a tavern from her farm in Bruntsfield on the south side of Edinburgh and was famed for the quality of her ale. Her death in 1711 moved the poet Allan Ramsay (1684–1758) to pen an elegy in her memory which reveals the 'democratic' nature of taverns in the rural suburbs of Edinburgh, where 'lairds' and 'souters' (shoemakers) intermingled:

> Auld Reekie mourn in sable hue!
> Let forth o' tears dreep like May dewe!
> To braw tipenny bid adieu
> Which we wi' greed
> Bended as fast as she could brew
> But ah! She's dead
> To tell the truth now Maggy dang
> O' Customers she had a bang
> For Lairds and Souters a' did gang
> To drink bedeen,
> The barn and yard was aft sae thrang
> We took the green[113]

Other well-known Edinburgh 'Luckies' in the early years of the eighteenth century, who were celebrated in Ramsay's poetry, included the notorious Lucky Spence, who ran a tavern/brothel in the Canongate near Holyrood House, and the much more respectable Lucky Wood who kept a well-run ale house in the Canongate.[114] Ramsay's *Elegy on Lucky Wood in the Canongate* is dated 1717 and praises her hospitality, honesty and neat appearance:

> She gae'd as fait as a new prin,
> And kept her housie snod and been;
> Her peuther glanc'd upo' your een
> Like siller plate;
> She was a donsie wife and clean,
> Without debate.[115]

Compared to Ramsay, Robert Fergusson (1750–74) had a less romanticised view of the qualities of Edinburgh landladies. His poem *Leith Races* (1773) satirises the 'browster wives' who cut corners on quality when brewing ale to increase their profits:

> The browster wives thegither harl
> A' trash that they can fa' on;
> They rake the ground o' ilka barrel,
> To profit by the lawen:
> For weel wat they a skin leal het
> For drinking needs nae hire;
> At drumbly gear they take nae pet;
> Foul water slockens fire
> And drouth their days.[116]
>
> 'browster' = brewer
> 'harl' = scrape
> 'lawen' = tavern bill

'Luckies' were also prominent in Aberdeen[117] and Perth in the eighteenth century. There were about sixty brewers in Perth in the 1760s, each known for their skill in brewing ale which was 'greatly relished by all classes' and, in the days before tea became fashionable, 'was in high favour with the wives'. Looking back to his youth, the Perth weaver and journalist, George Penny (1771–*c*.1850?) fondly remembered a hospitable Perth landlady, 'Lucky' Kettles:

who that has visited the Turk's Head of an evening and tasted Lucky Kettles' extra and her salt herring and oat cakes, can ever forget the happiness and devotion of the company in applying themselves to the business of the evening. Everybody in Perth, whether soldier or civilian, knew Lucky Kettles.[118]

Robert Reid ('Senex') (1773–1865) remembered a formidable Glasgow landlady, Mrs Currie of the Black Boy Tavern in the Gallowgate (afterwards Mrs Jardine of the Buck's Head Inn) washing or bleaching in an old house or barn in Fleshers' Close, on the edge of Glasgow Green. While she was doing this, she bantered with groups of nude male bathers in the Clyde 'with whom she delighted to give and take jokes'. She was noted for 'the size and rotundity of her person' and served 'excellent Burgundy' and chops to her favoured clients. Another well-known Glasgow landlady was Mrs Hunter in the Trongate near the Tontine Inn. She served 'rizzard haddies, Welsh rabbits or poached eggs', washed down by pots of ale. She was described as 'a fine matronly old person' but the main attraction for young men was 'Bonnie Jean' the barmaid.[119]

When James Graham of the Saracen Head and the Black Bull in Glasgow died in 1771, his widow Jean (formerly Leckie) took over the business. She was a person of some consequence 'who was highly respected in Glasgow, who visited the first families in the city and who also received visits from them on a footing of equality'.' Her social status was put at risk, however, when she made an unfortunate second marriage to a penniless young man called Buchanan who claimed 'genteel connections'.[120]

Another widowed landlady featured in John Galt's *Annals of the Parish* (1821) set in the fictional Ayrshire parish of Dalmailing. Galt recounts the activities of the widowed Mrs McVicar, in the year 1779, who

> kept a cloth shop and sold plaidings and flannels, besides Yorkshire super-fines, and was used to the sudden incoming of strangers, especially visitants, both from the West and the North Highlands, and was withal a gawsy furthy woman, taking great pleasure in hospitality . . . She would not allow of such a thing as our being lodgers in her house, but was so cagey to see us . . . that nothing less would content her that we must live upon her.[121]

In the Fife burgh of Cupar, there were significant numbers of female brewers (eight) and innkeepers throughout the eighteenth century. There were some twenty-five female innkeepers or vintners, and at least eight of them were the widows of innkeepers. Mary Anderson, a former innkeeper, left five decanters, twenty-one horn spoons and three punch ladles in her 1797 inventory. Another female innkeeper, Mary Ross, had twenty-five chairs, eighteen stone plates, fifteen decanters, and three punchbowls in her inventory of 1797. When the town council held its annual election dinner, in twenty-five years out of sixty it was held in an inn run by a woman, and a recent historian of Cupar concluded 'some of the best inns seem to have been kept by women'.[122]

Some landladies were accused of using their good looks to their advantage in their business. In West Lothian, the Bonny Lass of Livingstone 'kept a public house at a place called the High House of Livingstone ... she was esteemed handsome and knew how to turn her charms to the best account'.[123] A French traveller stayed in 'a dreadful inn' in Oldmeldrum, Aberdeenshire, in 1786, which was redeemed for him by the attractive landlady and her daughter, 'our hostess is beautiful, with a very pretty daughter, who waits on us very good natured. So, although we are extremely ill-accommodated, we pass the time very good-natured.'[124]

WOMEN USING PUBS AND TAVERNS

At the beginning of the century, Edinburgh taverns catered for a wide clientele, from tradesmen and shopkeepers to anti-Union politicians who met in Patrick Steil's Cross Keys Tavern in the High Street, colloquially known as Pate Steil's Parliament. It was here that the Edinburgh Musical Society, the first regular society of amateur musicians in Scotland, was founded in 1728, and it was claimed that 'ladies of good rank' occasionally joined 'oyster parties' in these taverns.[125] Edward Topham, an English visitor, described being invited to an oyster cellar by an Edinburgh lady in 1779 where he joined a large mixed party of men and women who were drinking porter and eating oysters. After supper, the tables were cleared and a large bowl of brandy punch was produced. This was followed by a dance, the reel being the most popular choice of dance. At smaller supper parties, Topham found that elite Edinburgh women drank more than English women of a similar social status, 'During the supper, which continues for some time, the Scotch Ladies drink more wine than an English woman could well bear; but the climate requires it, and probably in some measure it may enliven their natural vivacity.' He was charmed by the women singing at the end of the meal.[126]

Elite women were also associated with a select group of inns in Glasgow in the second half of the eighteenth century, along with members of the aristocracy and landed gentry. Glasgow merchants sent their daughters to receive lessons in cookery from the head chefs at the Saracen Head and the Black Bull Inn. Each girl paid the considerable sum of 5 shillings a head to learn how to cook and serve a dinner. A great charity dinner took place at the Saracen Head in 1779 'at which many of the neighbouring nobility and country gentry were present'. They were surprised to see 'fifteen or sixteen elegant young cooks, with white aprons' acting as waitresses. On being informed 'they were all young ladies', some of the younger male guests began to flirt with them and went down to the kitchens to help out.[127]

'LEWD AND IMMORAL PRACTICES' – CRIME AND MISBEHAVIOUR

Rather like heavy drug use spawning theft and crime to pay for an expensive addiction, dram shops, tippling huts and ale houses, which sold cheap whisky, could have the same effect, and provided meeting places for petty criminals and others. In urban areas, such as Edinburgh, they could also be used as bases for prostitution, often accompanied by petty theft. The link between drinking houses and prostitution was a Europe-wide phenomenon, with cities such as Venice, Florence, Siena, Seville, Augsburg, Dijon and London all opening official brothels between 1350 and 1500.[128] Allan Ramsay's remarkably explicit poem *Lucky Spence's Last Advice* (1718) is set in the form of the dying words of an Edinburgh 'Lucky' who kept a well-known brothel/tavern in the Canongate, near Holyrood.[129] It is a biting social satire in vernacular Scots, written in the 'habbie' stanza, but stands in a long European literary tradition of drawing comparisons between the workings of high society and the brothel.[130] The dying 'Lucky' exhorts her 'girls' to get the customer drunk and unconscious as quickly as possible, then rob him, using such broad sexual euphemisms as, 'light his match at your spunk box':

> Whan he's asleep, then dive and catch
> His ready cash, his rings or watch;
> And gin he likes to light his match
> At your spunk box,
> Ne'er stand to let the fumbling wretch
> E'en take the pox.
>
> Cleek a' ye can be hook or crook,
> Ryp ilky poutch frae nook to nook;
> Be sure to truff his pocket-book,
> Saxty pounds Scots,
> Is nae deaf nits:*
> In little book
> Lie great bank-notes.[131]
>
> * 'is nae deaf nits' = is no small thing

The reality behind Ramsay's poetry is revealed in court cases such as that of Elisabeth Alexander, an Edinburgh tavern or lodging-house keeper, who in 1737 was accused of robbery by George de Jardeen, a Frenchman. He and two 'loose vagrant women' had been housed in a private room in Alexander's tavern where he was plied with drink until he passed out, then robbed of twelve guineas, which was shared between the three women. Earlier in the century, the church was concerned about Edinburgh taverners 'who keep cellars and women servants therein [the cellars being in one part of the city and their dwelling houses at a considerable distance in another part of the city]' because they would be unable to supervise what went on.[132]

This is the world of Robert Burns's poem, 'The Jolly Beggars', written some time after 1785, and set in Poosie Nansie's Inn in Mauchline, Ayrshire, with a cast of down-and-outs, 'randie gangrel bodies', including a disabled soldier, his lover, a Highland widow, a fiddler, a tinker and 'a bard of no regard'. The penultimate verse of the poem and its chorus mocks accepted Presbyterian virtues such as self-denial, sobriety, moderation and industriousness, which have little meaning for the dispossessed:

> Life is all a variorum,
> We regard not how it goes;
> Let them cant about decorum,
> Who have character to lose,
> *Chorus*
> A fig for those by law protected!
> Liberty's a glorious feast!
> Courts for Cowards were erected,
> Churches built to please the priest.[133]

The reality behind this fictionalised account of Ayrshire lowlife could be brutal and misogynistic. In March 1786, Jean Armour's fifteen-year-old brother, Adam, was involved in a violent assault on Agnes Wilson, a prostitute working at Poosie Nansie's Inn in Mauchline. Agnes was forced to 'Ride the Stang', a form of mob justice that made the victim ride through the streets on a wooden pole, a practice reserved for cuckolds, henpecked husbands, prostitutes or adulterers. The assault was recorded in the minutes of the local kirk session which condemned Agnes Wilson, who seems to have been injured during the event, for 'lewd and immoral practices'.[134]

CONTROL, LICENSING AND REGULATION

There were obvious dangers of crime, misbehaviour and public disorder if drinking places were badly run, and they also offered valuable

Figure 2.4 Interior, Poosie Nansie's Inn, Mauchline, Ayrshire. The setting for Burns's poem, *The Jolly Beggars*. © Anthony and Judith Cooke.

opportunities for raising revenue through taxing drink and drink-related businesses. Because of this, public houses, inns, ale houses and taverns were controlled through a system of licensing by burgh magistrates in towns and by Justices of the Peace in the countryside. After the Union, licensing laws were imposed on Scotland by an Act of 1756 which brought Scotland into line with England where licences from JPs were required to sell ale, beer or other liquors.[135] Spirit licences were particular targets for control by the authorities, though their application to the task varied greatly from parish to parish. Sometimes, restrictions were brought about by pricing the licence fee too highly for many licensees, though there was always the danger of spirit houses going underground without a licence. In the burgh of Stirling, there was a reduction in the number of licensed ale houses from ninety-four in 1782 to sixty-eight in 1790, caused by an increase in the licence fee from £1/1s in 1782 to £1/11s in 1790.[136]

In the Highlands, a paternalistic landowner could have a considerable effect on the drinking behaviour of his tenants through control of licences. On Speyside, in the parish of Duthil and Rothiemurchus, the proprietor, Sir James Grant, intervened in the late 1780s to restrict sales of whisky, 'a beverage which seems fit only for demons'. Though there were still ten houses selling whisky in a thinly populated parish, the numbers had been considerably reduced, as 'they were suppressed by the proprietor' on seeing their bad effects.[137] The Grant family was involved in a similar exercise in social control in the planned village of Grantown in Inverness-shire where 'many public houses, by the general resolution of the counties concerned, have of late been suppressed; and there are at present only 4 ... Two of these are on the turnpike road, for the accommodation of travellers.'[138]

CLUBS AND SOCIETIES

One response to the problems created by rapid social and cultural change was the formation of clubs, associations and societies which often arose out of informal networks in taverns and pubs. The defining characteristics of these organisations were 'a set of rules, a declared purpose and a membership defined by some formal act of joining'.[139] They provided mutual support, friendship, information networks and, for recently arrived migrants, a public space where they could meet others of a similar background and find work or accommodation. For young men, they could provide an entry ticket into the world of work and, for older ones, inside information on new jobs and promotion in their chosen trade or profession.

Clark has claimed that in this period, 'inns, taverns, coffee houses and alehouses lodged an ever increasing number and variety of clubs and societies'. He argued that, in both Scotland and Ireland, societies for improvement were motivated, at least in part, by the desire to catch up with England both economically and culturally. Dublin copied Scotland, as did colonial North America, where the Scot, Alexander Hamilton, who moved to Annapolis, founded a Tuesday Club along the lines of the Whinbush Club in Glasgow. Scotland also had considerable influence on the associational life of Philadelphia.[140] In other words, clubs, societies and associations played an important role in the formation and development of civil society on both sides of the Atlantic.[141]

From 1750 onwards, there was a rapid growth in the number of clubs, associations and societies in urban centres such as Aberdeen, Edinburgh and Glasgow. In Edinburgh, there were as many as two hundred or more societies, many of which met in inns or taverns. Their social composition ranged from the aristocratic Society for the Improvers of Knowledge of Agriculture (1723), through the Select Society for Promoting the

Reading and Speaking of the English Language in Scotland (1754), largely composed of lawyers, clergymen, university staff, students and doctors, to the Lawnmarket Club, an organisation of Edinburgh wool traders which met at seven in the morning in a tavern to exchange gossip and market news over brandy.[142] Alexander Carlyle claimed that the conversation at the Select Society 'rubbed off all corners ... and made the literati of Edinburgh less captious and pedantic than they were elsewhere'.[143]

Clubs and associations often began in taverns, then moved out and purchased or rented their own premises as they became more formalised and socially exclusive. This was the case with the Musical Society of Edinburgh, instituted in 1728 with seventy members, which had its origins in a weekly music club that met at the Cross Keys Tavern where they played 'concertos and sonatas of Corelli' and 'the overtures of Handel'. The tavern was kept by Patrick Steil 'a great lover of musick and a good singer of Scots songs'. Eventually the weekly concerts became so successful that, in 1762, the Musical Society was able to build its own concert hall which could seat five hundred people in exclusive 'ticket only' concerts.[144]

Edinburgh pubs and taverns were not as 'democratic' as has sometimes been claimed. There was a recognised hierarchy of drinking places, and certain occupations frequently predominated in a particular inn or tavern. Even within taverns, there was often a hierarchy of rooms, such as at Dawney Douglas's tavern in Anchor Close where the rooms reflected a socially varied clientele who were kept apart in different rooms. Top of the hierarchy was the Crown Room, 'a fine apartment lit by two large windows and adorned with a handsome fireplace'. Ceremonial dinners were held here, and the Crochallan Fencibles held their meetings here. Their members included Adam Smith, Adam Fergusson, the law lords Hailes and Mondboddo, and Robert Burns who wrote the *Merry Muses of Caledonia* for this group.[145]

In Glasgow, there was also a rapid growth in the number of associations, clubs and societies.[146] Alexander Carlyle arrived in Glasgow in 1743 at the age of twenty-one to study theology, having previously studied in Edinburgh. He joined a literary club which met once a week 'in Mr Dugald's tavern near the Cross' and was patronised by students, merchants and visiting ministers. The members 'drank a little punch after our beefsteaks and pancakes and the expense never exceeded 1s 6d, seldom 1s'.[147] The Glasgow tobacco merchants formed the Hodge Podge Club in May 1752 which met in a tavern once a fortnight at 7.00 p.m. The club members played whist and the meeting time was moved forward to 5.00 p.m., with a hot supper of sirloin, accompanied by rum punch, served at 9.00 p.m.[148] Further down the social scale, the records of the Weavers' Society of Anderston, Glasgow reveal that, in 1773, the Deacon provided a double glass of whisky for members at the close of meetings and the Collector served a whisky rum at his house.[149]

In Aberdeen, the Philosophical Society (the Wise Club) was founded in 1758 and met in taverns once a fortnight. Its membership was mainly composed of the professoriat at King's and Marischal Colleges, and included Dr Thomas Reid, Dr John Gregory and the poet, James Beattie. The bills record payment for punch, port, porter, supper and pipes and tobacco.[150]

Clubs, associations and societies, together with subscription hospitals, missionary or benevolent societies, were important elements in the formation of middle-class identity and, together with higher-status housing and landownership, often helped to negotiate access to urban municipal power.[151] Though the period saw rapid urban growth, by the end of the eighteenth century, Scottish towns and cities were still relatively compact geographically, culturally and socially. Most of the urban elite, as well as artisans and craftsmen, still lived close to the centre of the burgh and were linked to each other through family networks or a common educational or occupational background.[152] In addition, the cramped living conditions in many Scottish towns, meant that men from both elite and artisan backgrounds were anxious to escape their homes and seek male conviviality in taverns, alehouses and coffee houses. Change was on the way, however.

NOTES

1. N. Tranter, 'Demography', in A. J. Cooke, I. Donnachie, A. MacSween and C. A. Whatley (eds), *Modern Scottish History, 1707 to the Present*, Vol. I, *The Transformation of Scotland, 1707–1850* (2nd edition, East Linton, 2001), pp. 112–13.
2. I. D. Whyte, *Scotland Before the Industrial Revolution, c.1050–c.1750* (London, 1995), p. 172.
3. J. de Vries, *European Urbanisation, 1500–1800* (London, 1984), p. 39. See also T. M. Devine, 'Scotland', in P. Clark (ed.), *Cambridge Urban History of Britain*, Vol. II, *1540–1840* (Cambridge, 2000), pp. 151–66.
4. T. C. Smout, *A History of the Scottish People, 1560–1830* (London, 1969), p. 260.
5. S. Nenadic, 'Necessities: Food and Clothing in the Long Eighteenth Century', in E. Foyster and C. A. Whatley (eds), *A History of Everyday Life in Scotland, 1600 to 1800* (Edinburgh, 2010), p. 137.

6. D. Defoe, *A Tour Through the Whole Island of Great Britain* (London, 1971), pp. 578, 604–6, 632–3, 651 and 654. See also T. C. Smout, *Scottish Trade on the Eve of the Union* (Edinburgh, 1963).

7. I. Donnachie, *A History of the Brewing Industry in Scotland* (Edinburgh, 1979), p. 6.

8. National Records of Scotland (NRS), Court of Session Papers, CS 236/A/1/19, James Auchmouty and John Veitch *v.* The Brewers of Fife, 1698.

9. A. K. Bell Library, Perth, Perth and Kinross Archives (PKA), B 59/29/42/3, List of brewers in Perth, 31 October 1718.

10. R. A. Houston, *Social Change in the Age of Enlightenment: Edinburgh, 1660–1760* (Oxford, 1994), p. 368.

11. P. Martin, *Cupar, The History of a Small Scottish Town* (Edinburgh, 2006), p. 85.

12. R. Chambers, *Domestic Annals of Scotland*, Vol. III, *From the Revolution to the Rebellion of 1745* (Edinburgh, 1861), pp. 271–3. On the different and competing legal and administrative boundaries in Edinburgh see Houston, *Social Change in the Age of Enlightenment*, pp. 105–21.

13. For the power of the Argyll dynasty at this time see M. Fry, 'Politics', in Cooke et al. (eds), *Modern Scottish History 1707 to the Present*, Vol. I, *The Transformation of Scotland, 1707–1850* (East Linton, 1998), pp. 43–62; and A. I. Macinnes, *Clanship, Commerce and the House of Stuart, 1603–1788* (East Linton, 1996), pp. 164–5.

14. *Domestic Annals of Scotland*, Vol. III, p. 271.

15. R. Crawford, *The Bard. Robert Burns, a Biography* (London, 2009), p. 93.

16. Houston, *Social Change in the Age of Enlightenment*, p. 212.

17. Sir J. Sinclair (ed.), *The (Old) Statistical Account of Scotland (OSA)*, Vol. X, *Fife* (Bradford, 1978), p. 131.

18. *OSA*, Vol. VIII, *Argyll* (Bradford, 1983), pp. 78–9.

19. *OSA*, Vol. XVI, *Banffshire, Moray and Nairnshire* (Bradford, 1982), p. 164.

20. A. J. Cooke, I. Donnachie, A. MacSween and C. A. Whatley (eds), *Modern Scottish History, 1707 to the Present*, Vol. 5, *Major Documents* (East Linton, 1998), p. 7, The Articles of the Treaty of Union, 1707.

21. J. B. Salmond, *Wade in Scotland* (Edinburgh, 1934), p. 56.

22. R. Reid (Senex), *Glasgow Past and Present*, Vol. 1 (Glasgow, 1884); Smout, *History of the Scottish People*, p. 226; and C. A. Whatley, *Scottish Society, 1707–1830* (Manchester, 2000), pp. 60–1, 162–3 and 204.

23. J. Gibson, *A History of Glasgow* (Glasgow, 1777), pp. 156–61.

24. T. C. F. Brotchie, *The History of Govan* (Govan, 1905), p. 59.

25. *Glasgow Past and Present*, Vol. II (1884), p. 170.

26. OSA, Vol. XIV, *Kincardineshire and South and West Aberdeenshire* (Bradford, 1982), p. 339.

27. NRS, Campbell of Jura Papers, GD 64/1/86/7, Rental of Archibald Campbell of Jura, 1764.
28. R. A. Dodgshon, 'Everyday Structures, Rhythms and Spaces in the Scottish Countryside', in E. Foyster and C. A. Whatley (eds), *A History of Everyday Life in Scotland, 1600 to 1800* (Edinburgh, 2010), p. 34.
29. Dundee City Archives (DCA), Maltmen Incorporation of Dundee, GD HF/M/8/3, Letter from Maltmen of Dundee to Mr James Smyth, WS, regarding multures on malt, 24 November 1744.
30. DCA, GD HF/M/8/3, Letter dated 24 November 1744.
31. NRS, Court of Session, CS 233/M/2/27, Maltmen of Glasgow *v.* Robert Tennant, 1749. See also Glasgow University Archives, Scottish Brewing Archives, T29/23, Testament of Robert Tennent, Maltman of Glasgow, 1749.
32. H. Arnot, *The History of Edinburgh* (Edinburgh, 1779), p. 354.
33. Interview with Jonathan Stewart, Dundee, 4 and 13 September 2013.
34. G. Stewart, *Curiosities of Glasgow Citizenship* (Glasgow, 1881), pp. 101–2. See also A. Hook and R. B. Sher (eds), *The Glasgow Enlightenment* (East Linton, 1995); and T. M. Devine and G. Jackson (eds), *Glasgow* Vol. 1, *Beginnings to 1830* (Manchester, 1995).
35. Houston, *Social Change in the Age of Enlightenment*, pp. 40–1.
36. J. Strang, *Glasgow and Its Clubs* (Glasgow, 1864), pp. 1–2.
37. Barrie, *City of Dundee*, p. 91; and Hartwich, *Ale an' A'Thing*, p. 25.
38. A. Hopkins, *The Aberdeen Pub Companion* (Aberdeen, 1975), pp. 80–1.
39. A. Gibson and T. C. Smout, 'Scottish Food and Scottish history', in R. A. Houston and I. D. Whyte (eds), *Scottish Society, 1500–1800* (Cambridge, 1989), p. 67.
40. PKA, Perth Burgh Records, PE 23 Bundle 26, Account of the Commissioners for the Bridge of Perth, 1767. A Chopin is an old Scots measure containing about an English quart (1.13 litres), a Mutchkin three-quarters of an imperial pint (0.43 litre) and a Gill a small measure of spirits. See also I. A. Robertson, 'The Earl of Kinnoull's Bridge: the construction of the Bridge of Tay at Perth, 1763–72', *Scottish Economic and Social History*, Vol. 6, 1986, pp. 18–32.
41. J. Myles, *Rambles in Forfarshire* (Dundee, 1850), p. 23.
42. W. Scott, *Guy Mannering* (Edinburgh, 1886), p. 34.
43. T. Pennant, *A Tour in Scotland and Voyage to the Hebrides 1772* (Edinburgh, 1998), p. 415.
44. T Pennant, *A Tour in Scotland, 1769* (Perth, 1979), pp. 186–7.
45. *OSA*, Vol. XIX, *Orkney and Shetland* (Bradford, 1978), p. 271.
46. Pennant, *Tour in Scotland 1772*, p. 272.
47. *Traditions of Perth*, pp. 32–3.
48. *OSA*, Vol. IX, *Dunbartonshire, Stirlingshire and Clackmannanshire*, p. 375.
49. *OSA*, Vol. VII, *Lanarkshire and Renfrewshire*, pp. 210–11.

50. J. de Vries, *The Industrious Revolution, Consumer Behavior and the Household Economy, 1650 to the Present* (Cambridge, 2008), p. 165.
51. P. Clark (ed.), *European Cities and Towns, 400–2000* (Oxford, 2009), p. 147.
52. *OSA*, Vol. II, *Lothian*, p. 47.
53. *OSA*, Vol. II, p. 33.
54. D. McLaren, *The Rise and Progress of Whisky Drinking in Scotland* (Glasgow, 1858), pp. 21–2.
55. A. Brown, *A History of Glasgow* (Glasgow, 1795), p. 272.
56. Brown, *History of Glasgow*, p. 73.
57. Pennant, *Tour in Scotland, 1769*, p. 231.
58. *Glasgow Past and Present*, Vol. II (1884), p. 177.
59. Gibson, *History of Glasgow*, pp. 224–32.
60. Arnot, *History of Edinburgh*, pp. 520–1.
61. Brown, *History of Glasgow*, pp. 128–9.
62. J. D. Marwick, *The River Clyde and the Clyde Burghs* (Glasgow, 1909), p. 140.
63. A. Carlyle, *Autobiography* (Edinburgh, 1860), pp. 308–9.
64. Arnot, *History of Edinburgh*, pp. 348 and 586.
65. Gibson, *History of Glasgow*, pp. 213–22.
66. Nenadic, 'Food and Clothing in the Long Eighteenth Century', in Foyster and Whatley (eds), *A History of Everyday Life in Scotland*, Vol. 2, p. 154.
67. H. Cockburn, *Memorials of his Time* (Edinburgh, 1856), p. 35.
68. D. G. Lockhart, 'Planned Village Development in Scotland and Ireland', in T. M. Devine and D. Dickson (eds), *Ireland and Scotland, 1600–1850; Parallels and Contrasts in Economic and Social Development* (Edinburgh, 1983).
69. D. G. Lockhart, *Scottish Planned Villages* (Edinburgh, 2012), p. 37.
70. *OSA*, Vol. V, *Stewartry of Kirkcudbrightshire and Wigtownshire*, pp. 138–41.
71. T. C. Smout, 'The Landowner and the Planned Village in Scotland, 1730–1830', in N. Phillipson and R. Mitchison (eds), *Scotland in the Age of Improvement* (Edinburgh, 1970), p. 94.
72. *OSA*, Vol. XIV, *Kincardineshire and South and West Aberdeenshire*, p. 166.
73. *OSA*, Vol. XVII, *Inverness-shire, Ross and Cromarty* (Bradford, 1981), p. 42.
74. T. C. Smout, 'Lead-mining in Scotland, 1650–1850', in P. L. Payne (ed.), *Studies in Scottish Business History* (London, 1967), pp. 103–35.
75. *OSA*, Vol. VII, *Lanarkshire*, pp. 215–16.
76. *OSA*, Vol. V, *Kirkcudbrightshire*, p. 155.
77. But see I. McCraw, *The Fairs of Dundee* (Dundee, 1994); and D. K. Cameron, *The Ballad and the Plough* (Edinburgh, 1997), pp. 94–101.

78. A. M. Kinghorn and A. Law (eds), *Poems by Allan Ramsay and Robert Fergusson* (Edinburgh, 1985), p. 133. See also C. MacLachlan (ed.), *Before Burns, Eighteenth Century Scottish Poetry* (Edinburgh, 2000), p. 225.
79. Baron Faujas de St Fond, *A Journey Through England and Scotland to the Hebrides in 1784* (Glasgow, 1907), Vol. 1, p. 224.
80. Scarfe, *To the Highlands in 1786*, p. 219.
81. M. Martin, *A Description of the Western Islands of Scotland, c.1695* (Edinburgh, 1994), pp. 146 and 294–5.
82. E. Burt, *Letters from a Gentleman in the North of Scotland, 1754* (Edinburgh, 1998).
83. Reid, *Glasgow Past and Present*, Vol. II, p. 172.
84. Burt, *Letters,* p. 297.
85. D. Walker, 'Inns, hotels and related building types', in G. Stell, J. Shaw and S. Stonier (eds), *Scottish Life and Society. A Compendium of Scottish Ethnology*, Vol. 3, *Scotland's Buildings* (East Linton, 2003), p. 131.
86. A. Fenton, 'The Food of the Scots', in Fenton (ed.), *Scottish Life and Society. A Compendium of Scottish Ethnology*, Vol. 5 (Edinburgh, 2007), p. 128.
87. Pennant, *A Tour in Scotland, 1769*, p. 80.
88. H. Jackson, *Neil Gow's Inver* (Perth, 2000), pp. 102–3.
89. A. I. Macinnes, *Clanship, Commerce and the House of Stuart, 1603–1788* (East Linton, 1996), pp. 210–21.
90. S. Johnson, *A Journey to the Western Islands, 1773* (London, 1984), pp. 57–8, 66–7 and 71.
91. Pennant, *Tour in Scotland 1772*, p. 418.
92. See L. Leneman, *Living in Atholl: A Social History of the Estates, 1685–1785* (Edinburgh, 1986); and A. J. Cooke, *Stanley. From Arkwright Village to Commuter Suburb, 1784–2003* (Perth, 2003), pp. 13–18.
93. NRS, Breadalbane Estate Papers, GD 112/11/1/4/75, Memorial by John Thomson for the proposed change house at Ardeonaig, Lochtayside, 1786.
94. St Fond, *Journey Through England and Scotland*, Vol. 1, pp. 230–1.
95. M. S. Moss and J. R. Hume, *The Making of Scotch Whisky* (Edinburgh, 1981), p. 37.
96. *Complete Works of Burns*, p. 137.
97. Scarfe (ed.), *To the Highlands in 1786*, pp. 166–7, 184 and 189.
98. A. J. Durie (ed.), *Travels in Scotland, 1788–1881* (Woodbridge, 2012), p. 39.
99. Perth and Kinross Archives (PKA), PE 42/Bundle 65, Perth Burgh Licensing Court, Licences allowing the sale of ale, beer etc. In Perth, 1772.
100. Martin, *Cupar*, p. 72.
101. Martin, *Cupar*, pp. 72–3.
102. See Crawford, *The Bard*, p. 208.

103. *The Works and Correspondence of Robert Burns* (Glasgow, n.d.), p. 138.
104. L. Colley, *Captives. Britain, Empire and the World, 1600–1850* (London, 2002), p. 188.
105. Stuart, *Old Edinburgh Taverns*, p. 35.
106. Stuart, *Old Edinburgh Taverns*, p. 43.
107. *Works and Correspondence of Robert Burns*, p. 89.
108. NRS, Glasgow Commissary Court, Wills and Probate Inventories, CC 9/7/68/247, Principal Will and Testament of James Graham, vintner in Glasgow, 12 March 1772, CC 9/7/68/371, Probate Inventory of James Graham, 20 August 1772, CC 9/7/71/158, Principal Probate Inventory of James Graham, 1 November 1779.
109. R. Reid (Senex), *Glasgow Past and Present*, Vol. I (Glasgow, 1884), pp. 90–1.
110. Reid, *Glasgow Past and Present*, Vol. I, pp. 81–4.
111. P. Clark, *British Clubs and Societies, 1580–1800. The Origins of an Associational World* (Oxford, 2000), p. ix. See also C. Withers, *Urban Highlanders: Highland–Lowland Migration and Urban Gaelic Culture* (East Linton, 1998).
112. Stuart, *Old Edinburgh Taverns*, p. 90.
113. MacLachlan (ed.), *Eighteenth Century Scottish Poetry*, p. 34. See also J. Bruce-Gardyne and J. Skinner, *Rebus's Favourite. The Deuchars Guide to Edinburgh Pubs* (London, 2007), p. 9; and Stuart, *Old Edinburgh Taverns*, p. 135.
114. MacLachlan (ed.), *Eighteenth Century Scottish Poetry*, pp. x and 31; Stuart, *Old Edinburgh Taverns*, pp. 92 and 103; and Carruthers, 'Culture', in Cooke et al. (eds), *Modern Scottish History*, Vol. I, pp. 253–74.
115. Kinghorn and Law (eds), *Poems by Allan Ramsay and Robert Fergusson*, p. 11.
116. Kinghorn and Law (eds), p. 177.
117. Hopkins, *Aberdeen Pub Companion*, p. 5.
118. Penny, *Traditions of Perth*, p. 25.
119. Reid, *Glasgow Past and Present*, Vol. II, pp. 171–5; and *Minute Book of the Board of Green Cloth, 1809–1820* (Glasgow, 1891), pp. 166–7. See also the autobiography of Robert Reid in *Glasgow Past and Present*, Vol. III, pp. 489–96.
120. Reid, *Glasgow Past and Present*, Vol. I, pp. 343–4.
121. J. Galt, *Annals of the Parish* (Edinburgh, 1919), p. 134.
122. Martin, *Cupar*, pp. 72–3.
123. *OSA*, Vol. II, *Lothian*, pp. 800–1.
124. Scarfe (ed.), *To the Highlands in 1786*, p. 154.
125. Chambers, *Traditions of Edinburgh*, p. 156; Chambers, *Domestic Annals of Scotland*, Vol. III, p. 576; and Clark, *British Clubs and Societies*, p. 80.
126. E. Topham, *Letters from Edinburgh, 1774 and 1775* (Edinburgh, 2003), pp. 28 and 51–3.

127. Reid, *Glasgow Past and Present*, Vol. I, p. 344

128. Clark (ed.), *European Cities and Towns*, pp. 55–6.

129. For a commentary on this poem, see Carruthers, 'Culture', in Cooke et al. (eds), *Modern Scottish History*, Vol. 1, pp. 255–6.

130. See, for example, the work of the great French poet François Villon (1431–*c*.1460?), in A. Bonner (trans.), *The Complete Works of François Villon* (New York, 1960), particularly his 'Ballade de la Grosse Margot' ('Ballad for Fat Margot'), or Lear's speech in *King Lear*, Act 4, Scene 6.

131. The poem is reprinted in full as Document 68 in Cooke, et al. (eds), *Modern Scottish History*, Vol. 5, *Major Documents* (East Linton, 1998), pp. 137–9.

132. Houston, *Social Change in the Age of Enlightenment: Edinburgh*, pp. 95 and 160.

133. Quoted in Crawford, *The Bard*, pp. 199–200. The poem is given in full as 'The Jolly Beggars. A Cantata', in *The Complete Works of Robert Burns Illustrated* (Glasgow, n.d.), pp. 132–6.

134. Crawford, *The Bard*, pp. 208–9. For 'Riding the Stang' see Cooke, *From Popular Enlightenment to Lifelong Learning*, p. 73; and E. P. Thompson, *Customs in Common* (London, 1991), pp. 472–9.

135. G. B. Wilson, *Alcohol and the Nation* (London, 1940), pp. 117–18.

136. *OSA*, Vol. IX, *Dunbartonshire, Stirlingshire and Clackmannanshire*, p. 628.

137. *OSA*, Vol. XVI, *Banffshire, Moray and Nairnshire*, p. 520.

138. *OSA*, Vol. XVII, *Inverness-shire, Ross and Cromarty*, p. 43.

139. R. J. Morris, 'Clubs, societies and associations', in F. M. L. Thompson (ed.), *The Cambridge Social History of Britain, 1750–1950*, Vol. 3, *Social agencies and institutions* (Cambridge, 1990), p. 395.

140. Clark, *British Clubs and Societies*, pp. ix and 85–7.

141. R. B. Sher and J. R. Smithers (eds), *Scotland and America in the Age of Enlightenment* (Edinburgh, 1990).

142. Stuart, *Old Edinburgh Taverns*, p. 20.

143. Carlyle, *Autobiography*, p. 298.

144. Arnot, *History of Edinburgh*, p. 379.

145. R. Chambers, *Traditions of Edinburgh* (Edinburgh, 1856 edition), p. 159.

146. See A. Hook and R. B. Sher (eds), *The Glasgow Enlightenment* (East Linton, 1995). See also S. Nenadic, 'The middle ranks and modernisation', and R. B. Sher, 'Commerce, religion and the enlightenment in eighteenth century Glasgow', both in T. M. Devine and G. Jackson (eds), *Glasgow*. Vol. I, *Beginnings to 1830* (Manchester, 1995), pp. 278–311 and 312–59.

147. Carlyle, *Autobiography*, p. 77.

148. Strang, *Glasgow and its Clubs*, pp. 38–40.

149. J. M. Taylor (ed.), *Weavers' Society of Anderston* (Glasgow, 1879), p. 22.

150. Hopkins, *Aberdeen Pub Companion*, pp. 4–5.

151. S. Nenadic, 'The Rise of the Urban Middle Class', in T. M. Devine and R. Mitchison (eds), *People and Society in Scotland*, Vol. I, *1760–1830* (Edinburgh, 1988), pp. 109–26. See also A. J. Cooke, 'The Scottish Cotton Masters, 1780–1914', *Textile History,* Vol. XL, No. 1, 2009, pp. 29–50.

152. R. B. Sher, *Church and University in the Scottish Enlightenment. The Moderate Literati of Edinburgh* (Edinburgh, 1985), p. 28; and A. Murdoch and R. Sher, 'Literary and Learned Culture', in Devine and Mitchison (eds), *People and Society in Scotland, 1760–1830*, pp. 127–42.

3

'Politeness and Agreeable Conviviality': Scottish Pubs and Increasing Social Segregation, 1790–1830

INTRODUCTION

FOR MOST OF THE period between 1790 and 1815 Britain was at war with France. This led to the recruitment of large numbers of men for the army and navy and the disruption of supplies of food and drink, including wine, brandy and rum, as well as other goods from mainland Europe, the Caribbean and North America. With the deposition of Louis XVI in September 1792, his execution the following year, and the formation of a French Republic along revolutionary principles, the authorities in Britain came down hard on any attempts by the lower orders or the middle classes to campaign for social and political change. The end of the French wars brought economic depression and hardship, as large numbers of demobilised soldiers and sailors returned home. This was the background to events, such as Peterloo (1819) and the Cato Street Conspiracy (1820) in England, and the Radical War (1820) in Scotland.

The fear of foreign invasion during the Napoleonic period led, in 1805, to an outburst of patriotism among the licensed trade in Perth. An association of Perth landlords was formed called 'The Loyal Perth Landlords' Defence against Invasion or No Accommodation for Napoleon'. Most of the pubs in the centre of Perth were members of this patriotic organisation, including the Ship Inn, the Salutation, the Black Cow, the Bluebell, the Ewe and Lamb, the King's Arms and no less than four Lions, Black, White, Red and Golden.[1]

RISING LIVING STANDARDS AND CHANGING TASTES

As living standards rose in the late eighteenth century, significant changes were taking place in the consumption of alcohol in Scotland. The consumption of whisky and strong ale increased at the expense of weak two-penny ale, and more wine and rum were drunk in middle-class households and taverns. By the 1790s, there was an increasing number of commercial breweries in Glasgow, and Glasgow-brewed porter was 'now much more drunk in public houses by tradesmen, than formerly' which had 'diminished the consumption of whisky'.[2] Porter was popular in Perth but mainly 'among the higher classes for their forenoon refreshment'.[3] A similar situation was found in Stirling where the poor drank small beer, 'a thin vapid, sour stuff', or whisky and 'the more opulent' drank English porter.[4] In Forfar, it was claimed that porter was now drunk by all levels of society down to the poorest. There had been a change in the 1770s from the widespread brewing of table beer by private families to the use of London porter which 'is now brought from London in great quantities and is becoming a common beverage with the lowest of the people'.[5]

The Reverend Abercromby Gordon, minister of Banff, boasted that the local brewery was well known for its strong ale, and that their porter, when bottled for a year, 'has been known to deceive the taste of a connoisseur'.[6] Porter was also enjoyed as a fashionable drink by the better-off in rural parishes, such as Kirkmichael in Ayrshire, where whisky was 'not esteemed a genteel drink in this corner. The general beverage, of late, among the better sort of farmer, is good porter, which they find to afford nourishment, as well as chearfulness, when moderately used.'[7]

By the late eighteenth century, brewing was becoming an integral part of the cash-based, market economy on a British-wide scale, with London-brewed porter enjoying pole position and becoming the fashionable drink of choice for more affluent beer drinkers across Britain.[8] Aberdeen had a large brewery, the Devanha, which, by the late 1790s, was brewing table beer, strong ale and superior porter. Aberdonians preferred to drink London porter, however, when they could afford it, 'such is the effect of prejudice'. Market specialisation was increasing, as Devanha strong ale was mainly exported to London and abroad, whereas Aberdeen was drinking London porter in preference to the home-brewed variety.[9]

Specialisation was also found on a more local and regional level, as at Inveresk in Midlothian, where the brewing of beer locally had declined in the 1790s, 'many families being now supplied with table beer from Leith or Prestonpans, which they find superior to that brewed here'.[10] From Forfar in Angus, it was reported in the same period that the local brewers were 'a flourishing class of men' but that their consumption of malt had declined since the recent rise in the drinking of London porter, 'from 1600 to 2000 bolls of malt are consumed annually but the consumpt of this article is lessened since the introduction of porter'.[11]

Contemporaries remarked on these changes in eating and drinking patterns, often but not always, censoriously. The Reverend Henry Stevenson of Blantyre in Lanarkshire commented in 1791 that there were now eight ale houses in the parish, whereas 'before the cotton and iron works found their way to us, there were only two or three alehouses', though he did not believe that they had had a detrimental effect on his parishioners who remained 'industrious, sober and contented'.[12] In the rapidly growing Barony parish of Glasgow, with a population of 18,451 in 1791, there were no less than 169 public houses selling ale and spirits. The Reverend John Burns attributed this to rising living standards but was more critical about their effects, 'from the great increase of wealth and the number of public houses for retailing spirituous liquors, intemperance, with its long train of evils, is becoming more prevalent amongst the labouring people'.[13] The Reverend John Bower, writing from the Lanarkshire textile, iron-smelting and mining centre of Old West Monkland, condemned the large number (thirty) of 'inns or public houses in the parish' but also believed they were an inevitable result of increasing wealth: 'Trade produces affluence: Affluence is the parent of luxury and dissipation, which infallibly undermines and dissolves the fabric.'[14] In the Ayrshire parish of Dalry, where there were over a hundred cotton weavers at work and where a hundred women and children prepared yarn for the loom, the local minister condemned the rising consumption of beer and whisky by 'those who can with ease earn from 2s to 3s a day; the prosperity of such persons often destroys them'.[15] Another Ayrshire weaving parish, Fenwick, had seen rising living standards, 'we are much more expensive in dress than 10 years ago', accompanied by an 'amazing' rise in the consumption of whisky.[16]

Ian Donnachie estimated that beer production in Scotland rose from 246,000 barrels [a barrel of beer is around 164 litres] in 1787 to peak at 437,000 barrels in 1799. Output then fell to average around 350,000 barrels a year until 1830. As the Scottish population was rising, this meant that per capita consumption of beer, which was 70 pints per head in 1795, reached a peak of 80 pints in 1800, then fell steadily to 48 pints by 1830. By contrast, the consumption of spirits in Scotland rose from an estimated 189,000 gallons (859, 950 litres) in 1780 to 1,670,000 (7,598,500) in 1800, 5,777,000 (26,285,350) in 1830, peaking at 6,935,000 (31,554,250) in 1850.[17]

Middle-class patterns of eating and drinking were also changing in line with rising living standards. In Edinburgh, wine was seldom seen at the tables of the 'middle rank of people' in 1763 but, thirty years later, 'every tradesman in decent circumstances presents wine after dinner; and many in plenty and variety'.[18] Increasing wine consumption might be expected in the affluent settings of the capital or in Glasgow's Merchant City but it was also found in small burghs, such as Lanark, where the magistrates formerly used to take 'a moderate meal with a few bottles of ale or porter and a dram or two; and in gala days, a little punch. Now [in 1792] they have superb entertainments, with punch, port or even claret.'[19] In Kelso in Roxburghshire, with a population of 4,324 in 1793, the annual consumption of excisable wines and spirits included 220 gallons (1,000 litres) of French wine and 2,560 gallons (11,648 litres) of 'Foreign wine, not French'.[20] Imports of French wine in this period were restricted by the French wars though import figures for Glasgow in the 1770s show a similar preponderance of non-French wine, mainly Portuguese. From the Angus burgh of Forfar, it was reported in 1792 that 'wine of various sorts, which was formerly brought from Dundee in dozens, and seldom used but as a medicine, is now imported in pipes [a pipe is about 105 imperial gallons], and is a very common drink at private as well as at public entertainments.'[21]

Inventories of Scottish inns in the early nineteenth century give details of stocks of drink which suggest that spirits, such as rum, brandy, gin and whisky, were more popular than wine or even beer. An inventory for John Begbie, an innkeeper in Kilmarnock, dated 1811, includes 36 gallons (164 litres) of rum, valued at £29, 30 gallons (136.5 litres) of brandy at £37, 10 gallons (45.5 litres) of Geneva (gin) at £12 and 56 gallons (255 litres) of whisky at £28. This contrasted with a modest eleven bottles of wine at just under £2 and thirteen bottles of claret at just under £4. Fortified wine was popular, with 270 bottles of port at £47, thirty-six of Madeira at £10 and 105 of sherry at £18. The cellars also contained a hogshead (238 litres) of rum valued at £51 and 5 hogs-heads (1,190 litres) of porter at £27, as well as bottled beer. This was a substantial inn with nine bedrooms and stables with three chaises, thirteen horses, a cow, a gig and harness. The inn displayed symbols of affluence, such as a looking glass, a sofa, a mahogany desk and an 'Eight day Clock and Case', together with a dozen silver spoons, a silver tureen, eighteen silver tea spoons and four dozen wine glasses. Begbie's debts came to a substantial £2,256.[22]

PUBS AS SPACES FOR COMMERCIAL AND BUSINESS TRANSACTIONS

Ale houses continued to provide space for commercial transactions in the countryside where there were few other public meeting places. From the Angus parish of Monikie, it was reported in 1790 that 'no business of any consequence can be transacted by the common people but in the ale-house'.[23] Another Angus parish, that of Dron on the outskirts of Dundee, had only three ale houses 'and these are at smiths' shops, places of general resort, where both the idle and the active meet. Everywhere they are the coffee houses of the parish, where all the news and reports in circulation . . . .are brought together from every quarter. Even the politics of the nation, are at times discussed here with freedom and decided on with confidence.'[24]

Taverns fulfilled the same role in towns, allowing people to trans-act their agricultural business, such as the sale of animals or grain. In Perth, Patrick Campbell of Edenchip, Lochearnhead, brought an action in 1790 against Charles Craigie, ale seller and drover in Perth, for £9 sterling over the price of a horse which Craigie had bought from John Campbell, vintner in Perth, who had been keeping the animal in his stables. In a complicated business transaction, the horse had not been sold by Patrick Campbell himself but by a relative, 'Mr Campbell younger of Achalader'. The two Campbells were high-status Highland landowners, who dealt with the affair through lawyers in Edinburgh. At the heart of the dispute was what price had been agreed for the horse between Charles Craigie, Perth ale seller and drover, and the intermedi-ary for the deal, the Perth vintner, John Campbell. The deal included a 'luck penny', a small sum returned for luck to the buyer by the seller. Another feature of the sale was drink being offered to seal the bargain. Achalader had said that, if Craigie paid £9 for the horse instead of his initial offer of £8/10s, he would give him 'as much out of that sum as would fill him drunk' to which Craigie had retorted 'the quantity of wine that would fill him drunk . . . would cost more than the odds that was betwixt them'.[25] This shows how urban centres acted as market-places for those living in the countryside, in this case from a considerable distance, and that wine, rather than ale or whisky, was the drink offered to seal the deal.

This period saw significant social changes taking place in the more economically advanced parts of the Scottish Lowlands, with higher-status groups withdrawing from the ale house into their own improved and enlarged private houses. In Kirkliston parish in West Lothian, it was claimed in 1792 that, in the last forty years, farmers 'have entirely departed from the pernicious custom of having their meetings for busi-ness or amusement in the public houses of the parish'. In this advanced and prosperous farming area, where farmers were building increas-ingly larger and more expensive houses, socially removed from their

workforce, 'they now meet in the family stile and conduct their entertainments with the sobriety and delicacy becoming family members'.[26]

Those lower down the social scale, however, continued to use pubs
and ale houses as places in which to transact business. Kilmacolm, in
Renfrewshire, had six ale houses in the village and three in the rest of
the parish, where 'the country people meet to transact their business and
spend the social hour. Their drink is generally small beer and whisky.'[27]
Similarly, in Neilston in Renfrewshire, there were nineteen inns or ale
houses, of which eight were in the village of Neilston. Their functions
were described as firstly 'to accommodate public meetings, or private
companies on necessary business' and secondly 'to entertain travellers
by day, and to lodge them and their horses, when overtaken by night'.[28]
Duffus, in Moray, had five or six houses for the sale of ale and whisky
in the parish, where 'the people resort when they are to transact business
either in selling or buying'.[29]

LIFE, COMMUNITY AND WORKPLACE RITUALS

In many rural areas of Scotland, the public house continued to play
an important role in life rituals such as births, courtship, marriage and
death. From Galston in Ayrshire, it was reported in the 1790s that:

> when a young man wishes to pay his addresses to his sweetheart, instead
> of going to her father's and asking his approval, he goes to a public house;
> and having let the landlady into the secret of his attachment, the object of
> his affection is immediately sent for, who never almost refuses to come.
> She is entertained with ale and whisky, or brandy; and the marriage is con-
> cluded on.[30]

In rural Perthshire, marriage contracts 'among the lower orders' were
generally drawn up in a public house. Country weddings often involved
inviting the whole parish to the ceremony and the guests had to ride
considerable distances on horseback to attend. When the bridal party
started out 'there was a halt made at every public house on the way, and
a quantity of spirits distributed'.[31] This was confirmed by the Reverend
James M'Diarmid, of Weem in Highland Perthshire, who reported that
the five ale or whisky houses in the parish in the 1790s were 'very little
frequented but at weddings, markets and other public meetings'.[32]

In the Aberdeenshire parish of Montquhitter, the Reverend Alexander
Johnston remembered the old-style penny bridal where two or three
hundred people convened at a tavern to celebrate a wedding 'at their
own expence for two or three days'. This had now gone out of fashion:

'the penny bridal is reprobated as an index of want of money and of want of taste'.[33] Similar customs were still to be found in the Highland parish of Kincardine, in Ross and Cromarty, where weddings and baptisms were a cause of great expense 'for the open hearted Highlander would not pass a public house, without entertaining those who attended him, to the number, perhaps of two thirds of a village, made up of his relatives and acquaintances'.[34]

Highland funerals and burial ceremonies were generally conducted on a large scale. In the parish of Alvie in Inverness-shire, the Reverend John Gordon condemned the heavy use of whisky by his parishioners, which meant that 'at their public meetings (such as burials &c) squabbles are too frequent; their fondness for spirits is owing to the easy access to it, there being no fewer than 13 houses in the parish where drams are sold without a county or excise licence'.[35] Funerals at Gairloch in Ross-shire were marked by people stopping work and the general dispensation of whisky.[36] At funerals at Tongue in Sutherland, refreshments were given out of whisky 'or some foreign liquor', while the food consisted of 'butter and cheese without bread'.[37]

Community rituals connecting pubs with the farming year included customs, such as that observed in New Machar, on the edge of Aberdeen, of holding 'malt feasts', in the local ale houses, where 'the farmers convened when the price of the malt became due and spent part of it encouraging their customers. This custom is now done away with, as there is little brewing done at home.' In another sign of the growth of a more affluent and market-based economy, it had been replaced by 'the gin shop in Aberdeen, when the people attend the weekly market'.[38] Work rituals involving alcohol could involve women as well as men. From Stornaway, in the Western Isles, it was reported that, every morning, the mistress of the house gave the servant girls 'a wine glass full of whisky'. Since the stoppage of the distilleries had taken place, this custom had been largely superseded by cash payments but 'in some families the dram is still given privately, to preserve peace and good order'.[39]

Pubs and ale houses also featured prominently in the work rituals of those employed in the 'new' manufacturing industries that were springing up across Scotland. Calico printing began to develop in favoured areas of Scotland towards the end of the eighteenth century. It was an industry dependent on taste and fashion and paid high wages to a skilled male elite of well-organised and unionised workers.[40] Campsie, in Stirlingshire, which had plentiful water supplies, was a centre of calico printing and, in 1793, it was reported that 'the quantity of liquor drunk in the seventeen public houses in the parish must be very great indeed; as I have been told that four or five pounds, at a reckoning, have been collected from a company of journeymen and apprentices on a pay night'.[41]

Chapters in the Life of a Dundee Factory Boy, the fictionalised but well-informed account of life on the factory floor, written by James Myles, a Dundee stonemason, bookseller and Chartist, describes working life in Dundee flax mills in the 1820s. On Saturday evenings, 'the females, with a view of courting the favours of the overseers, were in the custom of inviting them to public houses and treating them'. Myles also claimed that 'intemperate overseers, after a debauch beg whisky from females during working hours, and for fear of offending them, they would take a can in their hand, go out as if for water to drink, then proceed to a tavern where they were known and get a credit of whisky until Saturday night'.[42]

This is confirmed by the weaver poet, William Thom, remembering his unhappy youth in the School Hill weaving factory of Gordon, Barron and Co. in Aberdeen, ' a prime nursery of vice and sorrow', which he entered in 1814 at the age of sixteen. Thom recalled how children were used to smuggle drink into the workplace, 'Weaving commenced gradually on Wednesday; then were little children pirn fillers, and such were taught to steal warily past the gate keeper, concealing the bottle.'[43] It was even claimed that small girls smuggled whisky into cotton mills by floating bottles down the mill lade [leat] using strings to guide them.[44]

PUBS AND INNS FOR TRAVELLERS

Rising living standards and growing commercial and industrial activity led to many more people travelling about on business, requiring food, drink and accommodation for them and their horses. Heriot, in Midlothian, was situated on one of the main London-to-Edinburgh roads and Heriot public house had formerly been very popular as the ancient stage from Edinburgh. By 1794, however, changing fashion meant that it was 'now deserted by genteel and fashionable company, in consequence of the erection of two new inns at Middleton and Bankhouse'.[45] Henry Cockburn (1779–1854) remembered visiting the inns at both Heriot and Middleton when he was a schoolboy in the company of his father who was convener of the county of Edinburgh and attending a meeting of the road trustees. Cockburn recalled an enjoyable time at the old Heriot Inn, 'the power of ringing the bell as we chose; the ordering of our own dinner; blowing the peat fire, laughing as often and as loud as we liked'. The inn at Middleton, where the party stopped in the evening on the way home, was even more memorable, with a gathering of 'the aristocracy of Midlothian', including the Duke of Buccleuch, Henry Dundas (Cockburn's uncle), Robert Dundas, the Lord Advocate, all 'congregated in this wretched ale house for a day of freedom and jollity'. They were drinking claret and a 'huge bowl of hot whisky punch'.[46] Cockburn's account shows the 'democratic' nature of the rural Scottish ale house in the late eighteenth century, with the male members of the aristocratic and political elite patronising country ale houses, before increasing class segregation and the rise of teetotalism.

This type of accommodation for travellers and their horses was increasingly found all over the country. Newlands, in Peeblesshire, with a modest population of 891, boasted 'established weekly carriers between this parish and Edinburgh', as well as an innkeeper 'having a considerable farm and keeping post chaises' and an ale house 'keeping provender for horses'.[47] Similarly, Ecclefechan in Dumfriesshire, a tiny market town of five hundred, where the mail coach between London and Glasgow had been coming through every day since 1788, and the post office generated an income of £120 a year, had two 'well furnished inns, where passengers meet with good accommodation and may be provided with post chaises and post horses'.[48] Considerable investment could be involved in catering for the increase in the number and affluence of travellers. The Dunbartonshire parish of Cumbernauld was situated on the new turnpike road from Edinburgh to Glasgow 'near which a large commodious inn was erected at the expense of £1,000'.[49] Similar changes were taking place in Longforgan, in the Carse of Gowrie, on the Perth to Dundee road, where there were two inns, 'one at the west end of the village, very convenient for the accommodation of country passengers; and another one about the middle of the town, upon a much larger scale, with a brew house, malt-barn, bake-house and good stabling attached to it'.[50] This suggests that it was worthwhile investing considerable sums of money into providing facilities for travellers.

The growth in the number of turnpike roads was another reflection of the increasing amount of travel throughout the Scottish Lowlands and the degree to which it was possible to raise revenue for road maintenance and improvement by charging tolls for travellers and the growing number of vehicles on the roads. Turnpike toll houses were let to toll keepers by the turnpike trustees who often turned a blind eye to the sale of alcohol by toll keepers as it helped them to pay the rent. In Fenwick in Ayrshire, a weaving parish, where the minister complained about the amount of whisky consumed by his parishioners, there were '2 toll bars, beside 1 side bar; at two of them whisky is also sold, not always for the good of the neighbours'.[51] In Sprouston in Roxburghshire, there were three ale houses for a modest population of a thousand people, 'one at the ferryboat, one at a toll bar, another lately in Sprouston'.[52]

Some observers were highly critical of allowing toll houses to sell alcohol, particularly spirits. At Cleish parish in Kinross, where there were five inns and alehouses, the Reverend Daling noted that 'It has been found, by experience, very prejudicial to suffer spirits to be sold at the turnpike houses.'[53] Selling whisky at toll houses could be a highly profitable business and earn more for the toll keeper than the tolls themselves. In 1819, Robert Southey came across a toll house at Helmsdale in Sutherland, where the toll keeper 'never demands toll: the house and the privilege of selling whiskey are considered by him as well worth the rent he pays, and he gives up his toll as not worth the trouble of collecting it'.[54]

The choice of route for a turnpike road could mean prosperity or ruin for a village and its accompanying inns, ale houses and taverns. At Kilsyth in Stirlingshire, the Glasgow to Edinburgh turnpike via Cumbernauld had bypassed the village, with disastrous consequences for all concerned. The village had become almost deserted and, whereas

Figure 3.1 The Old Basin Tavern, Port Dundas, Glasgow, c.1900. © Mitchell Library, Glasgow.

formerly: 'The chief inn in Kilsyth, though almost never clean or commodious, was much frequented. The publican used to keep one, two, or
sometimes four post chaises, and from 6 to 12 post horses. Now there
is neither chaise, nor almost a post horse, to be found.'[55]

Another growth point for travellers, and the accommodation to
house and feed them, was the development of canals and the expansion
of ferries which were important in a country such as Scotland, with a
long and indented coastline and numerous large rivers, like the Clyde,
the Tay, the Dee and the Spey. Portpatrick in Wigtownshire was a major
and growing port for Ireland. The expansion of the town was encouraged by the local landowner, Sir James Hunter Blair, and the population grew from 611 in 1755 to 996 in 1790, accompanied by rising
imports of Irish cattle and Irish linen. This had spawned an expansion
in the number of inns and ale houses: 'almost every house is an inn,
where strangers may find accommodation suited to their circumstances.
The money they leave is the great fund out of which the inhabitants
pay their rents, and support their families.' This could bring its own
problems of social disorder, however, and it was claimed that 'the Irish
sailors are riotous in Portpatrick and the Scotch sailors in Donaghadee'
(the Irish port on the other side of the ferry route).[56] Another rapidly
growing Wigtownshire port was Stranraer which was similarly dependent on the Irish trade and had grown in population from 610 in 1755 to

Figure 3.2 The Old Ship Inn, North Ness, Hoy, Orkney, *c.*1890. © RCAHMS.

1,602 in 1791. This led to an explosion in the sales of spirits. In 1790, 24,426 gallons (111,138 litres) of whisky and other British spirits were imported into Stranraer and nearly £5,000 had been spent on whisky in that year in Stranraer and its neighbouring parishes.[57]

INNS, PUBS, TAVERNS AND TOURISM

The period saw the development of a leisure and tourist trade in Scotland, though it was initially confined to a small and wealthy elite.[58] Penicuik, in Midlothian, was situated on the edge of Edinburgh, and 'a small neat inn' in the middle of the town was patronised by 'parties of pleasure from Edinburgh, in summer, to see the House of Pennycuick'.[59] At Lanark in 1792, 'a neat additional Inn has lately been built, which was much needed, as the resort of strangers to see the Falls of Clyde, the Cotton works, &c is very considerable'.[60] Further north, in the royal burgh of Nairn, sea bathing was beginning to be marketed to elite tourists as early as the 1790s. The burgh had 'two very good inns, commodiously fitted up, and well kept'. At one of them, the proprietor, James Brander, had 'a bathing machine provided' for sea bathing.[61] This must have been a recent development as a few years earlier a French traveller had stayed in Nairn and had been unimpressed 'it seems a poor sort of capital. In the middle of the town, the houses are fairly well built: I noticed one or two fine ones but the rest not up to much . . . There's neither port nor trade, and not very much farming.'[62]

By the time Dorothy Wordsworth and her brother William were travelling through Scotland in 1803, the 'Grand Tour' of the Highlands was becoming well established. Shortly after the Wordsworths crossed the Scottish border at Dumfries on Wednesday, 17 August 1803, they met an English couple, 'Mr Rogers and his sister', whom they had encountered at their own cottage in Grasmere a few days before. The Rogers's were 'on their way to the Highlands'.[63] Dorothy Wordsworth found the condition of Highland inns something of a trial. Kingshouse, on the edge of the Moor of Rannoch guarding the descent into Glencoe, she described as 'a wretched place – as dirty as a house after a sale on a rainy day'. Others agreed. A traveller in 1791 reported that Kingshouse had 'not a bed fit for a decent person to sleep in nor any provisions but what are absolutely necessary for the family'. James Donaldson, Surveyor of the Military Roads, complained in 1802 that Kingshouse, 'has more the appearance of a hog sty than an inn'. Dorothy Wordsworth found the inn at Inveroran slightly more cheerful, with 'seven or eight travellers probably drovers, with as many dogs, sitting in a complete circle around a large peat fire in the middle of the floor, each with a mess of porridge in a wooden vessel on his knee'.[64]

In the same year as Dorothy Wordsworth's visit, the poet James Hogg, the Ettrick Shepherd, inspired by his friend and patron Walter Scott, visited the Trossachs as a tourist, though twelve years earlier, in his previous life as a shepherd, he had driven a flock of sheep through Glen Gyle.[65] Hogg's experiences of Highland inns were mixed. At Kinlochewe, he stayed at the local inn where 'the floor was well sanded as is the custom in that country. The windows were broken, and the bed was as hard as a stone. They had however, plenty of whisky, oatmeal cakes, tea and sugar, with some eggs and stinking fish, on which I fared sumptuously.' At Stornaway, on Lewis, where he stayed at 'the head inn', a ferocious fight broke out late at night in the next room, involving 'several respectable men, the collector and one of the bailiffs'. The fight was a full-blooded affair involving a ship's captain who 'wrought terrible devastation', and 'desperate wounds were given and received'. The next day, however, the visitors were offered 'very good loaves' baked by the landlady and at dinners or suppers they had 'fish, fowl or eggs' at sixpence a meal. At the inn at Inverslich, there was only one room for visitors which was invaded by 'a whole band of Highlanders, both male and female, who entered my room and fell to drinking whisky with great freedom'. Hogg described them as a 'party of vagabonds' and managed to foil their attempts to pickpocket his waistcoat in the dark.[66]

By 1819, tourism in the Trossachs was in full swing, thanks to the influence of Walter Scott. At Loch Achray, Robert Southey came across 'a small inn where carriages stop and guides are in residence. This was a farm house until Walter Scott brought the Trossachs and Loch Katrin into fashion.' At the 'very good inn' at Lochearnhead, Southey found for sale a pamphlet on the scenery of Loch Earn by Angus McDiarmid, the ground officer on the Earl of Breadalbane's estate of Edinample. The pamphlet, written in what Southey considered to be 'a flowery style', was highly priced at 2/9d for a modest forty-two pages.[67] As the Highland economy grew, not all Highland inns were full of tourists but were catering increasingly for drovers dealing in the growing trade in black cattle and the burgeoning government bureaucracy concerned with the Highlands. When visiting Skye, John McCulloch complained in 1824 that, 'the inn at Portree is a laudable enough inn, but of what use is an inn when you cannot get into it or if, when in, it is to be at a meeting of drovers or of Commissioners of taxes, roads or excise'.[68]

Another feature of the increasing tourist trade was the growth of spas and the construction of hotels to house their visitors. At Pitkeathly

Figure 3.3 Stein Inn, Waternish, Skye. Typical old waterside inn on Skye.
© Alistair and Louise Cooke.

Figure 3.4 Interior, Stein Inn, Waternish, Skye © Alistair and Louise Cooke.

Wells, near Bridge of Earn, Perthshire, the Moncrieffe Arms catered for an affluent clientele, advertising in 1827 that, 'excellent Piano Fortes are provided for the Ladies, and a Billiard Table in a spacious apartment for the Gentlemen'.[69] Edinburgh was also increasingly emerging as a tourist destination, with improved accommodation to match. Patrick Heron praised the quality of Edinburgh hotels in 1799, 'the hotels and inns of Edinburgh also merit notice. The elegant accommodation and ready service, we find in there, are scarcely exceeded in the metropolis of Britain.'[70]

PUBS IN FACTORY VILLAGES

A number of planned villages in Scotland were designed as factory villages for producing cotton in water-powered mills or as mining or iron-smelting settlements. They generally involved greenfield sites, situated close to reliable water supplies or supplies of iron ore or coal, and required purpose-built housing for their workers who had to be recruited either from the local area or from further afield. As the company controlled both housing and employment, a large degree of social control over the lives of the villagers was possible and, as well as providing schools and places of worship, the company usually took great care to ban, limit or control sales of alcohol in their village.[71] Catrine in Ayrshire was founded in 1787 by Claude Alexander and David Dale as a cotton-spinning village. Claude Alexander was praised for his efforts to reduce whisky consumption by building a brewery in the village:

> A brewery was built in the year 1793, by the proprietor of the village and let to a very respectable gentleman in Kilmarnock, with a view to introduce malt liquor in place of whisky, which has so baneful effect on the morals of the people. It gives me great pleasure to add that this benevolent scheme has, in a great degree, answered its purpose; for nearly 500 bolls of malt are brewed annually.[72]

At New Lanark cotton mills, a considerable number of the workforce were displaced Highlanders who were

> naturally generous, hospitable and fond of strangers, which induces them sometimes to make free with the bottle; but drunkenness, among the better class of inhabitants, is of late rather unusual. It is less so among other inhabitants but on the whole, they are a decent and orderly people.[73]

The New Lanark Company took good care to keep it that way and 'pot houses and public houses were gradually removed from the immediate vicinity of their dwellings'.[74]

Another planned cotton factory village, at Blantyre in Lanarkshire, saw a growth in the number of ale houses from two or three, before the building of the cotton mills and iron works, to eight by the early 1790s. The local minister, however, believed they had had a minimal effect on his parishioners who remained 'industrious, sober and contented'.[75] By 1816, when Blantyre was being run by Henry Monteith and Company, the company controlled the sale of liquor by buying taverns and closing them down. Only one public house had survived and that was strictly regulated, being closed every night at 11.00 p.m. and on Sundays. No sale of liquor was allowed during working hours. This contrasted with New Lanark where it was claimed that liquor was easy to buy.[76] At Wilsontown Ironworks in Lanarkshire, the owners built an inn near the company store which sold 'beer but not whisky'.[77]

FAIRS AND MARKETS

Pubs and ale houses performed an invaluable function during fairs and markets by providing a public space where farmers, grain merchants, horse dealers, butchers and others could meet to transact business. Rutherglen, on the outskirts of Glasgow, had no fewer than twenty-six public houses in 1792 for its modest population of 1,860. The burgh held six horse fairs a year, however, 'famous for the best draught horses in Europe'. As a result, the Rutherglen pubs were 'not able to accommodate strangers that frequent the fairs. To supply the deficiency, every inhabitant claims a right, established by immemorial practice, of selling ale and whisky, licence free, during the time of the fairs.'[78] Similar arrangements were found in the Perthshire parish of Monzie where there was 'one yearly market in the parish, when every house, hut and shed, is converted into a dram shop; it is held in the middle of August'.[79] Another Highland Perthshire parish, Moulin, reported that the people 'hardly know how to make a bargain or pay a debt, except over a dram of whisky' and that at the fairs 'every house, hut and shed in the respective villages is converted into a dram shop'.[80]

Similar behaviour was found in the Stirlingshire parish of Gargunnock where 'there is one prevailing custom among our country people . . . Everything is bought and sold over a bottle. The people who go to the fair, in the full possession of their faculties, do not always transact their business, or return to their homes, in the same state.'[81] In the Fife coal-mining parish of Auchterderran, there were six ale houses or inns 'chiefly supported by the trysts at Lochgellie, i.e. fairs or markets' which were held five times a year, mainly for the sale of black cattle.[82]

At Colmonell in Ayrshire in 1790 there were '2 inns, with very indifferent accommodation for so frequented a road, as this is likely to become; and 4 public houses for the lower ranks of people; particularly during the four great fairs, which are held here the first Monday of every quarter, at which a good deal of common country business is transacted'.[83] The Colmonell account suggests that social divisions were widening in this period as wealthier landowners, farmers and merchants withdrew from using the ale house.

Govan Fair in Renfrewshire was held on the first Friday in June, the last one being held in 1881. It took the form of a procession through the village led by a sheep's head. The ritual also involved the village band which paraded through the streets and was rewarded by a bottle of whisky from each public house on the route. The election of the Deacon of the Weaver's Society was held during the fair and was accompanied by all sorts of trickery – voters were often 'closeted in a pub, or locked in seclusion if opponents'.[84]

David Webster (1787–1837) was a Paisley weaver-poet who 'was fond of company and frequently with his companions he joined in the public house, indulged to excess'.[85] Webster was the last of the Paisley weaver-poets to celebrate alcohol. Those who came after him, such as other nineteenth-century working-class poets, wrote from a temperance viewpoint. His poem 'Paisley Fair' sums up the bacchanalian nature of Scottish fairs before their gradual decline in the mid nineteenth century as the temperance movement took hold.

> But some roar'd the race was beginning
> Hech Sirs sic a hullibaloo;
> Frae taverns and tents they were rinning
> Some sober and ithers blin' fou[86]

Fairs, trysts and markets were not just about buying and selling. They fulfilled an important social function by providing a meeting place, assignments with the opposite sex, and a rare opportunity for celebration in the otherwise monotonous and humdrum lives of farm servants, weavers, domestic servants and so on. The temptations of the fair are celebrated in the anonymous ballad, 'Lowrin' Fair':

> The ale wife an' her barrelies,
> The ale wife she grieves me.
> The ale wife and her barrelies
> She'll ruin me entirely.
>
> She's ta'en her barrelies on her back,
> Her pint stoup in her han'

An' she's awa' to Lowrin Fair
Tae haud a rantin' stan'.

But I hae owsen I' the pleuch,
An' plenty o' gweed corn;
Fesh ben to me anither pint,
Though I should beg the morn.[87]

BREWERS AND VINTNERS

In thinly populated rural areas, it was likely that licensees would need another job to earn a living and support a family. Dailly in rural Ayrshire, had a population of 1,607 in 1791 and supported no less than eighteen ale house keepers and retailers of spirits 'most of whom follow a separate occupation'.[88] It was obviously hard to make a living in many rural areas. In the thinly populated Lanarkshire parish of Glassford, there were 'four houses where ale and British spirits are sold; but it is not probable that any of the landlords shall become rich in the trade'.[89] Duns in Berwickshire, had a population of 3,324 in 1788 and no fewer than twenty-seven ale houses 'many of which are kept by low people, who do not depend upon their retail altogether, but also carry on, at the same time, some other profession, or rather from a spirit of indolence, they keep an alehouse, to help the emoluments of the profession they followed'.[90] A similar tale came from Cullen in Banffshire where, before 1748, the inhabitants 'were as poor and idle as any sett of people in the north'. Their only occupation was agriculture and 'to keep tippling houses; and often to drink with one another, to consume the beer for want of customers'.[91]

Keeping an inn could be a precarious occupation dependent on the state of the local economy, the location of the inn, the business skills of the licensee or even the health of the livestock, if the owner ran a carrier's business. William Cuthbert, an innkeeper and dealer in meal at Newton in Ayr, ran a carrier service between Ayr and Glasgow and went bankrupt in 1809, owing debts of £702. His losses included no less than ten horses 'having died through old age' at £16 each, amounting to £160. His creditors were scattered widely over the West of Scotland and included two in Glasgow, one in Greenock, one in Dalmellington and one in Auchencruive.[92]

There were particular problems keeping an inn in the Highlands because of the short length of the tourist season and the difficulty of obtaining supplies of food and drink. James Hope claimed in 1814 that, 'No inn-keeper can exist without some farm at least.'[93] At Beauly, the

Irishman who kept the inn at the time of Southey's tour 'speculates in road building', and the party were served 'salted ling, eggs, mutton chops, and excellent potatoes, with ginger beer and good port wine at what had appeared no better than an English ale house'. Even in the Highlands, however, some prime locations on the main tourist trail were highly profitable. The Kingshouse, on the edge of Rannoch Moor, guarding the entrance to Glencoe, was one of these. Southey reported that the landlord had taken over there ten years earlier, with a capital of only £70, 'This year, he has taken over a large farm and laid out £1,500 in stocking it.' There were rumours, however, that the landlord had made most of his money smuggling salt, rather than from legitimate business.[94]

John Dowie was a vintner who kept the well-known Dowie's Tavern in Libberton's Wynd, Edinburgh, patronised by many of the leading lights of the Edinburgh Enlightenment. Dowie died in February 1816 and left a modest estate of £243/9s, not the inflated figure of £6,000 claimed in *Old Edinburgh Taverns*,[95] though he did own various tenement properties around Libberton's Wynd. His son, who predeceased him, had been a lieutenant in the 55th Regiment of Foot, and had died in Jamaica. Dowie's trustees were William Aitchison, an Edinburgh jeweller, and John Young, 'Junior Solicitor to the Supreme Court of Scotland'. Two of his three daughters were married, one to an Edinburgh hairdresser, another to 'a wright at Causeway side'. A hint of Dowie's political sympathies is contained in the name of his unmarried daughter – Jacobina.[96]

The wills and inventories of brewers and vintners sometimes show the close links between their businesses and the surrounding agricultural area. Thomas Hood, brewer and vintner in the Murraygate, Dundee, who died in 1823 and left an estate of £881, acted as an agent for no fewer than sixteen carriers operating between Dundee and Aberdeen, the Carse of Gowrie, Kirriemuir, Forfar and Montrose. His will and inventory reveal a complex pattern of debt and credit, with members of his own family prominent among his debtors. The largest debt was a substantial £656.12.2d sterling owed by William Hood, a farmer from Invergowrie, presumably a family member. John Hood of Balmyle owed £45, James Abbott, shipmaster in Dundee, £32 and James Young, vintner in Dundee, £28. Other debtors included Catherine and Martha Abbott of Broughty Ferry and Dundee, two Dundee vintners, a female vintner from Kirriemuir, three Dundee excise officers, a miller from Glen Ogilvie and the minister of Mains Church on the edge of Dundee. Most debts were local – Forfar, Tealing, Inverarity, Woodhaven, Kirriemuir – though there was one to a Stirling wood merchant.[97]

Charles Oman, a hotel keeper and vintner, who owned the Waterloo
Hotel in Edinburgh, left the substantial estate of £4,990 when he died
on 16 August 1825. Oman dealt with an elite and aristocratic clientele. His debtors included Viscount Arbuthnot, the Society of Scottish
Antiquaries, Robert Dundas of Arniston, and J. Mansfield, Esq. Oman's
share of the Waterloo Hotel amounted to £60; he held £309 on deposit
with his Edinburgh bankers, Sir W. Hardie and Co.; his household furniture, silver plate, wines and spirits were valued at £2,180; and he was
due £1,975 by the Eagle Insurance Company, London. His trustees were
drawn from the hotel trade across Scotland, including George Burns
of the Black Bull Inn, Glasgow and William Drumbreck and James
McGregor, both hotel keepers in Edinburgh.[98]

'BREWSTER WIVES' AND LANDLADIES

Widows of brewers or maltmen frequently carried on in business after
their husbands died. Janet Sharp, widow of John Hutton, baker in
Perth, took action in 1790 against John Scott, maltman, who kept a
brewseat (ale house) on the Watergate, Perth. She let the property to
him and, when she raised the rent, he refused to pay the increase or to
leave the property. This was in spite of the fact that business was brisk
at the brewseat, according to Scott's nineteen-year-old female servant,
Margaret Dunn, who testified that, when Mrs Hutton visited to collect
the rent, the house 'was then throng with Company'.[99]

Keeping a pub was a common survival strategy for the widows of
maltmen or publicans, and the female landlady often had considerable
social status. In rural Aberdeenshire, the Reverend Alexander Johnston
of Montquhitter parish remembered the pivotal role played by female
landladies in rural parishes, 'the brewster wife [the hostess of the tavern]
who in those days, was always a person of parochial consequence'.[100]
This was especially true in the isolated village of Tomintoul, in the
Banffshire uplands, where Mrs M'Kenzie ran 'the best inn' after a colourful and eventful life spanning many countries. The village, which
consisted of some thirty-seven families, was a Roman Catholic stronghold whose spiritual needs were met by a priest in 'an elegant meeting
house':

> All of them sell whisky and all of them drink it. When disengaged from
> this business, the women spin yarn, kiss their inamoratas, or dance to the
> discordant sounds of an old fiddle ... In personal respect and fortune, at
> the head of the inhabitants, must be ranked Mrs M'Kenzie, of the best inn,

at the sign of the horns. This heroine began her career of celebrity, in the accommodating disposition, at the age of 14, in the year 1745. That year saw her in a regiment in Flanders, caressing and caressed.

She soon attached herself to an aristocratic protector 'high in the military department', then returned to Scotland, married and 'made her husband enlist in the Royal Highlanders, at the commencement of the war in 1756'. She travelled to Germany, France, Holland, England, Ireland, America and the West Indies but eventually settled in Tomintoul. She bore twenty-four children but still appeared 'as fit for her usual active life as ever' and, in appearance, 'still retains all the apparent freshness and vigour of youth', though she was sixty-three in 1793.[101] This narrative reveals the opportunities created for ordinary Scots by the growth of Empire, provided one could survive the rigours of travel and a military life.[102] It also shows the close links between Scottish inns and taverns and the military, whether pubs close to barracks, naval bases or ports, or havens for retired or half-pay soldiers or sailors and their female companions. 'The horns' is a long-established symbol for a cuckold and may reflect Mrs M'Kenzie's (or the Reverend John Grant's) sense of humour/irony.[103]

The landlady at Luss Inn on Loch Lomond, whom Dorothy Wordsworth, her brother and Coleridge encountered in 1803, was a very different figure:

> she was the most cruel and hateful looking woman I ever saw. She was overgrown with fat, and was sitting with her feet in a tub of water for the dropsy – probably brought about by whisky drinking. The sympathy which I felt and expressed for her, on seeing her in this condition – for her legs were swollen as thick as mill-posts – seemed to produce no effect.

The landlady was reluctant to light a fire for her guests and even to offer a bed 'notwithstanding the house was empty and there were at least half a dozen spare beds'.[104]

At Grantown on Spey, a planned village in Inverness-shire, the Grant Arms was being run by a former army sergeant and his wife when Robert Southey visited in 1819. The wife, 'a forward, vulgar, handsome woman from Portsmouth', apologised for not having enough wheaten bread to feed Southey's party of twenty. A group of soldiers had stayed the previous night and eaten everything in the inn. The landlady expected wheat bread from Nairn but 'I never depends for anything upon this place'. At Tain, in Ross-shire, however, Southey was full of praise for the landlady of the inn whom he described in glowing terms as a 'rememberable person, an elderly woman, somewhat Flemish in figure. From real kindness of nature and not with any design of enhancing her charges, she loads the table for her guests with whatever her larder can supply.' When she was addressed as 'my good lady', she replied, 'Nay, I'se nae gude Lady, na' but a poor woman'.[105]

Historians of gender in Scotland have not paid sufficient attention to Scottish drinking places, their staffing and clientele. For example, there is little mention of brewing as an important 'women's occupation' in a recent publication on *Gender in Scottish History*.[106] Women played a major role in the licensed trade in Scotland, from the Edinburgh 'Luckies' in the early eighteenth century to the 'brewster wives' who supplied drink to fairs and markets around Scotland. In rural Aberdeenshire, 'the brewster wife [the hostess of the tavern] . . . was always a person of parochial consequence'[107] while, in Cupar, Fife, 'some of the best inns seem to have been kept by women'.[108] The remarkable Mrs M'Kenzie, of the Horns Inn in Tomintoul, Banffshire, was the leading individual in the village, while Jean Leckie of the Black Bull Inn, Glasgow 'visited the first families in the city and also received visits from them' though her status was put at risk when she married a younger man.[109] Women. such as Janet Sharp in Perth, the widow of a Perth baker, owned property, including a brewseat, and were able to take legal action against their defaulting tenants.[110] In 1789, the Perth vintner, Thomas Marshall, appointed his wife, Catherine Law, as sole executor of his estate which included a dwelling house and the farm of Knoweheads, as well as 'my Tenements of land Gardens Stables vaults cellars'.[111]

WOMEN USING PUBS AND TAVERNS

By the 1790s, as a result of rising living standards, women further down the social scale were patronising Scottish ale houses, dram shops and taverns in increasing numbers. The change in the alcohol consumption of the masses from ale to whisky affected women as well as men. In the growing and industrialising burgh of Hamilton in Lanarkshire, with a population of 5,017 in 1791, including some 450 cotton weavers, there had been a change in mass tastes from drinking 'a lively malt liquor, of moderate strength, which was thought to be well made here' to the use of whisky as 'a common beverage' by all sorts of people, adding 'even women of the lower ranks are not ashamed, as often as they have an opportunity, to drink it to intoxication'.[112] Another rapidly industrialising textile-manufacturing parish was Neilston in Renfrewshire which had no less than twelve, often isolated, bleachfields, staffed by a 'migratory class' of women, often from the Highlands or Ireland, who lived in 'woman houses' during the bleaching season, going to the towns during the winter. The Reverend John Monteith complained that the female bleachfield workers were 'much exposed to wetness and cold, which in the high parts of the country is often intense, and is apt to lead to the too frequent use of spirituous liquors'.[113]

Similar behaviour was reported from New Port Glasgow which boasted eighty-one licensed houses for its 4,036 inhabitants, 'besides several others which deal clandestinely in these articles' (ale and whisky). Here it was claimed 'It is almost incredible what quantities of spirituous liquors, and especially of the worst species of whisky, are consumed in this town; and it is painful to add, but truth requires it, that not a little of it is consumed by women.'[114] Larbert and Dunipace in Stirlingshire was a rapidly industrialising parish with printfields, a cotton mill and the Carron Ironworks which, in 1790, employed a thousand workmen. From here, it was reported that:

> ale houses, or rather what may be called whisky houses, are very numerous in both these parishes. In these houses a drink of good ale cannot be got; but aquavitae is to be had in abundance. It has even got the better of some of the female sex, who instead of being admired, then become the abhorrence of sober men.[115]

In Stirling, alehouses were frequently used by women, often domestic servants or former servants. The Reverend James Sommerville lamented the effects of alcohol use on family life: 'if the mothers of families are corrupted, virtue must be gone'. He added 'the labourers take whisky, with a little bread to their breakfast. It inebriates and subverts the minds of men, women and children.'[116] The phenomenon of women drinking whisky was not confined to urban areas but could be found in rural and Highland parts of the country. The Reverend Paul Fraser, from the Campbell stronghold of Inverary, Argyllshire, complained that dram drinking was 'still too much practised, particularly by women of the lowest class', though it was less widespread in 1792 than it had been.[117]

In the 'woman's town' of Dundee, a centre of coarse linen manufacturing, many working-class women were no strangers to drinking and to pubs. On Sunday, 17 September 1821, a brawl broke out in a pub in the Overgate, an old street at the heart of the medieval burgh, lined with pubs and drinking dens. Most of the combatants were women.[118]

Drinking behaviour in Scotland was judged by gender but also by social class and status. Heavy drinking by male members of the aristocracy or by Edinburgh lawyers was looked on with indulgence, and the ability to 'hold one's drink' was highly rated in these circles. Similarly, high-status women in Edinburgh were not condemned for patronising oyster cellars where drink was freely available. *The Edinburgh Magazine* for August 1817 recounts: 'though it was a disgrace for ladies to be seen drunk, yet it was none to be a little intoxicated in good company'.[119] By contrast, observers were quick to condemn lower-class men or women who patronised dram shops and ale houses. The unfortunate Agnes Wilson, a prostitute who was injured in an assault at Poosie Nansie's Inn in Mauchline, Ayrshire, was condemned for 'lewd and immoral practices', while women who patronised ale houses in Larbert, Stirlingshire, a textile- and iron-manufacturing parish, were said to attract 'the abhorrence of sober men'.[120]

'THE PROFLIGATE OF BOTH SEXES': CRIME AND MISBEHAVIOUR

In the eastern Borders, there was a number of small burghs, where it was claimed, the local ale houses acted as sanctuaries or dens for petty criminals. At Duns in Berwickshire, a parish with a population of 3,324 in 1788 and containing twenty-seven ale houses, it was alleged not only that 'the profligate of both sexes find lodging, where they get intoxicated, and from where they sally forth, in the dark hours of the night, to commit depredations on the innocent, virtuous and unsuspecting members of the community' but also that Duns publicans acted as receivers of stolen goods in return for supplying alcohol.[121] A similar situation prevailed in Kelso in Roxburghshire where 17,690 gallons (80,490 litres) of British spirits were sold in 1792 to a population of 4,324. Kelso's town square was 'the harbour of vagabonds, who here lay their plans of depredation, which are too frequent among the idle and low class of whisky companions'.[122] In Selkirk in 1800, an outbreak of attacks on property was blamed on 'clubs of tradesmen who met either in public houses or in companies for bathing in the river'.[123]

Further north, Dingwall in Ross and Cromarty, with a population of 1,379 in 1791, had two inns and nineteen 'ale or whisky houses', of which only seven were licensed. Whereas the inns were kept by 'well behaving respectable people', the ale houses were described as 'the worst of nuisances' and were accused of 'encouraging theft in servants and by diverting the earnings of mechanics and labourers and the productions of farmers, for the support of their families'.[124]

This world is reflected in the records of burgh courts which provide 'microhistories' with rich details of everyday life in eighteenth-century Scotland, including low-level violence in pubs. In Perth, for example,

John Campbell Jr, the manager of a porter cellar in the Watergate, brought an action in 1790 against James Thomson, a sailor, for 'assaulting and beating' him in the cellar 'without provocation'. John Campbell managed the porter business for his father and partners. Watergate was close to the River Tay and the old Perth harbour, and housed a riverside community, with waterside-based occupations. Witnesses who gave evidence included John Imrie, a thirty-three-year-old boatman, Elspeth Anderson, the thirty-year-old widow of John Anderson, sailor, William McIntosh, twenty, 'residenter' and James Wilkie, sixty-six, merchant and innkeeper.[125]

James Wilkie was buying porter in the cellar when Thomson and a friend came in and had an argument with John Campbell about them 'spoiling the ramrod of his gun which he then had in his hand'. Campbell pushed Thomson to the door 'at the same time giving him a kick upon the bretch upon which the defender damned the pursuer and bid him come out and kick his arse again and he would show him what he could do'. A fight ensued outside the porter cellar, in which Campbell came out much the worse, being knocked to the ground twice and having a cut to his mouth.[126]

Inns and taverns were regularly used by Scottish judges when on circuit. They were often heavy drinkers and were sometimes incapable of carrying out their duties because they were drunk. The diaries of Dr Tomas Lucas of Stirling record how on 25 April 1810:

> The Justiciary Judge came here to hold the circuit court but strange to tell . . . owing to the effects of intemperance he could not proceed on his arrival from Glasgow at Gibb's Inn in this town. He asked where he was and could not recollect he had been in Glasgow. The next day he went to the court in his own carriage but could not do anything or say scarce a word except to call for wine and of which he drank twice.[127]

CONTROL, LICENSING AND REGULATION

Because of the dangers of drunkenness and crime in unregulated drinking places, and the opportunities they offered for revenue raising, places that sold alcohol were regulated by the authorities, though there was much evasion of duties and licences. By the late eighteenth century, there was growing concern about the proliferation of premises selling cheap, often poor quality, whisky to the poor. In many places, the county JPs or the burgh authorities tried to reduce or restrict numbers by charging a high licence fee or issuing fewer licences. Cardross parish, in Dunbartonshire, was a rapidly industrialising area, with bleachfields, dyeworks and printfields, 'by far the most considerable and extensive of any in Scotland'. Here, in an area of high employment and high male wages, the number of whisky shops had decreased because 'the Trustees have this year [1793] given licences to only two in the village of Rentoun, to sell spirits of home produce'.[128]

Not all magistrates and JPs were successful in controlling the number of licensed premises, particularly in the burgeoning towns and cities. The Reverend John Burns deplored the growing number of public houses in the Barony parish of Glasgow, a rapidly growing urban area with a population of 18,451 in 1791. Here, there were '169 public houses for retailing malt and spirituous liquors. The vast increase of these houses is one of the greatest injuries to the morals, the health and the prosperity of the inhabitants.' He recommended the 'suppression of many of these houses'.[129] In Dundee, with a population of 24,000 in 1792, there were no less than 179 licensed houses and 'the number of unlicensed ones, where they [spirits] may be procured is said to be very great'. The Reverend James Small complained that ale 'ceases to be the drink used in social meetings, or for refreshment from the fatigues of labour' in favour of 'intoxicating and enervating spirituous liquors'.[130] Similar complaints were made in the Abbey parish of Paisley, with a population of 10,792 in 1793, where 'dram drinking is common, alehouses numerous'. They had a bad effect on 'the health, the morals and the domestic comfort of the people', which could be stopped by limiting the number of ale houses and the hours they were open. The Renfrewshire Justices of the Peace already had these powers but 'the steady exertion of these powers is what is wanting'.[131]

CLUBS, SOCIETIES AND ASSOCIATIONS: THE ASSOCIATIONAL WORLD

Clubs, associations and societies continued to meet in inns and taverns in this period, though there was a growing degree of social segregation as newer and more exclusive and expensive hotels and taverns were built. Glasgow West India merchants socialised in the Pig Club, an exclusive club limited to twenty members, which met in a tavern once a week during the winter to dine together, drink rum and play whist. The club began in 1798 and ran until 1807 when it was replaced by the more formal Glasgow West India Association which met in the exclusive Tontine Hotel, a members-only institution.[132] This was part of a trend whereby elite groups began to abandon informal gatherings in inns and taverns and meet in more formal associations and more socially exclusive settings, away from the gaze of the general public. Elaborate codes of 'politeness' governed behaviour in clubs and coffee houses, providing 'access to status and social acceptability' for the growing urban middle classes.[133]

Another exclusive organisation which met in a tavern and drew its membership from the Glasgow merchant elite was the Board of Green Cloth. This was a Whist and Supper Club, which formed between 1780 and 1790 and came to an end about 1820. Club membership was limited to eighteen and was drawn from 'a small exclusive elite who knew each other well but no one else at all'. Members met at 5.00 p.m. and drank rum punch and whisky toddy, and, at 10.15 p.m., had a supper of 'Welsh rabbits, Finnan haddies or tripe'. By 1810 the Board was meeting in the Buckshead Inn, Argyle Street, Glasgow, and, on 3 March 1812, 'Mr Connell beats agt. Mr Finlay a bottle of Rum that Mr Jas Dennistoun will rout as a Cow louder and better than Mr Henry Monteith'.[134] Of those involved in the bet, Henry Monteith became Lord Provost of Glasgow (twice) and MP for Linlithgow burghs; Kirkman Finlay became Lord Provost and MP for Glasgow; James Dennistoun became Vice Lieutenant of Dunbartonshire; and David and James Connell were prominent West India merchants.

This type of 'high spirited' or drunken behaviour by elite males was fondly recalled by Walter Scott in *Guy Mannering*, published in 1829 but set in 1746, after the Jacobite Rebellion, when the Edinburgh lawyer, Paulus Pleydell, 'otherwise a good scholar, an excellent lawyer, and a worthy man', is tracked down by the English Colonel Mannering and Dandy Dinmont on a Saturday night to Clerihugh's Tavern, a favoured haunt of Edinburgh lawyers, surrounded by his drinking cronies, engaged in 'the ancient and now forgotten pastime of High Jinks'.[135]

Clubs and associations were widespread in the Scottish provinces. When Robert Southey, the Poet Laureate, arrived at Loudon's Hotel in Nairn in 1819, he found waiting there for him a diploma from the Literary Society of Banff appointing him an honorary member. When Southey and his travelling companion, the engineer Thomas Telford, retired for the night, they were kept awake by a lot of noise from the room upstairs, where the Nairn Freemasons were holding a meeting to admit new members, which went on until one o'clock in the morning.[136] The Salutation Inn in Perth was patronised by the local elite. The first meeting of the Perth Golfing Society was held in the Salutation on 5 April 1824 when thirteen gentlemen 'convened for considering the propriety of instituting a Golf Society' and established an expensive dress code, 'the uniform to be worn by the members on Field Days shall be a

Figure 3.5 The Salutation Hotel, Perth. A coaching inn dating from 1699. Used by Charles Edward Stuart when the Jacobite army occupied Perth in 1745. © Anthony and Judith Cooke.

Scarlet Golfing Jacket with appropriate buttons'. The first club dinner was held in the inn the following year.[137]

Pubs also offered public space for groups further down the social ladder, including radical groups and self-help groups for artisans. Walter Freer was a Glasgow powerloom tenter and trade union official who became a pillar of the temperance movement, a member of the Band of Hope, and eventually manager of the Public Halls in Glasgow. Freer's father was a handloom weaver and a Radical, a friend of Baird and Hardie, during the Radical War of 1820. Freer described how his father and two other Radicals were holding a committee meeting in the parlour of the Tun Public House in Glasgow when a government spy, who had betrayed two friends of the trio, came in. He greeted them as friends but one of the Radicals threw 'a vial of vitriol in his face, causing the loss of both eyes'.[138] In *The Young South Country Weaver*, published in 1821, the evangelical Reverend Henry Duncan of Ruthwell in Dumfrieshire denounced Glasgow pubs as 'hotbeds of sedition and infidelity'.[139]

The Glasgow handloom weaver, William Hammond, claimed that 'book clubs or subscription reading societies were first started in Glasgow about 1795, and afterwards spread throughout Scotland and into many English towns. These clubs generally met in taverns.' John Urie, a Glasgow wood engraver, remembered joining a book club in Paisley in 1830. The president of the club was a Paisley blacksmith, and members included weavers, a barber and a tailor. The club met in a tavern and each man ordered 'a gill and a bottle of sma' yill'. Books and politics were discussed, and the general character of the meeting was that of a debating society.[140]

CHANGES IN SCOTTISH DRINKING PLACES, 1790–1830

By the end of the eighteenth century and the early years of the nineteenth, class segregation in leisure was increasing – the upper and middle classes were becoming more wary about drinking in public spaces, and inns and taverns were becoming less fashionable. The upper- and middle-class clubs, associations and societies that had met in urban inns and taverns began to use private, sometimes purpose-built, spaces to store their increasing amount of furniture and regalia.[141] Similar changes took place in the countryside. In the rural Fife parish of Kilconquhar, for example, the minister reported that, in the 1760s and the 1770s, 'public houses here were frequented by people of all ranks'. By the 1790s, gentlemen and farmers drank at home and consumed 'milder and less intoxicating liquors and in greater moderation: the society of the female sex, securing decency, politeness and agreeable conviviality'.[142] Maxine Berg has argued that in the late eighteenth century, 'politeness, civility and taste became social markers more significant than material wealth'.[143] Women were at the heart of these changes and their influence became more pronounced with the rise of the temperance movement in the early nineteenth century.

In the Fife coastal burgh of Kirkcaldy, there were two brewers and thirty-one licensed inns and alehouses in 1790, together with thirty-one houses and nineteen shops licensed to sell spirits, making a ratio of one licensed house for every thirteen families in the burgh. This had been accompanied by great changes in the clientele of licensed premises, 'Far down in the present century, it was the practice, even among citizens of some character, to take a regular whet in the forenoon, and most commonly to spend the evening in the public house.' This type of 'democratic' drinking behaviour had now been given up and the habit of drinking spirits was now confined to a few, 'these generally of the very lowest order'.[144]

Further north, in the Inverness-shire Highland parish of Boleskine and Abertarf on the south side of Loch Ness, the heritor remembered the days when 'it was reckoned no disparagement for the gentlemen to sit with commoners in the inns, such as the country then afforded, where one cap and afterwards a single glass, went round the whole company'. Now this type of 'democratic' behaviour had disappeared and 'gentlemen' drank in their own houses.[145] Ale houses and dram shops, in particular, were increasingly becoming the refuge of those at the bottom of the social scale, a situation that would intensify in the nineteenth century with the growth of the temperance movement. It was the beginning of a change in the nature of the public house from 'a place for transact-

Figure 3.6 The Golden Lion, Stirling. Coaching inn built in 1786. Robert Burns stayed there the following year. © Anthony and Judith Cooke.

ing business and a setting for sports fixtures, to a space devoted to the consumption of alcohol'.[146]

The important function of providing public space for people, however, particularly young men and groups, to meet in the increasingly crowded, stressful and anonymous cities and large towns of nineteenth-century Scotland continued despite the pressures exerted by the temperance movement and its allies in central and local government. Similarly, urban inns and hotels began to provide more expensive and upmarket accommodation and facilities, such as ballrooms, for an elite clientele on occasions such as the local races. In Stirling, for example, during Stirling Races in 1810, Gibb's Inn, in the centre of town, was 'packed with gay and brilliant company, bringing together the beauty and fashion, the rank and the wealth of the Scottish Midlands'.[147]

Nonetheless, a sea change was about to take place with the foundation of Britain's first temperance (anti-spirits) society at Greenock in Renfrewshire in 1829, and the emergence of John Dunlop, a Greenock lawyer and philanthropist, and the Glasgow publisher, William Collins, as central figures in the British temperance movement. The movement grew rapidly and, by June 1830, the Temperance Society Record claimed a Scottish membership of 3,322 and an Irish one of 3,500.[148] The temperance movement will form one of the main subjects of the next chapter.

NOTES

1. *Perthshire Advertiser*, 6 August 1932.
2. OSA, Vol. VII, *Lanarkshire and Renfrewshire* (Bradford, 1973), pp. 298–9.
3. G. Penny, *Traditions of Perth* (Perth, 1836), p. 25.
4. OSA, Vol. IX, *Dunbartonshire, Stirlingshire and Clackmannan* (Bradford, 1978), pp. 698–9.
5. OSA, Vol. XIII, *Angus* (Bradford, 1976), p. 259.
6. OSA, Vol. XVI, *Banffshire, Moray and Nairnshire*, p. 53.
7. OSA, Vol. VI, *Ayrshire* (Bradford, 1982), pp. 382–3.
8. P. Mathias, *The Brewing Industry in England, 1700–1830* (Cambridge, 1959).
9. OSA, Vol. XIV, *Aberdeenshire*, p. 339; and A. Hopkins, *The Aberdeen Pub Companion* (Aberdeen, 1975), p. 8.
10. OSA, Vol. II, *Lothian* (Bradford, 1975), pp. 292–3.
11. OSA, Vol. XIII, *Angus*, p. 259.
12. OSA, Vol. VII, *Lanarkshire and Renfrewshire*, p. 27.
13. OSA, Vol. VII, pp. 349 and 354–5.

14. *OSA*, Vol. VII, pp. 530–1.
15. *OSA*, Vol. VI, *Ayrshire*, p. 158.
16. *OSA*, Vol. VI, p. 211.
17. I. Donnachie, 'Drink and Society, 1750–1850', *Journal of the Scottish Labour History Society*, No. 13, May 1979, pp. 9–11.
18. *OSA*, Vol. II, *Lothian*, p. 47.
19. *OSA*, Vol. VII, *Lanarkshire and Renfrewshire*, p. 472.
20. *OSA*, Vol. III, *Eastern Borders*, p. 515.
21. *OSA*, Vol. XIII, *Angus*, pp. 258–9.
22. National Records of Scotland, Edinburgh (NRS); Court of Session Records, CS 96/3485; Sederunt Books of John Begbie, innkeeper, Kilmarnock, Inventory, 26 April 1811.
23. *OSA*, Vol. XIII, *Angus*, p. 534.
24. *OSA, Vol. XIII, Angus*, p. 136.
25. Perth and Kinross Archives (PKA), Perth Burgh Court Records, B59/26/5/49, Bundle 4A, No. 4, Patrick Campbell of Edenchip against Charles Craigie, ale seller and drover, Perth for £9 sterling on the price of a horse, 1790.
26. *OSA*, Vol. II, *Lothian*, p. 747.
27. *OSA*, Vol. VII, *Lanarkshire and Renfrewshire*, p. 779.
28. *OSA*, Vol. VII, p. 816.
29. *OSA*, Vol. XVI, *Banffshire, Moray and Nairnshire*, p. 509.
30. *OSA*, Vol. VI, *Ayrshire*, p. 224.
31. Penny, *Traditions of Perth*, pp. 30–1.
32. *OSA*, Vol. XII, *North and West Perthshire* (Bradford, 1977), p. 813.
33. *OSA*, Vol. XV, *North and East Aberdeenshire*, p. 344. See also M. Bennett, *Scottish Customs from the Cradle to the Grave* (Edinburgh, 1992), pp. 121–59.
34. *OSA*, Vol. XVII, *Inverness-shire, Ross and Cromarty* (Bradford, 1981), pp. 515–16.
35. *OSA*, Vol. XVII, *Inverness-shire, Ross and Cromarty*, p. 4.
36. J. H. Dixon, *Gairloch and Guide to Loch Maree* (Edinburgh, 1888), p. 115.
37. *OSA*, Vol. XVIII, *Sutherland and Caithness* (Bradford, 1979), p. 481.
38. *OSA*, Vol. XV, *North and East Aberdeenshire*, p. 359.
39. *OSA*, Vol. XX, *The Western Isles* (Bradford, 1983), pp. 35–6.
40. A. J. Cooke, *The Rise and Fall of the Scottish Cotton Industry, 1778–1914* (Manchester, 2010), pp. 128–9.
41. *OSA*, Vol. IX, *Dunbartonshire, Stirlingshire and Clackmannanshire*, p. 275.
42. D. Phillips (ed.), *Chapters in the Life of a Dundee Factory Boy* (Dundee, 1980), pp. 35–6. See also C. A. Whatley, 'Altering Images of the Industrial City: the case of James Myles, the "Factory Boy" and mid-Victorian

Dundee', in L. Miskell, C. A. Whatley and B. Harris (eds), *Victorian Dundee: Image and Realities* (East Linton, 2000), pp. 70–95.

43. W. Thom, *Rhymes and Recollections of a Handloom Weaver* (Paisley, 1880), p. 3.

44. J. Dunlop, *Artificial and Compulsory Drinking Usages of the UK* (London, 1844), p. 11.

45. *OSA*, Vol. II, p. 274.

46. H. Cockburn, *Memorials of his Time* (Edinburgh, 1856), pp. 13–15.

47. *OSA*, Vol. III, *The Eastern Borders* (Bradford, 1979), p. 841.

48. *OSA*, Vol. IV, *Dumfriesshire* (Bradford, 1978), p. 199.

49. *OSA*, Vol. IX, *Stirlingshire*, pp. 37–8.

50. *OSA*, Vol. XI, *South and East Perthshire, Kinross* (Bradford, 1976), pp. 325–6.

51. *OSA*, Vol. VI, *Ayrshire*, p. 211.

52. *OSA*, Vol. III, *The Eastern Borders*, p. 652.

53. *OSA*, Vol. XI, *South and East Perthshire, Kinross*, p. 642.

54. R. Southey, *Journal of a Tour in Scotland in 1819* (London, 1929), p. 130.

55. *OSA*, Vol. IX, *Stirlingshire*, p. 505.

56. *OSA*, Vol. V, *Stewartry of Kirkcudbright and Wigtownshire* (Bradford, 1983), pp. 487 and 495.

57. *OSA*, Vol. V, p. 524.

58. A. Durie, *Scotland for the Holidays: tourism in Scotland, 1780–1939* (East Linton, 2003).

59. *OSA*, Vol. II, *Lothian*, p. 372.

60. *OSA*, Vol. VII, *Lanarkshire and Renfrewshire*, p. 451.

61. *OSA*, Vol. XVI, *Banffshire, Moray and Nairnshire*, p. 753. See also A. Durie (ed.), *Travels in Scotland, 1788–1881* (Woodbridge, 2012).

62. N. Scarfe (ed.), *To the Highlands in 1786. The Inquisitive Journey of a Young French Aristocrat* (Woodbridge, 2001), pp. 160–1.

63. D. Wordsworth, *Recollections of a Tour Made in Scotland, 1803* (Edinburgh, 1874), p. 5.

64. A. R. B. Haldane, *The Drove Roads of Scotland* (Edinburgh, 1971), p. 42.

65. J. Hogg, *A Tour in the Highlands in 1803* (Paisley, 1888), p. 15.

66. Hogg, *Tour in the Highlands*, pp. 54–5, 77 and 102–6.

67. Southey, *Journal of a Tour in Scotland*, pp, 29 and 37.

68. A. R. B. Haldane, *New Ways Through the Glens* (Newton Abbot, 1973), p. 187.

69. J. W. and R. E. Seath, *Dunbarney. A Parish with a Past* (Perth, 1991), pp. 64–5.

70. P. Heron, *Scotland Delineated, 1799* (Edinburgh, 1975), p. 358.

71. Cooke, *Scottish Cotton Industry,* pp. 36–9.

72. *OSA*, Vol. VI, *Ayrshire*, pp. 562–4.

73. *OSA*, Vol. VII, *Lanarkshire*, p. 467.

74. Smout, 'The Landowner and the Planned Village', p. 96.
75. *OSA*, Vol. VII, *Lanarkshire*, p. 27. See also Cooke, *Scottish Cotton Industry*, pp. 34–9.
76. Report of Select Committee on State of Children Employed in Manufactures, *Parliamentary Papers, 1816*, Vol. III, pp. 164 and 168.
77. Donnachie, 'Drink and Society', p. 16.
78. *OSA*, Vol. VII, *Lanarkshire*, p. 564.
79. *OSA*, Vol. XII, *North and West Perthshire*, p. 741.
80. *OSA*, Vol. XII, pp. 766–7.
81. *OSA*, Vol. IX, *Stirlingshire*, p. 375.
82. *OSA*, Vol. X, *Fife*, p. 52.
83. *OSA*, Vol. VI, *Ayrshire*, p. 91.
84. T. C. F. Brotchie, *The History of Govan* (Govan, 1905), pp. 271–2.
85. T. Leonard, *Radical Renfrew. Poetry from the French Revolution to the First World War* (Edinburgh, 1990), p. 91.
86. *Radical Renfrew*, p. 98.
87. D. K. Cameron, *The Ballad and the Plough* (Edinburgh, 1997), p. 98.
88. *OSA*, Vol. VI, *Ayrshire*, p. 135.
89. *OSA*, Vol. VII, *Lanarkshire and Renfrewshire*, p. 280.
90. *OSA*, Vol. II, *The Eastern Borders*, p. 138.
91. *OSA*, Vol. XVI, *Banffshire, Moray and Nairn*, p. 123.
92. NRS, Court of Session, Sederunt Books, CS 96/3987, Inventory of William Cuthbert, 1809.
93. A. R. B. Haldane, *New Ways Through the Glens* (Newton Abbot, 1973 edition), p. 182.
94. Southey, *Journal of a Tour in Scotland*, pp. 118 and 234; and Haldane, *New Ways Through the Glens*, p. 182.
95. Stuart, *Old Edinburgh Taverns*, p. 46.
96. NRS, Edinburgh Sheriff Court, SC 70/1/26/119, Inventory of John Dowie, 26 October 1821.
97. NRS, Brechin Commissary Court, CC3/3/15/419, Will of Thomas Hood, 11 March 1823, and CC 3/5/7/102 Inventory, 8 July 1822.
98. NRS, Edinburgh Sheriff Court, SC 70/1/35/239, Inventory of Charles Oman, 8 August 1826.
99. PKA, Perth Burgh Court, B 59/26/5/49/ Bundle 4 No. 28, Janet Sharp against John Scott, 1790.
100. *OSA*, Vol. XV, *North and East Aberdeenshire* (Bradford, 1982), p. 342.
101. *OSA*, Vol. XVI, *Banffshire, Moray and Nairnshire*, pp. 279–80.
102. For an account of an upper class Scottish family's experience of Empire, see E. Rothschild, *The Inner Life of Empires* (Princeton, 2011).
103. See E. P. Thompson, *Customs in Common* (London, 1991), pp. 467–531.
104. Wordsworth, *Recollections of a Tour in Scotland*, pp. 70–1.
105. Southey, *Tour in Scotland*, pp. 98–9 and 123–4.

106. L. Abrams, E. Gordon, D. Simonton and E. J. Yeo (eds), *Gender in Scottish History since 1700* (Edinburgh, 2006).
107. *OSA*, Vol. XV, *North and East Aberdeenshire*, p. 342.
108. P. Martin, *Cupar* (Edinburgh, 2006), pp. 72–3.
109. *OSA*, Vol. XVI, *Banffshire, Moray and Nairn*, pp. 279–80; and R. Reid, *Glasgow Past and Present*, Vol. 1 (Glasgow, 1884), pp. 343–4.
110. PKA, B 59/26/5/49/4, No. 28, Janet Sharp against John Scott, 1790.
111. PKA, B 59/26/5/49/1/46 (1), Will of Thomas Marshall, vintner in Perth, 4 February 1789.
112. *OSA*, Vol. VII, *Lanarkshire and Renfrewshire*, pp. 394–5.
113. *OSA*, Vol. VII, pp. 807 and 823.
114. *OSA*, Vol. VII, pp. 691–2.
115. *OSA*, Vol. IX, *Stirlingshire*, pp. 555–8.
116. *OSA*, Vol. IX, pp. 628–30.
117. *OSA*, Vol. VII, *Argyllshire*, p. 157.
118. M. Archibald, *A Sink of Atrocity. Crime in 19th Century Dundee* (Edinburgh, 2012), p. 218.
119. Brotchie, *History of Govan*, p. 97.
120. R. Crawford, *The Bard, Robert Burns, A Biography* (London, 2009), pp. 208–9; and *OSA*, Vol. IX, *Stirlingshire*, pp. 555–8.
121. *OSA*, Vol. II, *The Eastern Borders*, p. 138.
122. *OSA*, Vol. II, pp. 515 and 524.
123. B. Harris and C. McKean, *The Scottish Town in the Age of the Enlightenment, 1740–1820* (Edinburgh, 2014), p. 430.
124. *OSA*, Vol. XVII, *Inverness-shire, Ross and Cromarty*, p. 370.
125. PKA, Perth Burgh Court, B59/26/5/49, Bundle 4B, 27, John Campbell, merchant, against James Thomson, sailor, who assaulted him in a porter cellar in Watergate, Perth, 1790.
126. Campbell *v.* Thomson, 1790.
127. *Stirling Observer*, 30 April 1986, p. 13.
128. *OSA*, Vol. IX, pp. 26–9.
129. *OSA*, Vol. VII, *Lanarkshire and Renfrewshire*, p. 349.
130. *OSA*, Vol. XIII, *Angus*, p. 169.
131. *OSA*, Vol. VII, *Lanarkshire and Renfrewshire*, pp. 851–2.
132. A. J. Cooke, 'An Elite Revisited: Glasgow West India Merchants, 1783–1877, *Journal of Scottish Historical Studies*, Vol. 32, No. 2, 2012, p. 140.
133. M. Berg, *Luxury & Pleasure in Eighteenth-Century Britain* (Oxford, 2007), p. 233.
134. *Minute Book of the Board of Green Cloth, 1809–1820* (Glasgow, 1891), pp. v–vii, 8–9 and 29.
135. W. Scott, *Guy Mannering or the Astrologer* (Edinburgh, 1886), pp. 252–3.
136. Southey, *Tour in Scotland*, pp. 106–8.
137. Plaque in the Stuart Room, Salutation Hotel, Perth.
138. W. Freer, *My Life and Memories* (Glasgow, 1929), p. 12.

139. H. Duncan, *The Young South Country Weaver; or a Journey to Glasgow: A Tale for the Radicals* (Glasgow, 1821), p. 64.
140. W. Hammond, *Recollections of a Glasgow Handloom Weaver* (Glasgow, 1904), pp. 87–8.
141. P. Clark, *British Clubs and Societies, 1580–1800, The Origins of an Associational World* (Oxford, 2000), p. 248.
142. *OSA*, Vol. X, *Fife*, pp. 458–9.
143. Berg, *Luxury and Pleasure*, p. 205.
144. *OSA*, Vol. X, pp. 512 and 560–1.
145. *OSA*, Vol. XVII, *Inverness-shire, Ross and Cromarty* (Bradford, 1981), p. 18.
146. T. Griffiths and G. Morton, 'Introduction', in Griffiths and Morton (eds), *A History of Everyday Life in Scotland, 1800 to 1900* (Edinburgh, 2010), p. 2.
147. *Stirling Observer*, 30 April 1986, p. 13
148. E. King, *Scotland Sober and Free. The Temperance Movement, 1829–1979* (Glasgow, 1979), p. 7; and B. Harrison, *Drink and the Victorians, The Temperance Question in England, 1815–1872* (Keele, 1994), pp. 94–100.

4

'People's Palaces':
Urbanisation, Temperance and Responses,
1830–1914

INTRODUCTION

THE NINETEENTH CENTURY IN Scotland was characterised by rapid population growth, population movement on a large scale and growing urbanisation, particularly in the west central Lowlands. The so called 'big four' – Glasgow, Edinburgh, Dundee and Aberdeen – dominated the urban landscape but some other places grew at even faster rates. Coatbridge in Lanarkshire grew from 742 people in 1831 to 30,034 in 1891, which was typical of some of the rapidly growing coal and iron centres.[1] Glasgow's population increased from 275,000 in 1841 to 784,000 in 1911, a nearly threefold increase. Edinburgh and Leith more than doubled from 164,000 in 1841 to 401,000 in 1911. In the same period, Aberdeen grew from 65,000 to 164,000 and Dundee from 60,000 to 165,000. The housing stock could not keep pace and overcrowding became endemic. In 1911, half of all Scots lived in one- or two-roomed households while for England and Wales the comparable figure was 7 per cent.[2] This degree of overcrowding helps to explain the attraction of urban pubs for the Scottish working man in the Victorian period.

TEMPERANCE

The first temperance society in Britain, an anti-spirits society, was founded in Greenock, Renfrewshire in 1829. Apart from the link with John Dunlop (1789–1868), a Greenock lawyer and temperance pioneer, the choice of Greenock is significant in other ways. Greenock was an expanding port, cotton-manufacturing and sugar-refining centre with a large immigrant population drawn originally from the Highlands and later from Ireland. In 1792, the population was 14,299, including 1,825 families with a Highland-born head of household, making around

9,000 people (63 per cent of the population) with Highland origins. The burgh population almost doubled from 14,299 in 1792 to 27,571 in 1831. It was a hard-drinking place. In 1792, there were 247 licences granted for the sale of spirits, one for every fifty-eight people. By 1840, there were thirty-one inns and taverns in Greenock, plus 275 houses selling ales and spirits, one for every twenty-five families.[3] There had been earlier attempts to promote 'moderate drinking' in Greenock – a Moderation Society, founded in 1818, and the Regular Society, which tried to promote the use of alcohol 'in moderation'.[4]

The second anti-spirits society in Britain was also founded in 1829, in Maryhill, an industrial suburb on the edge of Glasgow. A year later, the first anti-spirits society in England was founded in Bradford by Henry Forbes, a Scottish worsted manufacturer, and the first teetotal society in Preston in 1832.[5] These were all fast-growing manufacturing towns and suburbs which had experienced rapid economic, social and cultural change and were adjusting to large numbers of migrants looking for work. The anti-spirit movement emerged simultaneously in both Ireland and Scotland, where whisky rather than beer, as in England, was the drink of the masses. It was part of a more general movement across Britain 'to propagate the respectable way of life', including the Lord's Day Observation Society, the British and Foreign Temperance Society, both founded in 1831, and the Society for the Prevention of Cruelty to Animals (founded 1825).[6] Certainly, the Scots drank prodigious quantities of alcohol in the form of spirits, mainly whisky. In 1838, it was claimed that the annual average consumption of spirits in Scotland was 23 pints a head, compared to a mere 7 pints a head in England and 13 pints in Ireland.[7] Table 4.1 shows the ratio between population and the number of spirit shops in the West of Scotland in 1834.

Table 4.1 Ratio between the number of families and the number of spirit shops in six urban centres in the west of Scotland, 1834.

	Families	Spirit dealers	Ratio
Glasgow	40,000	2,198	1:18
Paisley	12,308	454	1:27
Renfrew	535	30	1:18
Greenock	6,353	327	1:19
Port Glasgow	1,279	81	1:15
Dumbarton	804	71	1:11

(Source: Report of the Select Committee on Drunkenness, *Parliamentary Papers*, 1834, Vol. VIII, pp. 136–7)

Many historians have seen the temperance movement as part of an attempt by employers to discipline the 'new' industrial workforce. E. P. Thompson argued that industrialists faced great challenges in getting their workforce to adapt to regular hours and the pace of the machine. The methods they adopted included temperance, 'the division of labour; the supervision of labour; fines; bells and clocks; money incentives; preachings and schoolings; the suppression of fairs and sports'.[8] Brian Harrison agreed that temperance 'helped to discipline the industrial workforce'.[9] For example, at the Houldsworth ironworks at Coltness, Lanarkshire, which employed eight hundred people in 1849, 'much loss and annoyance had frequently been occasioned by the negligent or wilful conduct of workmen under the influence of this habit (drunkenness)'.[10]

This is not the whole story, however. The temperance movement marks growing involvement by women with social issues and political campaigning, though they were excluded from the franchise. In this, it is similar to female involvement with the anti-slavery campaign which often met in the same premises and recruited similar individuals. Temperance also attracted 'respectable' working men and women who were looking to see moral improvement in the working class. Chartists, radical Liberals and early socialists were all hostile to heavy drinking by working men because they felt it demeaned the working class as a whole. The Reverend Patrick Brewster of Paisley (1788–1859), for example, was a leading Chartist, anti-slavery campaigner and poor law reformer as well as a temperance campaigner.[11] Another example of involvement in multiple reform campaigns was the anonymous 'Jacques' who, after a chequered career, became a flax dresser in Dundee in 1826. He was a member of a mutual improvement society, attended popular lectures of various kinds and took 'a subordinate role' in agitation for 'Reform, the Corn Laws and temperance'.[12]

In Scotland, however, there was a darker side to temperance. Many of the places it flourished were areas that had experienced high immigration from Ireland, and anti-Irish and, in particular, anti-Catholic sectarian feeling was widespread. In Greenock, the founding centre of temperance, the Reverend Patrick Macfarlan launched an attack in 1841 on 'intemperance and licentiousness', blaming 'the immigration from other quarters, of families unaccustomed in their infancy to the habits of a well-educated Scottish population [which] has tended not a bit to lower the standard by which they are wont to regulate their conduct'.[13] In the cotton-manufacturing village of Blantyre in Lanarkshire, where the majority of the workforce was Protestant Irish, the manager commented in 1835 that 'in a small community like this, the Irish do not associate much with the Scotch; they spend their evenings and Sundays together and in all cases whisky is consumed'.[14]

This type of sectarianism was found wherever there had been migration from Ireland. In the Ayrshire weaving parish of Maybole where, in 1837, Roman Catholics made up a modest 355 (fewer than 6 per cent) of 6,362 inhabitants, the Reverend George Gray fulminated against the 'drunken and filthy' habits of the Irish weavers.[15] Similarly, James Myles, Dundee Chartist and bookseller, attacked the social conditions in 1850 in the Scouringburn, one of the worst slums in the city, characterising the Irish who had settled there as 'the most debased and ignorant of their countrymen'. Myles added, 'The low Irish are not a very improvable race. They cling to their rags, their faith and their filth with all the besottedness of perfect ignorance and stupidity.'[16] It was partly to counter this sectarianism and to defend the reputation of Irish immigrants in Britain that the Catholic priest Father Mathew left Ireland on a temperance mission to Glasgow in 1842 and visited several English cities the following year.[17]

The Scottish temperance movement grew rapidly. By 1832, there were fourteen temperance societies in Glasgow alone with a membership of eight thousand. The Scottish Temperance League, which hoped to achieve change through education and persuasion rather than through restrictive legislation, formed in Falkirk in 1844 and grew rapidly to a membership of twelve thousand with an income of £7,000 over the century.[18] The Scottish Permissive Bill Association, founded in 1858, favoured legislation. It was heavily influenced by examples from the United States, where the first prohibition laws were passed in Maine in 1852.[19]

Temperance quickly moved down the social ladder and became a grass-roots movement. In the Ayrshire weaving village of Fenwick, the Improvement of Knowledge Society, a mutual improvement group for local weavers, passed a motion in September 1836 that 'Intemperance has been most hurtful to the human race for the past 100 years' and praised the value of abstinence over the use of 'ardent spirits'.[20] In Aberdeen, the Total Abstinence Society had a membership of three thousand, made up almost entirely of Chartists and other radicals.[21] Keir Hardie, born in 1856, started his working life in the Lanarkshire coalfields. His stepfather was a heavy drinker and Hardie reacted by becoming a temperance organiser and a member of the Band of Hope and the Good Templars.[22] Another political activist, David Kirkwood, was born the son of a labourer in Parkhead in the east end of Glasgow in 1872. He recalled that 'the drink habit was very strong amongst artisans in those days, and youths were started off drinking with a sort of

Temperance worker (paying a surprise visit to the home of his pet convert).
"Does Mr. MacMurdoch live here?"
Mrs. MacMurdoch. "Aye; carry him in!"

Figure 4.1 Cartoon, 'The Temperance Slacker' (*Punch*, nineteenth century).
Author's collection.

initiation ceremony'. Kirkwood joined a temperance group which used 'a Temperance Hall, where we met for lectures, concerts, socials and the rest of it'.[23] An interesting insight here is the way in which the temperance movement had to create alternative and attractive 'drink-free' spaces to the public house to counteract its attractions.

Like similar charitable and religious movements in the nineteenth century, the temperance movement acted as a ladder of upward social mobility for some of its working-class activists. In 1829, William Simpson, a coal carter, began a temperance society in Dundee which soon enrolled a thousand members. By 1833, he had moved on (having) 'lately been appointed a preacher to a meeting of Wesleyan Methodists at Leeds'.[24] Another example of upward social mobility is Robert Kettle (1791–1852), a former handloom weaver, who became a successful cotton yarn merchant, secretary of the Glasgow City Mission, editor of the *Scottish Temperance Journal* and President of the Scottish Temperance League in 1848.[25]

TEMPERANCE, RESPECTABILITY AND THE SUPPRESSION OF DRINK-RELATED CUSTOMS AND RITUALS

The temperance movement and its supporters were active in suppressing long-standing everyday life and community rituals in their localities if they involved alcoholic drink. The Reverend Henry Duncan of Ruthwell in Dumfriesshire was a prominent evangelical who pioneered the savings bank movement, ran popular science classes and was the author of *The South Country Weaver. A Tale for the Radicals* (1820).[26] Ruthwell was an agricultural parish that had retained customs such as 'a drinking' which raised money for a family experiencing hard times by holding 'a kind of rustic ball for which whisky and other refreshments were procured by those intended to be benefited. The custom was, for two individuals, furnished with a certificate by the minister, to go through all the respectable households in the parish, inviting the inhabitants to this festivity.' Those who could not attend were invited to make a charitable contribution. Duncan boasted of having ended this seemingly harmless custom by insisting that people made gifts of money instead of alcohol.[27]

Gretna, on the English border, was famous for its 'irregular marriages', celebrated mainly by runaway English couples, and involving some three or four hundred marriages a year in 1834. The weddings took place in dram shops, 'Tippling houses have each their rival priest', including 'one who breaks stones daily on the verge of England.'[28]

At the other end of the life cycle, it was reported in 1837 from Old Cumnock in Ayrshire that it had been the custom a few years ago 'to give half a dozen rounds, or more, of spirits, wine etc. at funerals' but that this custom had now largely been abandoned.[29] In Ruthwell, Dumfriesshire, the Reverend Henry Duncan was proud of having suppressed old-style funerals during which heavy drinking took place on multiple occasions 'among the lower and middle classes'. Now, only one service was allowed for each funeral, accompanied by a subscription paper signed by 'almost every head of a family in the parish'.[30] On Jura, it was claimed that, by 1843, drinking was much less prominent at 'weddings, funerals and public meetings'.[31]

The suppression of traditional blood sports, associated with 'rough culture', drink, betting and the public house, was part of a more general movement to 'propagate the respectable way of life', exemplified by the foundation of the Society for the Prevention of Cruelty to Animals in 1825. One historian has defined 'respectability' as based on 'regular earnings and employment, sobriety and thrift',[32] so that temperance played a crucial role in the attack on 'rough culture'. In the Dumfriesshire parish of Gretna, cockfighting had died out by 1834, having formerly been very popular in the village of Rigg.[33] Sometimes, the banned blood sport literally went underground, as Hugh Miller (1802–56), the Cromarty stonemason and Free Church journalist, found out during a masons' strike in Edinburgh, when he and his companions entered a public house where badger-baiting was taking place in a hidden underground chamber. Miller was revolted by the cruelty of the scene and left the pub to examine the geology of Arthur's Seat.[34]

A recent history of sport in Scotland makes the dubious claim that, 'The cruel animal sports which were common in England and much of Europe until the nineteenth century, are almost never found in Scotland after the Reformation,' adding 'the Calvinist reformers stopped animal sports'.[35] In fact, many popular customs in Scotland, including some blood sports, survived long after the Reformation, in spite of vigorous attempts by church and burgh authorities to suppress them.[36] As Burnett and Jarvie admit, cockfights were commonplace in rural Scottish parish schools on Shrove Tuesdays, from Applecross in the West Highlands to Cromarty on the Black Isle, Dornoch in Sutherland, Kirkmichael in Highland Perthshire and Liff, a rural parish on the edge of Dundee.[37] As late as 1835, a new cockpit, which could accommodate 280 people, was opened in Glasgow.[38] By 1850, however, Hugh Miller, who had witnessed school cockfights in his native Cromarty, could condemn them as 'a relic of a barbarous age'.[39] Much less opprobrium attached itself to aristocratic blood sports, such as fox hunting (until the late twentieth century), deer hunting, and grouse and pheasant shooting. The persistence of 'rough' blood sports, such as badger-baiting, in Scotland is discussed later in this chapter.

DRINK AND THE WORKPLACE

The temperance reformer, John Dunlop, became interested in temperance in 1828 when he visited France where he was astonished to find a Roman Catholic population much less given to public drunkenness than the Presbyterian Scots. His inspiration came from American temperance reformers and from evangelical Christians on both sides of the border, including John Wesley, William Wilberforce and the Reverend Doctor Thomas Chalmers.[40] Chalmers, the minister of St John's parish in the east end of Glasgow, a prominent evangelical who played a leading role in the Disruption of 1843, was an influential figure who tried to replicate the ideals of the rural Scottish parish in the unpromising closes and wynds of inner-city Glasgow.[41]

Dunlop made a close study of Scottish drinking habits, and this revealed how closely entwined were the worlds of manual work and the public house. One long-established practice that Dunlop campaigned against was the payment of wages in public houses and the pressures this placed on working men to spend their wages on drink before the wives received their housekeeping money. On pay nights,

> Many masters pay regularly in a public house; and many to save the trouble of procuring change, give pound notes among a number of their men, who adjourn statedly to the tavern, in order to change them and divide the wages. The public houses are provided accordingly on Saturday nights with change and drinks; and the ordinary rule is sixpence to be drunk for each pound changed. Sometimes besides the sixpence, a greater part of the wages is drunk.[42]

This often led to a frantic search around the pubs by wives, sometimes accompanied by small children, to track down their husbands before they had spent all their wages.[43] This practice was ended by the truck legislation of the 1870s.[44]

This is confirmed in a number of autobiographies written by working men. The anonymous 'Jacques' described how, 'my wages were invariably paid in a public house and the scenes of debauchery I there witnessed, the conversation, chiefly characterised by lewdness and profanity ... were too shocking to prove ... corrupting or to induce approval or imitation'.[45] Patrick Dollan, born into an Irish Catholic family in the mining village of Baillieston, Lanarkshire, described a similar custom, where the miners, 'who worked in groups of three or four with one man as a paymaster always met in the pub on Friday evenings to cut up the swag. Youths did not like these arrangements; although they were teetotallers, they were always expected to pay their share of drinks they did not consume.' Dollan was elected to Glasgow Town Council in 1913 as a councillor for Govan ward and eventually became Lord Provost of Glasgow and was knighted.[46]

In the new steam-powered cotton mills in Glasgow and Paisley, the well-paid and highly unionised male mule spinners had elaborate rules and rituals connecting work, life rituals and drink. They included payment 'on getting the first wheels [on the spinning mule], entry money for drink' (1 guinea), changing mills, changing machines, marriages, births (5 shillings for each).[47] Trade union committees routinely met in pubs, and the bitter Glasgow Cotton Spinners' Strike of 1837 ended when the strike committee was arrested in a secret room in the Black Boy Tavern in Glasgow.[48] Hugh Miller, the Cromarty stonemason, geologist and Free Church activist, described similar workplace drinking customs among the stonemasons:

> When a foundation was laid, the workmen were treated to drink; they were treated to drink when the walls were levelled for laying the joists; they were treated to drink when the building was finished; they were treated to drink when an apprentice joined the squad; treated to drink when 'his apron was washed'; treated to drink when 'his time was out'; and occasionally, they learned to treat one another to drink.[49]

In the Ayrshire weaving parish of Loudon in 1842, much whisky was consumed by 'trampers' who were 'young men who wander from village to village earning a miserable living at the loom'. Loudon had a population of 4,444 in 1841 and an average 4,000 gallons of whisky a year was drunk in the parish – a gallon for every man, woman and child. This was in the declining years of handloom weaving, and the itinerant weavers eked out a miserable existence living on 'a few potatoes and salt' and drinking whisky 'not only in public and private houses, but in the fields'.[50] The treating in pubs of foremen by dockworkers was a way of buying favour in the daily scramble for work at the dock gates.[51] Drink was used in work rituals in many trades – cabinetmakers and joiners, hatters, iron founders, shipwrights, sailmakers, coopers, sawyers, stocking makers, calico printers, herring fishers, cattle dealers and butchers, domestic servants.[52]

LEGISLATION AND REGULATION

Because of the growing strength of the temperance movement, the association of crime and prostitution with pubs, and the importance of
the licensed trade as a major revenue raiser for both local and central
government, it was subject to increasing legislation and regulation. The
Hume-Drummond Act of 1828 laid down the basis for licensing in
Scotland for the next century. It confirmed Justices of the Peace in
the counties and magistrates in burghs as the authorities for granting
certificates which controlled the issue of excise licences to pubs, inns,
ale houses and so on. Strict conditions were laid down for the issue
of licences, forbidding the sale of alcohol 'during the hours of Divine
Service on Sundays' and prohibiting opening 'at unreasonable hours'.[53]

   In Newton, a Midlothian mining parish, two local landowners halved
the number of public houses in the parish, from fourteen to seven, by
1845 by controlling the issue of licences. One landowner, Sir J. Hope,
was petitioned by the kirk session to bind his tenants, on pain of
dismissal, to close their pubs on Sundays. Two publicans had been
closed down for opening their pubs on Sundays, even though the licence
allowed them to open outside the hours of divine service.[54] Similar
pressures had been brought to bear at Prestonpans in East Lothian,
another mining area, where there were twenty-four spirit houses and
seven public houses in 1839. Here, the sale of spirits on the Sabbath
had been largely discontinued owing to 'a formal resolution against
the practice' by the dealers. The practice had involved women carrying
'vessels containing gallons of spirits, but partially, if at all, concealed'.[55]
From Gladsmuir in East Lothian in 1836, the Reverend John Ramsay
called for the abolition of the Act permitting Sunday-night opening for
pubs, 'one of the most ill-advised that was ever sanctioned by a British
Parliament'.[56]

   Local control and regulation through the issue of licences applied
to other premises where alcohol was sold, including turnpike tolls and
licensed grocers. From Jedburgh in the Borders, with a population of
5,647 in 1831, the Reverend John Purves complained that 'the road
trustees having resolved to grant a licence to toll keepers, there will
be in the country an increase in the number of alehouses, and it is to
be feared of dissipation'.[57] From the agricultural parish of Hobkirk, the
minister deplored, 'the practice of giving licences to the keepers of the
toll gates, stubbornly maintained by road trustees' and suggested that
the toll gate licences should be restricted to ale.[58] In Kelso, a burgh with
a population of 5,114 in 1835, there were sixty-three places licensed to

sell spirits, one for every eighteen males over twenty in the parish. The Reverend Macculloch observed 'there are few grocers who are not spirit dealers' and attacked 'the baleful practice of selling drams across their counter and in their back shops'. He blamed 'the pecuniary interests of landlords' who were anxious to receive their rents and 'had more weight with the court than the cause of temperance and good morals'.[59]

The temperance movement was closely associated with Liberalism and, out of 127 nineteenth-century teetotal leaders across Britain whose political allegiance is known, no less than 119 (94 per cent) were Liberals. In England, the temperance cause was linked with dissenting chapels, trade unions, co-operatives, and national reform movements, such as the anti-slavery movement and campaigns against prostitution. The Scottish support base was similar except that members of dissenting Presbyterian churches, the Free Church and the United Presbyterian (UP) Church featured much more prominently in the leadership than did the established Church of Scotland. Of Scottish teetotal leaders, only one was from the Church of Scotland, six from the Free Church and five from the UP Church. The Church of Scotland viewed the temperance movement with suspicion – they disliked laymen, particularly working-class laymen, preaching against the evils of drink. George Easton, a Dumfriesshire navvy, was sacked in 1849 for persistently addressing temperance meetings.[60]

After the 1832 Reform Act and the Burgh Reform Act of 1833 which extended the franchise in parliamentary and local elections, Scotland became a bastion of Liberalism[61] and active in both the temperance and anti-slavery movements. Scotland played a prominent role in the UK Alliance which campaigned for prohibition. In 1868/9, 234 prohibitionists gave £5 or more to the UK Alliance. The place of birth is known for ninety-six of these people, of whom twenty-one (22 per cent) came from Lancashire and nineteen (20 per cent) from Scotland.[62]

The UK Alliance was an effective lobbying organisation and, in 1853, sabbatarians and temperance reformers combined to get through Parliament the Forbes McKenzie Act which fixed licensing hours in Scotland from 8.00 a.m. to 11.00 p.m. and introduced Sunday closing, except for hotels and inns, which were open for 'bona fide' travellers. The Act laid down the basis of licensing laws in Scotland for the next 125 years. Forbes McKenzie was a Scot who was Conservative MP for Liverpool.[63] The effects of the Forbes McKenzie Act on drinking habits in Scotland were widely disputed at the time. In Dundee, arrests for Sunday drunkenness halved from 414 between 15 May and 24 October 1853 to 201 for the equivalent period in the following year.

Much Sunday drinking went underground, however, shebeens flourished and the Dundee courts held special courts purely for shebeens.[64]
James Smart, Superintendent of Police in Glasgow, claimed in 1855 that,
prior to the Act, 'the streets of the lower part of the City were kept in
a state of turmoil and disorder all Sunday morning, and frequently the
entire day'. Pubs were open on Sunday mornings until 11.00 a.m. when
'the customers are turned out onto the street, many of them in a state of
intoxication, and this while the people were passing to church'.[65]

This is what one historian has called 'the discipline of the streets' or
'the formal regulation of the streets', which was increasingly enforced
by the policeman as the century went on but in which control of the
drink trade played an important role.[66] Sometimes, the marginal and
dispossessed fought back and asserted the right to space in their own
neighbourhoods over the police. One of the worst slums in Dundee in
the 1850s was the Scouringburn area, dominated by Irish immigrants.
On one occasion, 'they tried to take possession of that unsavoury thoroughfare, and from the windows of the common stairs stoned the police,
shouting, "More stones, the town's our own."'[67]

Before the Forbes McKenzie Act, many Glasgow pubs stayed open all
night, and 'a raffle, a wedding or a dance was sufficient to keep a whole
neighbourhood from sleep the greater part of the morning'. Another
threat to public order came from unregulated 'Music and Dancing
Saloons, Billiard Rooms etc.' which were popular in Glasgow. During the
Glasgow Fair Week and at New Year, the pubs kept open continuously
from Monday morning until the following Sunday morning. The Glasgow
Superintendent of Police claimed that the new Act 'has produced a degree
of quiet and order on our Streets on week mornings and in particular on
Sabbath mornings'.[68] The following year he reported a reduction in the
number of licences granted, from over 2,000 in 1853 to 1,773 in 1856.
As in Dundee, however, they had been replaced by 'Shebeen Clubs, a
class of houses that open when the Licensed houses shut, and are kept
open generally till four or five in the morning and during the whole of
Sunday'. For the last twenty years, many brothels in Glasgow had sold
wine and spirits without any licence, as had 'Unlicensed Oyster Stores,
low Lodging Houses, low Eating Houses etc.'.[69]

The *Glasgow Herald* acknowledged that there were fewer 'open exhi-
bitions of public drunkenness, especially on Sundays', fewer riots and
less brawling. Much drinking, however, had gone underground, clubs
had taken over from pubs on Sundays and there were now no fewer than
1,600 unlicensed shebeens in Glasgow selling whisky. Further south,
in Dumfries, 'a teetotal Superintendent put on the screw so tightly that

Table 4.2 Drunkenness convictions and drink-related crime figures for six Scottish towns and cities, 1852–7.

	Population	Three years under Old Law, 1852–4	Three years under New Law, 1855–7
Glasgow	329,097	66,993	53,755
Edinburgh	160,302	28,905	23,903
Dundee	78,931	9,598	8,330
Aberdeen	71,973	13,744	10,357
Paisley	47,952	2,054	1,527
Greenock	36,689	9,042	6,287

(Source: D. McLaren, *The Rise and Progress of Whisky Drinking in Scotland and the Working of the Public Houses (Scotland) Act, 1853*, Scottish Temperance League, Glasgow, 1858, p. 40)

the inhabitants would bear it no longer' and brought about a change of magistracy which abandoned the strict enforcement of the Forbes McKenzie Act.[70]

Table 4.2 reveals some striking differences between Scottish cities and towns. Figures for drunkenness and drink-related crime fell consistently after the 1853 Act but more striking are the differences between Aberdeen and Dundee where Dundee, with a larger population, had lower rates of drunkenness and drink-related crime, and between Paisley, with a population larger than Greenock, but much lower rates of drunkenness and drink-related crime.

As well as national legislation, local authorities in Scotland tried to control the drink trade by regulating the issue of licences, controlling opening hours and by enforcing changes to the interiors of public houses and even the numbers of entrances and exits they had. When Thomas Wyness was appointed Chief Constable of Aberdeen in 1880, he became known as 'The Terror of the Trade'. He cracked down on back-shop drinking in licensed grocers' shops and insisted on the removal of compartments in pubs and the introduction of open counters. He also brought about the abolition of the 'treacle cask' or the 'trade cistern' in licensed grocers.[71]

The Dean of Guild Papers for cities such as Aberdeen, Dundee, Edinburgh, and Glasgow reveal sustained attempts in the 1880s and 1890s to regulate drinking behaviour and ease the job of the police by reducing the number of rooms in public houses, and the number of entrances and exits they had, so that control by licensees and the police was made easier. Numerous small rooms in a pub were frequently replaced by one large room with a centrally placed bar so that the

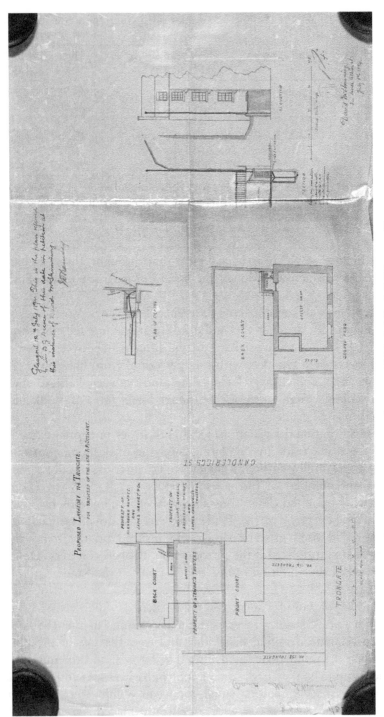

Figure 4.2 Alterations to a spirit shop at 114 Trongate, Glasgow, 1894. © Mitchell Library, Glasgow.

licensee could supervise drinking. A plan for alterations to a spirit shop at 114 Trongate, Glasgow, dated 1894, shows licensed premises situated up a narrow close off the Trongate and opening out on to a front and a back court, with exits to both.[72] Any police raid here stood a fair chance of seeing the suspects disappear into a maze of courts and closes.

It was not only in the larger Scottish cities where the magistrates disliked pubs situated down closes with multiple exits. In Perth in 1900, the magistrates suddenly denounced all bars which had their entrances in closes. One Perth bar made the waggish announcement, 'the Parliament Bar, following the example of the Volunteers, has been ordered to the front'.[73]

Scottish magistrates were heavily influenced by the example of Liverpool which had reduced public drunkenness through detailed regulation of the internal layout of pubs and by insisting that closing times were strictly enforced. Both Glasgow and Dundee sent delegations to Liverpool to investigate the changes that had taken place. The Glasgow magistrates reported in March 1902 that they had viewed Liverpool pubs from the 'top of a car' and could easily see into them, 'the windows of which are not obscured with figured glass or blinds, as is so common in Glasgow'. On looking in a pub door in Liverpool, one could 'see a considerable part of the interior', unlike Glasgow, where there was usually a porch at the entrance. The magistrates ascribed the reduction in drunkenness in Liverpool to closing all back and side doors of pubs, 'thus reducing secret drinking', and 'the stamping out of the harbouring of prostitutes'. The number of drunken prostitutes arrested in Liverpool fell from 2,009 in 1889 to 634 in 1901.[74]

The Dundee delegation to Liverpool in June 1902 consisted of Chief Constable Dewar, Bailie Robertson, Mr Wilson of the Town Clerk's office, and Lord Provost Hunter. The layout of Liverpool pubs was strikingly different from that in Dundee, 'as a general rule there are no semi-private small compartments such as we have in some of the Dundee public houses'. In Liverpool, 'back door entrances are not allowed' and pubs generally had 'two entrance and egress doors, one at each end of the bar, which tend to lessen jostling amongst customers passing in and out'. It was claimed that 'shebeening and Sunday clubs are almost unknown' in Liverpool and that penalties for shebeening were more severe than in Scotland. Cases of drunkenness in Liverpool had fallen from 16,042 in 1889 to 4,327 in 1901 owing to slum clearance, strict application of the law and 'the cheap facilities now offered by rail, steamer and car for excursions'. There was little sign of the evening promenade in Liverpool, compared to 'the throng of people' in working-class areas of Dundee such as the Overgate, the Scouringburn, Hilltown and the Greenmarket on Saturday nights. Most Liverpool pubs were situated on main thoroughfares, 'and not in back courts or closes', as in Dundee. They were 'largely owned by Brewery Companies' and the Liverpool police claimed these were easier to control than those owned by individual licensees, as was the norm in Scotland.[75]

TRAVELLERS AND ALCOHOL

One of the side effects of the Forbes McKenzie Act (1853) was the creation of the concept of the 'bona fide' traveller which produced some ingenious responses from the licensed trade. A clause in the Act made it illegal to serve alcohol on Sundays in Scotland, except to 'bona fide' travellers. The development of railways, trams and steamships made it cheaper, easier and quicker to travel around Scotland, and the 'day trip', often associated with heavy drinking, developed rapidly. One way of circumventing the Sunday drinking ban was to travel on steamers down the Clyde, until the Gladstone Government Act of 1882 prohibited the sale of liquor on passenger vessels in Scotland on Sundays.[76] Drunken behaviour on Clyde steamers predates the 1853 Act, however, and the word 'steaming' was coined for getting drunk. At Glasgow Fair in 1850, some twenty thousand people went down the Clyde on steamers, including a party of eight or ten people who, before they got to Rothesay, had had 'three bottles of whisky and a fight'.[77] Members of the licensed trade also travelled in large organised groups 'doon the watter'. In July 1898, the Scottish Wine and Spirit Merchants' Benevolent Association Annual Trip took six hundred people on a special train to Craignure, then on a sail to the Kyle and Arran, with music provided by the band of the Argyll and Sutherland Highlanders.[78]

This type of bacchanalian behaviour was not confined to the Clyde. An English solicitor came across a group of excursionists on a day trip from Elgin on the Loch Ness steamer in August 1868, accompanied by a brass band, some of whom 'had imbibed pretty freely'. There were complaints from North Berwick, East Lothian in 1873 that, 'Saturday after Saturday there are poured into the street excursion parties, the members of which have no other idea of passing a holiday than by swilling strong drink'.[79]

As tourism and travel expanded in the nineteenth century, better and more luxurious inns and hotels were built to meet the growing demand for accommodation. As early as 1839, Dumbarton boasted two good inns which 'are well filled in summer by travellers going to and returning from Loch Lomond'. The town was reached by steamers from Glasgow and Greenock, sailing three times a day in the summer.[80] At Rhu, the population 'is increased by more than a half, possibly two thirds of this number during about five months in the year, from the number of families who come for summer quarters and sea bathing'.[81] As well as sea bathing, Highland scenery also proved a potent attraction for visitors. In Arrochar, there were two inns at Tarbert for tourists in 1839, and also at Arrochar, 'a hotel lately built and opened'. These were for tourists, 'who come from all quarters to visit the splendid and beautiful scenery'.[82] Lowland towns also benefited from tourism. By 1858, the Golden Lion at Stirling was a recognised stop for Thomas Cook tours of Scotland, and offered 'hot, cold and shower baths' for weary travellers.[83]

Edinburgh saw a whole string of upmarket hotels built to meet the growing demand from tourists and business visitors. The two great Edinburgh railway hotels, the North British and the Caledonian, at opposite ends of Princes Street, opened in 1896 and 1903 respectively. Inverness, which claimed to be 'long celebrated for the excellency of its inns', boasted the Caledonian Hotel which, in 1835, had eighty bedrooms and a 'spacious ballroom'.[84] In Oban, the Great Western Hotel was built as early as 1863 and enlarged twenty years later.[85] An English solicitor who stayed there in August 1868 was impressed: 'the bedrooms are clean and roomy, the Coffee and drawing rooms large and handsomely decorated and furnished, the feeding good and plentiful and the attendance first rate'.[86] The growth of an increasingly affluent middle class saw the rise of the Scottish golf hotel on east and west coasts. At St Andrews, a raft of golfing hotels was built in the second half of the nineteenth century, beginning with the Golf in 1863. The Marine Hotel in Troon dates from 1897; the Turnberry Hotel, built by the Glasgow and South Western Railway Company, from 1904. In the Highlands, the Aviemore Station Hotel was built by the Highland Railway Company for £25,000 in 1899.[87] All these hotels catered for the 'bona fide' Sunday traveller, as well as affluent tourists.

At a lower social level, however, the authorities continued to intervene to enforce the provisions of the Forbes McKenzie Act, such as closing times and the bona fide traveller provision. In Perth, the police brought cases against four public houses in May 1889 for not enforcing closing time on a Tuesday night: the Liberal Club, the Parliament Close Inn, the Queen's Hotel and the Old Ship Hotel.[88] The following year, the Exchange Hotel, Perth was fined ten shillings for serving five 'persons belonging to Perth and neither travellers nor lodgers standing at the hotel bar' at 10.20 p.m.[89]

'BELOW THE RADAR': SHEBEENS AND UNLICENSED DRINKING PLACES

Though the unlicensed shebeen predated the Forbes McKenzie Act, the number of shebeens grew exponentially after 1853. In the Central District of Glasgow, around the Saltmarket, Gallowgate, Trongate area, there were upwards of '200 houses of ill fame' in 1870, with about 150 shebeens selling liquor illegally. The larger shebeens were situated on the main thoroughfares, and 'generally have one large room, capable of accommodating at a pinch from 30 to 40 people'. There was usually a smaller room for select customers, and the family kitchen took any overspill. They were fairly noisome places 'a conglomeration of fish bones and fragments of sodden pastry, in crowded low-roofed rooms, filled with clouds of bad tobacco smoke and the tainted breaths and perspiration of a most unprepossessing company'.[90]

A Glasgow shebeener started in 'the doctored drink' trade in 1850 'at a shebeen in my native Saltmarket'. The place was 'a dancing crib' and, when the dancers got too warm, they cooled themselves with doctored drink containing water, grain whisky, methylated spirits and raspberry vinegar to colour the drink. The daily takings were 96 shillings, of which 88 shillings was profit. Four years later, he was working 'at a Drum in King Street' where they served whisky punch which contained methylated spirits and was also highly profitable, with takings of 106 shillings and 6d and a profit of 85 shillings. The trade boomed when the Forbes McKenzie Act shut up licensed premises at 11.00 p.m. Five years later, he bought whisky from a publican on the south side of Glasgow who was distilling it at home from a mixture of 'molasses and sour beer'.[91]

Shebeens were not only to be found in the slums but in middle-class areas, too. The *Victualling Trade Review* for 1 June 1893 carried a gleeful report headed 'Vigilantes promoting a Shebeen' in Edinburgh. The Edinburgh Vigilance Society was set up by the temperance movement to 'disestablish liquor dealers' premises' but an undercover reporter had discovered members taking large quantities of liquor into an unlicensed hall on the south side used for dancing parties and Good Templar meetings and so on. Better still, the hall was owned by a member of the Vigilance Society. Beer and cold drinks were sold in an anteroom off the hall, and whisky was also available. The reporter left at 1.00 a.m. when several men were drunk, and the event, which included dancing, was planned to last until 5.00 a.m.[92] In Dundee, shebeens were known as 'cheeping shops', and the largest shebeen in the city in the late 1880s hid behind a veneer of respectability, calling itself the Kincardine Literary Club.[93]

A *Scotsman* reporter estimated there were five hundred shebeens in Glasgow in 1894. Most were situated in working-class areas but he described a visit to one in Garnethill, in Glasgow's middle-class West End, where drink was being served on a Sunday afternoon. There were seven or eight men in the room, and three respectable-looking young women served the drinks, consisting of beer and whisky. Another Glasgow shebeen he attended on a Sunday was a two-room and kitchen house on the south side, near Bridge Street station, a whisky-drinking place patronised by working men. The beer served was 'villainous stuff', the whisky of slightly better quality.[94] He also visited a disreputable shebeen, functioning as a brothel, in Candleriggs, run by a woman, a one-roomed hovel with two beds in it occupied by both men and women.[95]

'DARK CLOSES AND SECLUDED BUILDINGS': SENSATIONALISM AND THE SCOTTISH CITY

Reports like this reveal a deep vein of anxiety running through the temperance movement in Scotland. Temperance activists were concerned not only about the social conditions in the Victorian slums, where poverty, drunkenness, disease, overcrowding and crime were the norm, but by what they perceived as the moral failings of the poor and the threat they posed to respectable society and the maintenance of the social order. This explains the popularity of reports on the city slums that were published around this time: from George Bell's *Day and Night in the Wynds of Edinburgh* and *Blackfriars Wynd Analysed* (1849 and 1850) to Alexander Brown's *Shadow's Midnight Scenes and Social Photographs* (1858), an exposé of life in the Glasgow slums.[96] Other works in the same genre include: the fictional *Chapters in the Life of a Dundee Factory Boy* (1850) by James Myles, a Dundee stonemason, bookseller and Chartist; the *Recollections of a Police Officer in the Granite City* by the Aberdeen policeman Alexander Clark, published in 1873 but describing events in the 1840s; and the sensationalist series of articles 'The Dark Side of Glasgow' published in the *North British Daily Mail* in 1870.[97] Similar exposés were published in England around the same time. In 1857, the prohibitionist J. Ewing Ritchie published his *Night Side of London* which catered to the same middle-class 'mixture of fear and fascination' about the slums and the urban poor.[98]

George Bell was an Edinburgh physician, influenced by the Reverend Thomas Chalmers and the Reverend Thomas Guthrie, evangelicals who became pillars of the Free Church after the Disruption. Bell worked with Guthrie in the Edinburgh Ragged School movement and had similar anxieties over the moral state of the poor. In 1850 more than a thousand people lived in Blackfriars Wynd, many of them poor Irish migrants, and over a hundred of them caught typhus in the epidemic of 1847/8 brought by refugees from the Irish famine. Bell was virulently anti-Irish, comparing Irish immigration to a disease in the body politic: 'the migratory Irish are a pestilence as well as a pest'. He believed that poverty was caused by 'idleness and vice', adding 'Statistics prove that the Scots are the most drunken people on the face of the earth'. He noted that almost all the whisky shops were concentrated where the poor lived and that dram shops 'open before sunrise and they remain open until an hour short of midnight'. The profits on dram selling were so great that one Edinburgh dram seller could afford to give away in a year £400 of gingerbread or lozenges, as a 'snap' or incentive to those who bought drams.[99]

The Glasgow printer and journalist, Alexander Brown (Shadow), wrote from a similar evangelical viewpoint, though he was slightly less moralistic and censorious. His *Midnight Scenes* viewed the slums of Glasgow on a Sunday night in 1858 as foreign territory inhabited by hostile natives, 'the impression at once felt is that of intrusion. No nautical explorer ever fell among savages who looked with greater wonder at his approach.' Unlike Bell, Alexander Brown drew a distinction between different types of shebeen. One was run by 'a decently attired looking man' and its appearance was that of 'an old fashioned country inn, with a table before us and resting on a comfortable seat', where they were served 'a glass of very good ale [at] a very good price'. Another, near Eglinton Street, was full of drunken women. In Bridgeton, on a Friday night, they were struck by 'the inordinate number of public houses and the generally quiet, sober and respectable demeanour of the working population' and by 'numerous bands of well-dressed smart little factory girls' on the streets.[100]

All these publications played on the anxieties of what might be described, perhaps unfairly, as 'the meddling classes', the respectable middle and skilled artisan classes, who formed the backbone of nineteenth-century campaigns for temperance, anti-slavery, anti-Corn Laws, self-improvement, slum clearance, public health, control of prostitution and so on. This is sensationalist literature as 'poverty tourism' or 'poverty porn', tapping into a rich seam of anxiety but also into an equally rich seam of prurience about the behaviour of the lower classes. The development of photography around the same time also fed this market. Thomas Annan (1829–87), an activist in the Free Church of Scotland and a member of the Total Abstinence Society, was commissioned by the Glasgow City Improvement Trust to photograph the slums of Glasgow before and after the City Improvement Act of 1866 swept the worst slums away.[101] It was no accident that Alexander Brown's 1858 work was titled *Shadow's Midnight Scenes and Social Photographs*. Rodger has argued that 'newspaper sensationalism in no small part created the slum'.[102] In Scotland, however, the anxieties of the Presbyterian churches and their concern for the threat to the moral fabric of society, posed by the growth of the slums, predated newspaper sensationalism and, I would argue, informed a good deal of the journalism that came later.

Much of the leadership, and a good deal of the organisation for many of these reforming campaigns, were provided by the clergy, laymen and laywomen of the evangelical wing of the Church of Scotland and, after the Disruption, of the Free Church and the United Presbyterian Church. The activities of the Reverend Doctor Thomas Chalmers, minister of St John's parish in Glasgow, have been mentioned earlier. Chalmers had his counterparts in other Scottish cities, such as the Reverend Thomas Guthrie, minister of Greyfriars, Edinburgh and founder of the Ragged School movement, who was shocked by the gulf between the Edinburgh slums and the rural Angus parish of Arbirlot where he had worked until 1837. To Guthrie, one of the earliest church leaders to take the temperance pledge, the contrast was 'nothing less than the change from green fields and woods and the light of nature, to venting into the darkness and blackness of a coal pit'.[103] A similar reaction came from the minister of St David's parish, Dundee, the evangelical Reverend George Lewis, whose pamphlet *Scotland: A Half-Educated Nation*, published in 1834, was an impassioned attack on the failings of the parochial school system to meet the educational needs of the urban poor.[104]

Some popular novelists described Scottish cities in equally sensationalist terms. David Pae has been described as 'the leading popular novelist in Scotland'[105] though much of his work was published anonymously in serial form. Pae, a Dundee-based journalist and novelist, was a teetotaller who wrote for the *People's Journal* and became founding editor of the *People's Friend*. He was a prolific writer who, among his numerous novels, produced two, published in serial form, that examined the problems of the Victorian Scottish city: *Mary Paterson, or the Fatal Error* (1864), set in Edinburgh during the Burke and Hare murders, and

Lucy the Factory Girl or the Secrets of the Tontine Close (1858), set in
Glasgow during the cotton-manufacturing era. Both are morality tales
but with very different outcomes for their female protagonists. Mary
Patterson is a country girl who turns her back on her family, goes to
Edinburgh where she is seduced, takes to drink and turns to prostitution, becoming one of the victims of Burke and Hare.[106] Lucy Blair is
an heiress who has been swindled out of her inheritance and is forced
to earn her living as a weaver in a Glasgow power-loom factory. Unlike
Mary Patterson, she is a virtuous girl who falls in love with the factory
owner's son, eventually marries him and is restored to her inheritance.
In *Lucy the Factory Girl,* Pae promised his readers a 'dark and romantic
tale' which would transport them 'into the haunts of vice and crime,
wherein dark closes and secluded buildings are congregated those who
have bid farewell to honesty, sobriety and virtue'.[107]

There was a certain irony in teetotallers writing about the drink-
soaked Scottish city which did not escape J. G. Bertram, the editor of
the *North Briton,* who wrote to David Pae in August 1858, declining his
suggestion to use the newspaper to publicise the temperance message.
Bertram explained, 'if you mixed with *all classes* of the public of Edinr
as I do, and did not confine yourself to a few teetotal (friends) you
would long ago been of my opinion ... the kind of paper you would
like the *NB* to become is no doubt a good kind, but my dear friend *it
wouldn't pay'.*[108] One Scottish writer who was unencumbered by the
teetotal legacy was Robert Louis Stevenson who, in his youth in the
early 1870s, patronised an old Edinburgh pub frequented by sailors,
criminals and 'the lowest order of prostitutes – three penny whores'.
Stevenson reported, 'the girls were singularly decent creatures, not a bit
worse than anybody else'.[109]

'THIEVES AND LOOSE WOMEN': CRIME AND THE SCOTTISH PUB

Against this background, many writers and commentators, particularly
those from a temperance background, were quick to draw connections
between heavy alcohol use, pubs and drinking places, and crime. George
Bell pointed out the gap between the large sums spent on whisky in
Blackfriars Wynd, Edinburgh, where the average annual consumption
of whisky was 4 gallons (18 litres) per man, woman and child, and
the low earnings of the inhabitants, with an average income of 8/10d
per week, which could only be bridged by crime.[110] The Dundee Police
Commissioners claimed in 1834, 'There is hardly a crime committed
or a riot perpetrated but what may be referred to the intemperate use

of ardent spirits, and that mostly in the night time.'[111] Similarly, David Barrie, a temperance advocate who had been involved with licensing courts in Dundee and elsewhere, believed that 'nine tenths of the organised crime in Scotland can be traced either directly or indirectly to the immoderate indulgence in liquor'.[112]

Even rural areas were not exempt from whisky-related crime. From the Argyllshire parish of Glassary, where 5,600 gallons (25,480 litres) of whisky were sold every year to a population of 5,369, the Reverend Dugald Campbell claimed in 1844 that 'probably nine tenths of the criminal business here has its origins in whisky'.[113] In Glasgow, Alexander Brown described the infamous Tontine Close, with its high density of drinking places and reputation for crime and prostitution, as 'reputed the most dangerous of any in the city'.[114] The Tontine Close provided one of the settings for David Pae's *Lucy the Factory Girl*, and a set piece in the book describes a thieves' kitchen in the Close, accessed through a trapdoor in the ceiling.[115]

Nothing better illustrates the enormous gap between the rhetoric of Victorian morality, with its emphasis on female 'purity' and idealisation of the mother as the 'angel at the hearth', and the reality of life in the Victorian city, than the almost industrial scale of female prostitution. There were two hundred brothels in Edinburgh in 1842, with eight hundred girls working full-time and 1,200 'sly prostitutes' working part-time.[116] In Glasgow, the city missionary, William Logan (1813–79), estimated that there were 450 brothels in 1843, each employing four girls on average, a total of 1,800 prostitutes. Some 1,350 bullies or 'fancy men' lived on the proceeds of prostitution and 450 brothel madams, making a total of 3,600 people living on the earnings of prostitution in Glasgow.[117]

There were close links between the sale of alcohol and prostitution. Logan believed that the earnings from prostitution itself were easily exceeded by the amount spent on alcohol by each client and theft from clients. He estimated that each brothel had eighty clients a week, some 36,000 weekly visitors in total. On average, the girls received an average of a shilling (5 pence) per client, an average weekly income of £1,800. Each client spent an average of two shillings on alcohol, or £3,600 a week and money stolen from clients averaged 2/6d per head, a weekly total of £4,500. The average weekly income generated by prostitution in Glasgow came to £9,900, an annual total of £514,800. Of the 2 shillings a head spent by clients on alcohol, only half was spent while the client was there. The brothel madam sent out for drink but retained half for, what in England was called 'wack brass', but more genteelly in Scotland 'the goodwill of the house'. Streetwise regulars brought their own alcohol with them; Logan had seen 'several gentlemen drive up to a first class house in a four horse carriage filled with bottles'. The 'first class house', that is the expensive brothel, was where the world of the prosperous and 'respectable' (male) middle and upper classes overlapped with the life of the Victorian slum. The life of a Glasgow prostitute was nasty, brutish and short, blighted as it was by poverty, venereal disease, violence from pimps and clients, and alcohol and drug abuse. Logan estimated the working life of the average prostitute at a mere six years and claimed that some three hundred women died every year.[118]

Another 'underground' and 'invisible' sexual activity in the Victorian city was homosexual sex which, like female prostitution, was closely linked to public houses and the consumption of alcohol. Out of a sample of twenty sodomy cases tried in the Scottish courts between 1828 and 1875, eleven mentioned heavy alcohol consumption and three involved sexual encounters in the 'drinking boxes' of a public house. Examples include the trial of three journeymen stocking makers in Hawick in 1828, who were drinking on a November fair day, then went back to the accused's room to continue drinking whisky when the alleged (unsuccessful) assaults took place. The sentence was transportation for life. Another sodomy case in Edinburgh in 1845 revealed that the two men accused had engaged in sexual activity beforehand in a 'drinking box' in a pub in the Old Town, for which they had been put out by the landlord. In 1866, two young men, William Glen, a Glasgow slater aged twenty-one, and Maurice Broadley, a Londonderry picture dealer aged nineteen, were convicted of sodomy 'in or near a drinking box' in a public house in Bridgegate, Glasgow and sentenced to ten years' penal servitude. Similarly, Archibald Miller, a 'travelling tinsmith' aged thirty, was 'drinking in a box in a pub in Lanark High Street', when he was approached by three boys for money, after which he had sex with them. In Arbroath, John Kidd, a thirty-seven-year-old butcher, and Peter Rattray a nineteen-year-old mechanic, were accused of sodomy in Kidd's shop. They had spent the evening drinking in pubs in Arbroath and gone back to Kidd's shop to drink whisky when the pubs closed. They were found not guilty.[119] These cases provide some insight into why local authorities in Scotland were anxious to regulate the internal arrangements of public houses and abolish drinking boxes and private rooms.

In 1870, the *North British Daily Mail* ran a sensationalist exposure of 'the criminal and unfortunate classes in this city' which constituted 'a fearful anomaly in a Christian city'. In the Central District of Glasgow, there were 'upwards of 200 houses of ill fame' in which 'shebeening and thievery are likewise perpetrated'. Unlicensed shebeens were castigated as 'a fruitful source of evil' where drinking 'goes on during the greater part of the night and continuous relays of customers are coming and going'. The lowest shebeens were 'the rendez-vous of thieves and loose women' and were guarded by a network of scouts who warned the shebeeners of the approach of the police by a series of whistles.[120]

By 1890 the Glasgow magistrates were taking vigorous action against lotteries and betting shops and many forms of outdoor street life and popular amusements involving young people, in a conscious attempt at control of the streets. They wished to regulate a wide range of everyday social activities including lotteries, street betting and betting houses, theatres, shows, billiard rooms, unlicensed premises, street importuning, habitual drunkards, street obstructions, steam whistles, bicycles on streets, beggars and vagrants, public placards and so on. Bailie Graham was particularly incensed about *cafés chantants* (a cafe providing musical entertainment), of which there were two or three in the city, some open on Sundays. He had visited one with the Chief Constable and found 120 people, mostly young men, drinking coffee and lemonade 'and chaffing the waitresses in the most secular way'. He believed 'they ought not to be permitted in a city like Glasgow'.[121]

These sternly Presbyterian attitudes reflected the growing influence of the temperance and sabbatarian movements on the city fathers. In 1890, fifty out of seventy-five members of Glasgow Town Council were pro-temperance, thirty-two of the fifty were total abstainers and eleven out of fourteen magistrates were abstainers.[122] Two years later, fifteen of the twenty-six councillors recommended by the Scottish Permissive Bill Association were returned to Glasgow Town Council. Three Lord Provosts, Sir William Collins (1877–80), Sir Samuel Chisholm (1899–1902) and Sir Daniel Macaulay (1911–14) were notable temperance leaders. Women played a prominent role in the sabbatarian and temperance movements, and the Glasgow British Women's Temperance Association petitioned the Lord Provost in 1900 against the Sunday opening of ice cream shops. In Perth, the Provost fulminated against 'this ice cream pestilence'.[123] This was because of a widespread belief that many Italian-owned ice cream shops were selling alcohol under the counter. The *Scottish Licensed Trade News* for February 1910 carried a report that 'Many enterprising Italians, not content with the legitimate profits of the ice cream trade', were 'suspected of hastening the day of their return to a villa in sunny Italy, by doing a little shebeening'.[124]

The magistrates faced an uphill task, however. In 1900, of 179,281 people charged with criminal offences in Scotland, no less than 114,207 (63 per cent) were for offences directly connected with drink. In Aberdeen, out of 7,057 people prosecuted for crime in 1901, no fewer than 3,579 were prosecuted for breach of the peace and drunkenness, compared to 2,033 in 1897.[125]

MUSIC AND ENTERTAINMENT

The origins of music hall lie in the pubs. The 'free and easy' was a room fitted up in a public house with a chairman and generally volunteer performers. Some of the saloons were 'beautifully fitted up, finely painted and brilliantly illuminated'.[126] The home of the 'free and easies' in Glasgow was the Saltmarket and the more prominent ones were the Shakespeare, the Jupiter, the Oddfellows and the Sir Walter Scott which flourished in the 1840s and 1850s.[127] These were the precursors of the music halls.[128] The 'free and easies' continued to flourish into the 1870s. The *North British Daily Mail* discovered nineteen within five minutes' walk of Glasgow Cross. Their audiences were mainly young men aged between sixteen and twenty-two, with a smattering of young women. The entertainment consisted mainly of sentimental songs, clog dances and the occasional indecent song. The 'free and easies' held between 100 and 150 people at a time and the investigating journalist thought there were probably something like forty of them in the area.[129]

There were also drinking and dancing clubs organised by young men, often from the same factory or mill, who clubbed together to hire a room in a public house, for 9d to 1/6d a night. These clubs met on Friday nights and the young men brought girlfriends with them and provided the music themselves in the form of fiddles, flutes or whistles. One in the Gorbals had about twelve couples dancing on the night the reporter visited while, in another, the walls were decorated with greenery and the young men were shoemaking and tailoring apprentices and their girlfriends were shop girls dressed in their best clothes. The journalist was 'astonished by the decorum' of the dances.[130]

This type of harmless amusement, along with others less harmless, challenged and offended the temperance reformers and their allies in public life, and led them to create alternative alcohol-free attractions, removed from the temptations of the public house. Walter Freer, for example, the son of a handloom weaver, who remembered the old

singing saloons of the Saltmarket from his youth, became a passion-
ate advocate for temperance and, eventually in 1890, the manager of
Glasgow Corporation Halls. As a young man, Freer joined the Band of
Hope and the Glasgow Abstinence Union which organised concerts 'to
wean folks from the unhealthy atmosphere of the squalid public house
and the low down music hall'.[131] Temperance and urban clearance had
restricted many of these activities by the 1890s. The City Improvement
Act of 1866 was designed to clear the worst slums in the inner city,
which housed most of these singing saloons.

An alternative temperance culture sprang up of concerts and dances
with tea and pastries designed to 'counteract the pernicious influence
of the drinking and singing saloons, and to afford amusement to those
who had been wont to seek it amidst scenes of vice and dissipation'.[132]
This type of consciously respectable event, often presented under an
exotic-sounding title, such as soirée or *conversazione*, and aimed particularly at young men, was to be found all over Scotland and in
England, Wales and Ireland, too. It was also widespread in North
America and in the Protestant Scandinavian countries. It was linked
with self-improvement, literacy and the concept of bettering oneself and
'getting on' in life. In Edinburgh, the autodidact and popular journalist,
David Pae, a member of the Bristo Young Men's Mutual Improvement
Association, went to the association's annual Queen Street soirée on 15
December 1856 where tea and fruit were served, rather than alcohol,
and improving lectures delivered.[133] Sometimes, these events were
sponsored by employers, as in Dundee, where the young millwright
John Sturrock attended a soirée of employees of the Lilybank Foundry
at the Thistle Hall in November 1865. There were speeches delivered,
songs sung, and the evening ended at midnight after 'an hour and a
half's dancing'.[134]

By 1901, when three young men were recording their impressions
of Glasgow life under the pseudonym 'J. H. Muir', they claimed that
'the "sing songs" and "cosies" which you hear of in Manchester are
unknown in Glasgow. The magistrates will not grant a music licence to
a public house.' They believed that this type of municipal interference
had turned Glasgow pubs into unpleasant, male-only drinking dens,
'Singing may go with beer but not with whisky. So the public houses of
Glasgow are crowded, garish, inhuman, unmerry places, to which men
come from refuge from the rain.'[135]

The links between the theatrical tradition and the licensed trade
continued into the late nineteenth and early twentieth centuries when
commercial theatre was developing. Robert Robin, who died in 1905,

owned three pubs in Glasgow and the Argyle Hotel, Dunoon, and left
the substantial estate of £304,377. He also owned the New Century
Theatre in Motherwell, valued at £5,000.[136] Another wealthy Glasgow
wine and spirit merchant, Edward Taylor, who owned four licensed
'shops' in Glasgow, left an estate of £61,169 on his death in 1905. His
estate included shares valued at £1,056 in theatre owners Moss Empires
Limited and Howard and Wyndham Limited.[137]

PUBS AND SPORT

Many sporting activities were housed in, or connected with, pubs. A
number of publicans ran sparring matches on their premises and kept
cockpits and ratpits in their back courts. Jock Gowdie, a local boxer, ran
the Pugilist's Tavern, off the Gallowgate in Glasgow. He held boxing
matches there and also bulldog-fights, cockfights and badger-baiting,
colloquially known as 'drawing the badger'. One famous badger was
kept somewhere between Edinburgh and Glasgow so that the owner
could have it fight in both cities. Bets came to £100 a side.[138] Charles
Donaldson, sports writer with the *Evening Times,* bought the Coffin
public house in Whitevale Street, Glasgow in 1909. He turned it into 'a
shrine for boxing', and the world heavyweight champion, Jack Johnson,
visited it with his wife in 1915.[139] The popularity of boxing can be
gauged by the attendance figures of seven or eight thousand for an exhibition bout between the British and American champions at Glasgow
City Hall in 1860.[140]

   These figures, however, were dwarfed by the attendances at football
matches, particularly those between Celtic and Rangers, and interna-
tionals between Scotland and England. The first Hampden international in 1878 was watched by twenty thousand spectators, and an
astonishing 102,000 attended the inaugural international at the new
Hampden Park in 1902.[141] This was challenged only by attendances
for 'Old Firm' matches. The record attendance for a Scottish club game
was in September 1898, when 44,868 fans packed out Parkhead. By
1913, the game at Ibrox attracted 65,000 fans and many more were
locked out.[142]

   As professional football began to emerge in Scotland in the last
quarter of the nineteenth century, its affairs were often managed, not
by the players who 'are unfortunately, mainly incapable of managing the
various clubs and associations, and accordingly, they elect others, not
players, but chiefly publicans etc., to undertake this duty for them'.[143]
As football became big business and players became more affluent and

prominent public figures, a number of them took over the management and ownership of licensed premises, once they had ended their careers on the field. Archibald Vallance, of the Red Lion Vaults, West Nile Street, Glasgow, was a native of Garelochead, Dunbartonshire, who came to Glasgow in 1873 at the age of thirteen to play for Rangers. He was recruited through family and community networks, as Rangers Football Club had been founded in the previous year 'by a group of lads from the Gareloch', and Tom Vallance proposed the toast to 'the Rangers Football Club and Ibrox Park' at the banquet to mark the opening of the new stadium in 1887.[144] Archibald Vallance was elected Captain of Rangers in 1881. He was a dog breeder, an angler and a member of the Queen's Own Yeomanry.[145]

On the other side of the sectarian divide, Celtic Football Club was founded by Brother Walfred, a Catholic priest in the East End of Glasgow, in 1888. Its first chairman was John McLaughlin, a publican from Hamilton, who had been educated by the Jesuits at the prestigious Stonyhurst College in Lancashire. He served as chairman of Celtic from 1893 until his death in 1909 and was instrumental in converting the club into a limited liability company.[146] McLaughlin left an estate of £4,086, which included £162 in shares in Celtic Football Club, a £3 share in the Caledonian Bowling Club and two pubs – one in Hamilton, valued at £1,350, the other in Wishaw, valued at £500.[147] Outside the west of Scotland, Alfred Ward, of the Golden Bull, Dumfries, had been captain, secretary and general manager of Queen of the South Football Club and, in 1914, was 'a bowler and curler of repute'.[148]

Pubs were used, as they are today, as places where football teams and their supporters met up before and after matches, and where they would naturally turn for fundraising and financial support. Lilias Smith was a wine and spirit merchant who owned the James Watt Bar in East Hamilton Street, Greenock. When she died in 1898, leaving an estate of £4,474, the estate was carried on by trustees. In 1904, the trustees held twenty shares of £1 each in Morton Football Club, and the following year the Club approached the trustees for a financial contribution in connection with 'the reconstruction of the Football Club', which they agreed to consider.[149] The Glasgow wine and spirit merchant, Thomas Reid, who died in 1914, was Chairman of Partick Thistle.[150] By 1911, 11.3 per cent of shareholders in Scottish football clubs were proprietors or employees in the drink trade who owned 31.2 per cent of all shares issued. Three years later, the drink trade provided 21.8 per cent of directors of Scottish First Division clubs and 15.8 per cent of Second Division directors.[151]

Horse racing and the betting that went along with it were closely associated with pubs. Pubs were always busy during race meetings and a successful licensee might be affluent enough to own horses or to hold shares in a racecourse. When Hamilton Racecourse opened in 1888, it was funded mainly by businessmen and lower professionals, 'with over a quarter of the shares owned by members of the drinks trade'.[152] Association with the 'sport of kings', with its aristocratic and landed connections, gave status to those of uncertain social status, such as wine and spirit merchants, who could afford to enter the expensive world of racehorse ownership and breeding. George and John MacLachlan, from Strathallan in Perthshire, were Glasgow-based publicans who diversified into building breweries in Maryhill, Glasgow (the Castle in 1889), and at Duddingston, Edinburgh in 1900. In 1901, they bought Auchentoshan Distillery at Duntocher, Dunbartonshire. George MacLachlan lived at 8 Park Terrace in Glasgow's West End and maintained a stud of horses.[153]

Gray Edmiston, who owned the Lyceum Vaults in Glasgow, preferred to spend 'whatever time he has to spare in the bosom of his family, except for now and again, when he takes a run to the racecourse'.[154] Some pubs had an equine theme in their title, such as the trio of Glasgow pubs owned by John Scouller – the Horseshoe Bar in Drury Street, which he bought in 1884, the Spur Bar, Polmadie Street, and the Snaffle Bit, Howard Street. When Scouller remodelled the island bar at the Horseshoe, between 1885 and 1887, it became the longest continuous bar in Britain, and people in the trade travelled from Aberdeen, Dundee and Inverness to see it.[155]

Another popular sport with a strong connection with pubs and hotels was angling which appealed both to aristocrats and to artisans. Many inns and hotels were situated on lochs or rivers and, in July 1890, out of 167 angling events reported in the *Glasgow Herald,* sixty-two (37 per cent) were organised from, or took place at, inns and hotels.[156]

Some licensees were keen all-round amateur sportsmen. Archibald Lauder of the Royal Lochnagar Vaults, Sauchiehall Street, Glasgow entered the licensed trade at the age of 13, working his way up to become owner of the Vaults. He produced his own blend of whisky, 'Royal Northern Cream', which won prizes at the Edinburgh Exhibition in 1886 and at the Paris Exposition of 1889, exported whisky to Russia and France, and supplied the Royal Navy. Lauder was a keen sportsman – a bowler (Willowpark Bowling Club), golfer (Troon Golf Club) and curler (Kelvindale Curling Club). He was a mason (common for Protestants in the licensed trade) and a member of Anderston United

Presbyterian Church.[157] Lauder died in 1912, at Drumspillan, Pinwherry, Ayrshire, leaving an estate of £57, 287.[158]

WINE AND SPIRIT MERCHANTS AND LICENSEES

The Scottish licensee differed in significant ways from the English land-lord or publican. Firstly, his/her title was different, that of 'wine and spirit merchant' – a phrase that features in nineteenth-century wills and probate inventories, and which still appears over the door of many present-day pubs. Secondly, the choice of drink sold was very different between Scotland and England. In Scotland, the drink of choice in pubs was whisky, with beer sometimes drunk as a chaser, whereas in England, it was ale or beer. Thirdly, the system of ownership and control of pubs was different between the two countries. In England, the emergence of large-scale industrial brewing in the nineteenth century resulted in breweries competing to acquire pubs as an outlet for their product. This led to the growth of brewery chains and the landlord or publican becoming a tenant of the brewery in a 'tied house', restricted by conditions laid down by the brewery. By contrast, in Scotland most pubs were run by individual licensees, though not all of them owned the building. In Glasgow, for example, most licensees in the late nineteenth and early twentieth centuries leased their 'shops', paying from £15 to £1,000 a year in rent. The average rent was £96.18.6d a year. A pub property represented a good investment for the Victorian professional and commercial classes in Scotland. In the early 1900s, the owners of public house properties in Glasgow included MPs, magistrates, council-lors, doctors and clergymen, as well as institutions, such as the Bank of Scotland, the Clyde Trust and so on.[159]

Finally, while the English landlord typically lived over the premises, the Scottish urban licensee usually lived at a distance, travelling from his/her workplace in the centre of the city to the suburbs or even further out, using rail, tram and steamer networks. In Glasgow, the success-ful licensee might live in the middle-class West End or a Renfrewshire suburb such as Pollockshields on the south side of the city. Out of a sample of twenty-seven men and one woman involved in the licensed trade in Glasgow and its vicinity, who died between 1871 and 1925, seven lived in central Glasgow, seven in Renfrewshire, three in the West End of Glasgow, two each in Ayrshire, Dennistoun and Partick, one in Hamilton and the remaining four were scattered around the fringes of Glasgow suburbia.[160] In Dundee, prosperous licensees lived in the West End or in the seaside suburb of Broughty Ferry, reached by a fast and reliable rail network. Similar residential patterns applied to Aberdeen and Edinburgh. This was a common pattern among the rising middle classes in Victorian Scotland. The Paisley industrialist, James Clark, a member of the thread dynasty, boasted in 1844 that he could reach his country house in Dunoon from Paisley by rail and ferry in only an hour and 35 minutes for the modest sum of 6d.[161]

Despite all the efforts of the temperance reformers, 'drink was firmly intertwined into the economic and social base of all Scottish towns'. In Glasgow in 1861 there were 1,296 wine and spirit merchants, together with 118 publicans. Twenty years later, this had risen to 2,295 publicans and wine and spirit merchants, falling to 1,954 in 1911. Edinburgh had 474 wine and spirit merchants in 1861 and fifty-one publicans. In Dundee, the number of publicans and wine and spirit merchants rose from a modest fifty-six in 1861 to 270 in 1881, declining to 190 in 1911. A large proportion of those in the Scottish drink trade were employers or self-employed, with the exception of Glasgow. In Aberdeen 76 per cent of those in the drink trade were either employers or self-employed, in Dundee it was 70 per cent, in Edinburgh 52 per cent falling to 28 per cent in Glasgow where a large number of outlets were owned by businessmen in other occupations.[162]

The Scottish licensed trade was slow to organise against its powerful temperance opponents, unlike its English equivalent. In England, the wealthy brewers and the English publicans were among the bedrocks of support for the Conservative Party, and made formidable political opponents. When William Ewart Gladstone, the Liberal prime minister, lost the 1874 election, he complained, 'we have been borne down in a torrent of gin and beer'.[163] In Scotland, the first attempts at organisation of the licensed trade were at regional, rather than national, level. The Dundee Wine, Spirit and Beer Trade Protection Association was founded in June 1863, building up to a membership of 110 by 1889.[164] Regional lobbying had little effect on the Westminster Parliament, however, which is where the Scottish temperance organisations exercised much of their influence. A Scottish organisation had to wait until 1880, when the inaugural meeting of the Scottish Wine, Spirit and Beer Trade Defence Association (SWSBTDA) was held in the Athole Arms Hotel, Glasgow, attracting delegates from Glasgow, Edinburgh, Rothesay, Greenock, Dumfries, Dumbarton, Dumfermline and Coatbridge. Its first president was James McWilliam, a wealthy Glasgow wine and spirit merchant, its vice-president, James Watt, wine merchant and former Provost of Leith, treasurer, George Dalrymple of Pathhead Brewery, Glasgow, and its parliamentary agent and secretary (a key role), Alexander Wylie, WS, an Edinburgh solicitor.[165] Scottish licensees took the threat of temperance very seriously. By 1896, nearly 10,000 of the country's 11,006 license holders had signed up for the SWSBTDA, and the trade's own journals, the weekly *National Guardian* and the monthly *Victualling Trades Review*, carried regular anti-temperance articles.[166]

There were many pitfalls lying in wait for the inexperienced or unwary licensee: the temptation to sample too much of one's own stock; the attractions of the barmaid or barman; the need to supervise staff closely and watch out for pilfering; the drunken, possibly violent customer or customers; the need to keep underage drinkers and prostitutes out of the pub; and the need to keep an eye open for undercover betting or the sale of stolen goods. Some of these activities were unwise, others meant one could lose one's licence.

Some observers, particularly those with a temperance axe to grind, delighted in pointing out the contrast between the prosperous, well-fed licensees in the slums and their poverty-stricken clientele. In Edinburgh, the young evangelical Dr George Bell described the owner of one dram shop as 'rubicund, fat, jolly, with his white apron standing behind his counter'.[167] The crusading journalist Alexander Brown made a similar observation in a public house near Eglinton Street, in Glasgow, where the publican, 'is a stout, fresh, well fed man of a landlord ... with an exquisitely dressed white shirt, a highly coloured Valentia waistcoat, and a profusion of watch guards and rings, he is a perfect exquisite in his trade'.[168]

In the Highlands, the tenancy of inns was often in the gift of the local estate. In Glen Lyon, in Highland Perthshire, the inn at Innerwick was the provision that 'Old Culdares' (the local laird) made for 'his officer son's piper, who came with an Irish wife'.[169] The calibre of Highland licensees varied enormously. In the Invergarry Inn in July 1857, the mistress and her maids were unprepared for visitors at 2.00 p.m., 'neither she nor her maids were either washed or dressed' and the rooms were 'filthy with dirt and stench'. By contrast, in August 1868, the landlord of the hotel at Tarbert was 'a very superior young fellow, well educated, not above his business, but actively engaged in making his guests comfortable'.[170] At the other end of Scotland, Archibald Geikie remembered 'many quiet, unpretending, but remarkably comfortable little inns in Galloway' run by farmers who served their own 'fresh farm produce' to their guests.[171]

Wills and probate inventories have to be used with a degree of caution. They are frequently likely to underestimate wealth, and may even leave out completely the principal business the deceased founded if it had already been handed over to a son or other family member. Wills and probate inventories do, however, give some understanding of the wide range of business interests of some Glasgow wine and spirit merchants and of the enormous contrasts in the material rewards on offer, depending on the location of the pub and the licensee's personality and business ability. Table 4.3 hints at some of these contrasts in the different levels of wealth between Glasgow wine and spirit merchants.

Table 4.3 Wealth at death of twenty-nine Glasgow* wine and spirit merchants who died between 1871 and 1923.

	Dates of death			
	1871–1891	1891–1911	1911–1923	Total, 1871–1923
Number of wine and spirit merchants	10	13	6	29
Total wealth at death	£129,883	£559,298	£158,639	£847,820
Average wealth at death	£12,988	£43,023	£26,439	£29,235
Goodwill, stock and fixtures in w. and s. businesses	£41,461	£65,358	£54,498	£161,317
Av. value of w. and s. businesses	£4,146	£5,027	£9,083	£5,562
Total value of whisky in bond	–	£39,572 (4)	£13,389 (2)	£52,961 (6)
Av. value of whisky in bond	–	£9,893	£6,694	£8,826
Railway shares	£11,057 (4)	£43,524 (1)	£1,535 (1)	£56,116 (6)
Av. value of railway shares	£2,764	£43,524	£1,535	£9,352
Brewery and distillery shares	–	£23,800 (5)	£2,720 (1)	£26,520 (6)
–	–	£4,760	£2,720	£4,420
Charitable bequests	£212 (1)	£5,415 (3)	–	£5,627 (4)
Av. value of charitable bequests	£212	£1,805	–	£1,406
War bonds	–	–	£17,736 (1)	£17,736

(Sources: National Records of Scotland, Edinburgh, Sheriff Courts of Ayr, Glasgow, Hamilton and Paisley, Wills and Probate Inventories of 24 wine and spirit merchants; Mitchell Library, Glasgow, Sederunt Books of trusts of five wine and spirit merchants)

*Includes John Herbert McLaughlin, Chairman of Celtic Football Club, who lived in Strathmore Road, Hamilton, died on 11 August 1909 and owned pubs in Hamilton and Wishaw

A successful, second-generation owner who had diversified into other, often drink-related, areas could amass a fortune. Robert Robin, for example, inherited the Scotia Bar, Stockwell Street, Glasgow from his father Mathew. Mathew Robin, who died in 1876, leaving an estate of £61,000, had been Provost of Renfrew, JP for Renfrewshire and a pillar of St Vincent Street, United Presbyterian Church.[172] His son Robert built on the business and, when he died in 1905, leaving an estate valued at £304,377, he owned three pubs in Glasgow, the Argyll Hotel, Dunoon, and was a director of the Craigellachie Glenlivet Distillery Company.[173]

At the other end of the social and economic scale were those struggling to run a spirit shop in the Saltmarket or Calton, like John Brown, who left an estate of £149 on his death in 1888, of which £100 was goodwill in his spirit shop in Main Street, Calton, together with £20 stock-in-trade.[174] Somewhat better off was James Cush, born in County Tyrone, who ran the Whitevale Bar at 721 Gallowgate and died in 1892, leaving an estate of £1,518. The weekly takings of the Whitevale Bar were £36, with a weekly profit of £5, a yearly profit of £260. This was a comfortable living compared to many, however, and, in a touching gesture, Cush specified in his will that his children were to receive 'as liberal an education as the means at their disposal will permit'.[175] Other Irish-born publicans were more successful and able to return to Ireland to spend the money they had made in Scotland. On a visit to Ireland, Archibald Geikie noticed a prosperous 'new villa' being built outside Ballymena. It belonged to a man called O'Donnell who had made his fortune 'Keepin' public houses' in Scotland.[176]

BAR STAFF

Bar staff in Scottish pubs traditionally worked long hours for low pay. For those ambitious, hard working or unscrupulous enough, however, there was always the possibility of better rewards. A remarkable testimony survives from a Glasgow barman called O'Neill who worked in shebeens in the Saltmarket, serving cheap whisky laced with methylated spirits – a highly profitable business. In 1855, he was working at 'a rattler in the Saltmarket', where they quickly lost their licence but carried on as an unlicensed club, 'open night and day Saturday and Sunday, never shut at all, we had 13 waiters and relieved each other in night and day shifts'. Customers were charged a shilling entry fee and that money went to him as 'acting manager', by which time he was making £12 to £13 a week.[177]

In 1887, the *Scottish Wine, Spirit and Beer Trades Review* published an article 'The Girl Behind the Bar', a spirited defence of the Glasgow barmaid. Written by a *flâneur*, who claimed to know 'nearly every hotel, bar and restaurant in the city', it described how barmaids worked a fifteen-hour day and often slept on the premises.[178] The following week, the *Review* noted that Glasgow waiters had formed themselves into a union or association to regulate the trade, including remuneration levels and behaviour (no drunkenness was to be tolerated).[179] Four years later, there was a waiters' strike in Glasgow, after Mr Thiers of the Windsor Hotel tried to reduce wages for waiters for the Balfour banquet. They demanded 12/6d per day for day men and 10 shillings for night men. In Edinburgh, a meeting held in 1891, at Buchanan's Hotel, High Street to consider forming a waiter's union, claimed that waiters' wages in Edinburgh were lower than in Glasgow. The meeting proposed setting Edinburgh wage rates at 7/6d for day men and 5 shillings for evening men. For marriages, balls, and so on, they proposed 12/6d for day men and 7/6d for evening men. Entry money to the union was fixed at 2/6d, the weekly subscription at 3 pence.[180]

Long hours persisted, however, and the barman typically worked from 8.00 a.m. to 11.00 p.m., usually dressed in a long white apron and white shirt. In 1903, the Glasgow barman worked a sixty-five-hour week, with two or three hours a day off for meals and one afternoon and one evening off per week.[181] A year later, John Holmes remembered working in Glasgow bars 'from eight in the morning until eleven at night', adding 'we had no break and no half day and no night off'. They also worked on New Year's Day but, in 1904, 'ten o'clock closing was instituted and now we have an eight hour day practically speaking'.[182]

As the strength of the temperance movement increased, there was a determined attempt to ban barmaids in Scottish pubs, as an affront to the delicacy of the female sex and a threat to morality. Openings for unskilled women workers at this time were largely limited to domestic service, agricultural work, factory work or bar work. In 1903, the licensing magistrates in Glasgow tried to ban barmaids from Glasgow pubs. Kenna and Moody claim that this ban was regarded as absurd in England,[183] but an article headed 'The Barmaid Persecution' reported that the Licensing Magistrates in London, where something like eight or nine thousand barmaids were employed, had been approached by the National Union of Women Workers, lobbied by the British Women's Temperance Association, to consider the abolition of barmaids, along the lines attempted in Glasgow. It was proposed to begin by banning barmaids from theatres and music halls.[184]

CUSTOMERS

The clientele of Scottish pubs varied greatly, depending on whether the pub was in a rural or an urban area, in the Highlands or the Lowlands, in a port or an inland burgh. It also depended on the type of employment in the surrounding area and sometimes the ethnicity and prevailing religious beliefs of the locality. Some drinking places depended on football, boxing, horse racing or rugby supporters, while others relied on musical entertainments, such as the 'free and easies', and later the music hall and variety theatres. Still others depended on 'underground' activities, such as prostitution and crime, including the handling of stolen goods. Many pubs in rural areas or in small burghs still depended on agricultural business transacted at markets, trysts and fairs. As transport links improved, mass tourism began to take off in the second half of the century, initially along the Clyde and Forth coasts, and in favoured parts of the Highlands, such as Oban, Fort William, Aviemore, Inverness and Strathpeffer, bringing visitors to inns and hotels.

In Aberdeen in 1837, there were 870 licensed houses for a population under sixty thousand. Their customers included many transients: sailors, fishermen and visiting farmers in from the surrounding countryside for the markets.[185] Some licensed houses in Aberdeen catered for the local elite, however. The Lemon Tree in Aberdeen was 'a well-known and comfortable hostelry' with excellent food, presided over in 1859 by Mrs Ronald. Its clientele included 'leading members of the church' and even the city magistrates after 'a public execution'.[186] In Lochgilphead, Argyllshire where, in 1844, a gallon (4.55 litres) of whisky was consumed for every man, woman and child, there was condemnation of, 'the almost universal connection between herring fishing and whisky drinking'.[187]

In New Monkland, Lanarkshire, there were complaints in 1835 about union activities among weavers and colliers, and their close associations with 'inns, alehouses and spirit shops':

> The frequent associations and combinations which prevail here and are connected with similar combinations in different parts of the country to raise the price of labour . . . These combinations arise most amongst the colliers and the weavers. The great number of inns, alehouses and spirit shops that abound in Airdrie and other parts of the parish afford great temptation to idleness and dissipation, which involve many families in poverty and misery.[188]

The traditional picture of the Scottish pub in this period is of a male-only, stand-up place for drinking. In shebeens and licensed grocers, however, women often made up a high proportion of the clientele. A shebeen near Eglinton Street, Glasgow in 1858 offered a stark contrast between the 'exquisite' landlord and his clientele who included 'a wreck of a woman' who 'staggers, rather than walks towards the bar' and was charged 4 pence for filling a broken teacup with whisky. Apart from a 'dead drunk' young man, most of the other customers were women.[189] In 1890, there were fifteen thousand commitments of habitual drunkards to prison in Glasgow, of whom an astonishing two-thirds were women. They were described as 'like tangle drifting between the shebeen, the public house and the poor house'.[190] David Barrie remembered a 'very badly conducted public house' in a 'low lying neighbourhood' of Dundee in the late 1880s, where 'wretched men and women and very young children in dirt and rags poured out and in to the great disgust of many of the neighbours'.[191] The Dundee Inebriates' Register of 1905, with photographs of those convicted under the Inebriates' Act of 1898, shows that of the forty-two on the register, thirty-five (83 per cent) were women, of whom twenty-two were mill workers, four spinners and two factory workers.[192]

In garrison towns, soldiers provided much custom for local pubs. In 1836, the *Stirling Observer* reported that

> one of the soldiers now stationed in the Castle went into a public house in Broad Street and calling for some whisky, put a deleterious drug into a portion of it, offered it to the servant maid; but she having suspected all was not as it should be ... would not partake of it but immediately informed her master, who after severely reprimanding the valiant hero of the bayonet, turned him out.[193]

The drinking places in the inner cities hosted a wide variety of customers, from criminals and prostitutes to police, and 'respectable' middle-class men seeking low-life encounters. A Glasgow shebeener sold cheap adulterated whisky in a Saltmarket shebeen in 1855, and also served, 'champagne and sparkling hock, the chief customers for the fizz being the swell English thieves' who paid in notes. In 1862, he opened up his own place in the Saltmarket where he claimed his customers included, 'hundreds of respectable gentlemen, members of the police force and others'.[194]

In ports, there were pubs for dock workers, where men routinely treated foremen, to curry favour in the ferocious competition for work at the dock gates.[195] In Dundee, a number of dockland pubs in the Blackscroft area served a 'transient population' in the early 1900s, consisting of 'casual shore labourers, deserters from foreign vessels berthed at the docks and the drifting flotsam and jetsom [sic] always to be found in a port'. Dock labourers waited at the top of the 'Langstairs',

3

LIKENESS AND DESCRIPTION OF PERSON REFERRED TO

REGISTER No. **81**

Name and alias—**BRIDGET GLANCEY or BURKE.**

Residence—**18 Crescent Lane and East Poorhouse.**

Place of business or where employed—Manhattan Works.

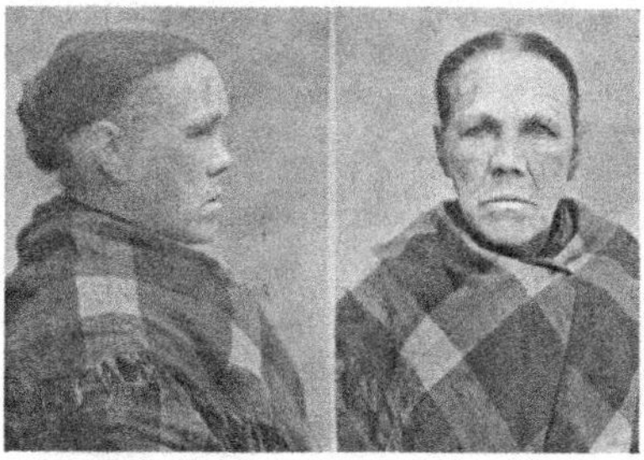

Age—60 Years.

Height—5 ft.

Build—Proportionate.

Complexion—Fresh.

Hair—Dark brown.

Eyes—Grey.

Peculiarities or marks—Broken nose, blue mark on brow, E. G. left forearm.

Profession or occupation—Millworker.

Date and nature of last conviction—31st July, 1905.—Contravention of Section 70 (1) of the "Licensing (Scotland) Act, 1903."—Found in a state of intoxication and incapable of taking care of herself, and not under the care or protection of some suitable person.

Court at which convicted—**Police Court, Dundee.**

N.B.—Should the above or any other known convicted person within the meaning of the previously quoted Section, attempt to purchase or obtain any exciseable liquor, it is requested that the licensed person, or the person refusing to supply the liquor, will, as soon as practicable, give information of such attempt to the Police in order that the law may be enforced.

To..

DUNDEE

Whose special attention is called to above.

This Notice served by me on the....................day of August, 1905.

John Burnett Constable

Figure 4.3 Bridget Glancey or Burke, Dundee, 1905. © Leisure and Culture, Dundee.

which led down to the docks, for word that a 'button boat' was ready to unload timber, or a 'coolie boat' with a cargo of jute had just landed. Children could be seen 'running the cutter' from pubs, with jugs of beer and flagons of porter for those who preferred to drink at home. These were 'singing pubs', where sentimental songs, such as 'Nellie Dean' and 'The Old Rustic Bridge by the Mill', were sung but also sectarian songs such as:

Figure 4.4 Interior, The Cromdale Bar, Hawkhill, Dundee, 1906. © Leisure and Culture, Dundee.

Ha! Ha! The bhoys, don't yez hear the noise?
The days of the Paddies bees coming.
They'll be coming up in lots
And they'll kill youse dhirty Scots
And you'll know what it is to be a Fenian.[196]

In late nineteenth-century Glasgow, the booming shipyards, factories and foundries provided plentiful and relatively well-paid employment for men which gave a distinctive character to the whole city. On Saturday nights, 'the streets are throbbing and pulsating with life [and] Glasgow presents a spectacle which can be witnessed nowhere else except in two cities – London and New York'. The explanation lay in 'the great shipyards, unique in their magnitude, [which] contribute largely to the boisterous scene', plus the factories and foundries. As a result, the Glasgow streets and bars were packed between 9.00 and 10.00 p.m. and the bars filled up even more after 11.00 p.m.[197]

Not all bars and pubs were patronised solely by manual workers. After the passing of the Forbes McKenzie Act, there were complaints by the Glasgow press, 'who require to be out of bed every publishing night, that they are denied necessary refreshment in respectable licensed houses

and are driven to seek it in unlicensed places'.[198] When the Exchange
Hotel in Perth was prosecuted in 1890 for not observing 10.00 p.m.
closing, those in the bar included a chimney sweep, a law clerk and
a music teacher, who had gone in to see some chess prizes.[199] Bicycle
ownership boomed towards the end of the century and, by 1890, there
were some 150,000 cyclists in Scotland.[200] Archibald Geikie thought
this benefited the trade in rural Scotland, 'a distinct revival of the roadside inn can be traced to the wide spread of bicycle-riding', as 'wheelmen
appeared to be "drouthy cronies", who are not sorry to halt for a few
minutes at an inviting change house'.[201]

FURTHER CONTROL OF THE LICENSED TRADE

Gothenburgs

The Gothenburg public house system originated in Sweden, an attempt
to reduce heavy drinking, and to use the profits of the drink trade for
municipal spending that would benefit the general population. In 1865,
the drinks trade in Gothenburg was placed in the hands of a trust
company and the town received most of the profits. In Scotland, the idea
was popular among mining communities in the Lothians and Fife, and
well-preserved examples of Gothenburg pubs survive at Newtongrange,
Midlothian and Prestonpans, East Lothian.[202] Critics of the system
unkindly pointed out that, in 1895, Gothenburg, with a population
four times smaller than Dundee, had four times as many drunks as the
Scottish city.[203]

The Public House Trust (Glasgow District) Ltd

Similar ideas of municipal control of the drinks trade lay behind the
creation of the Glasgow Public House Trust, based on the Earl Grey's
Public House Trust Company in Northumberland, and launched in
1901 with a capital of £25,000 in £1 shares. The managers were paid
fixed salaries with no commission on liquor sales but with incentives
to sell food and soft drinks. The scheme was not a great success. By
1904, the Glasgow Public House Trust held only four licences, two in
Glasgow, one in Stirling and one in Newton, on the edge of Glasgow.
Profits for the year were a paltry £103.[204] Around this time, compulsory acquisition powers were given to Glasgow Corporation, under the
Buildings Regulation Act, which led to fears in the licensed trade that
they could be used for compulsory purchase of pubs on street corners.[205]

Figure 4.5 Interior, Prestoungrange Gothenburg Tavern, Prestonpans, East Lothian, 1986. © RCAHMS.

The Temperance (Scotland) Act, 1913

The Scottish temperance movement continued to tighten the controls on the licensed trade in Scotland through local and national political action. John Wilson, MP for Govan, proposed the Liquor Traffic Local Veto (Scotland) Bill in 1899. It was rejected by Parliament but received majority support from Scottish MPs.[206] The Temperance (Scotland) Act of 1913 finally made it possible for local veto polls to close down licensed premises in any given area. Its implementation was delayed by the outbreak of World War I, however, which brought far-reaching changes to Scotland and the rest of Europe. This will be discussed further in the next chapter.

NOTES

1. R. J. Morris, 'Urbanisation', in A. Cooke, I. Donnachie, A. MacSween and C. A. Whatley (eds), *Modern Scottish History, 1707 to the Present,*

Vol. 2, *The Modernisation of Scotland, 1850 to the Present* (East Linton, 1998), pp. 119–21.

2. T. C. Smout, *A Century of the Scottish People, 1830–1950* (London, 1986), pp. 35 and 41.

3. J. Sinclair (ed.), *The (Old) Statistical Account of Scotland (OSA)*, Vol. VII, *Lanarkshire and Renfrewshire* (Wakefield, 1973), p. 710; and *New Statistical Account (NSA)*, Vol. VII, *Renfrew and Argyle* (Edinburgh, 1845), p. 490.

4. I. Donnachie, 'Drink and Society, 1750–1850,' *Journal of the Scottish Labour History Society*, No. 13, May 1979, p. 17.

5. E. King, *Scotland Sober and Free. The Temperance Movement, 1829–1979* (Glasgow, 1979), p. 7; and B. Harrison, *Drink and the Victorians, The Temperance Question in England, 1815–1872* (Keele, 1994), pp. 99–101.

6. Harrison, *Drink and the Victorians*, pp. 85–8.

7. Reports from the Assistant Hand-Loom Weavers' Commissioners, South of Scotland and East of Scotland, *Parliamentary Papers, 1838–39* (Irish University Press, Industrial Revolution, Textiles, Vol. IX, 1970 reprint), p. 51.

8. E. P. Thompson, 'Time, Work Discipline and Industrial Capitalism', in Thompson, *Customs in Common* (London, 1993), p. 394.

9. Harrison, *Drink and the Victorians*, p. 93.

10. *Parliamentary Papers, 1849*, Vol. XXII, Tremenheere Report on the Mining Districts, p. 14.

11. King, *Scotland Sober and Free*, p. 9.

12. *Saturday Evening Commonwealth*, 1 and 8 November 1856, 'Jacques, Glimpses of a Chequered Life'.

13. *NSA*, Vol. VII, *Renfrew and Argyle*, p. 429.

14. Report on the State of the Irish Poor in Great Britain, 1835, *Parliamentary Papers, 1836*, Vol. XXXIV, Appendix G, Scotland, p. 108.

15. *NSA, Vol. V, Ayrshire*, pp. 368 and 374.

16. J. Myles, *Rambles in Forfarshire* (Dundee, 1850), p. 25.

17. Harrison, *Drink and the Victorians*, p. 158.

18. T. Griffiths and G. Morton, 'Introduction', in Griffiths and Morton (eds), *A History of Everyday Life in Scotland, 1800 to 1900* (Edinburgh, 2010), p. 16.

19. King, *Scotland Sober and Free*, pp. 10–11; and J. R. Gusfield, *Symbolic Crusade, Status Politics and the American Temperance Movement* (Urbana Il, 1972), p. 103.

20. Anon., 'The Fenwick Improvement of Knowledge Society', *Scottish Historical Review (SHR)*, Vol. 17 (1920), pp. 121–4.

21. W. W. Knox, *Industrial Nation. Work, Culture and Society in Scotland, 1800–Present* (Edinburgh, 1999), p. 43.

22. W. H. Fraser, *Scottish Popular Politics* (Edinburgh, 2000), p. 93.

23. D. Kirkwood, *My Life of Revolt* (London, 1935), pp. 57–9.

24. *NSA*, Vol. XI, *Forfar and Kincardine*, p. 47.

25. Donnachie, 'Drink and Society', p. 18.

26. G. J. C. Duncan, *Memoir of Henry Duncan, Minister of Ruthwell* (Edinburgh, 1848).

27. *NSA*, Vol. IV, *Dumfriesshire* (Edinburgh, 1845), pp. 241–3.

28. *NSA*, Vol. IV, p. 273.

29. *NSA*, Vol. V, *Ayrshire* (Edinburgh, 1845), p. 491.

30. *NSA*, Vol. IV, *Dumfriesshire*, pp. 242–3.

31. *NSA*, Vol. VII, *Renfrew and Argyle*, p. 543.

32. Knox, *Industrial Nation* (Edinburgh, 1999), p. 94.

33. *NSA*, Vol. IV, p. 272.

34. H. Miller, *My Schools and Schoolmasters* (London, 1874), p. 333.

35. J. Burnett and G. Jarvie, 'Sport, Scotland and the Scots', in Jarvie and Burnett (eds), *Sport, Scotland and the Scots* (East Linton, 2000), p. 1.

36. See M. Bennett, *Scottish Customs from the Cradle to the Grave* (Edinburgh, 1992).

37. *OSA*, Vol. XII, *North and West Perthshire*, p. 678; Vol. XVII, *Inverness-shire, Ross and Cromarty*, p. 293; Miller, *My Schools and Schoolmasters*, pp. 45–9; J. G. Fyfe (ed.), *Scottish Diarists and Memoirs, 1746–1843* (Stirling, 1942), p. 447; and Myles, *Rambles in Forfarshire*, p. 22.

38. W. H. Fraser, 'Developments in Leisure', in Fraser and R. J. Morris (eds), *People and Society in Scotland*, Vol. II, *1830–1914* (Edinburgh, 1990), p. 239.

39. Miller, *My Schools and Schoolmasters*, pp. 45–9.

40. Harrison, *Drink and the Victorians*, pp. 99–100.

41. C. Brown, 'Religion', in Cooke, et al. (eds), *Modern Scottish History*, Vol. I: *1707–1850* (East Linton, 2001), pp. 63–85.

42. J. Dunlop, *Artificial and Compulsory Drinking Usages of the UK* (London, 1844), p. 23.

43. Dunlop, *Drinking Usages*, p. 27.

44. Fraser, 'Developments in Leisure', p. 240.

45. *Saturday Evening Commonwealth*, 1 and 8 November 1856.

46. Mitchell Library, Glasgow (ML), Dollan Mss, Autobiography, p. 12.

47. Dunlop, *Drinking Usages*, p. 9.

48. A. Alison, *Some Account of My Life and Writings* (Edinburgh, 1883), pp. 384–5; and W. H. Fraser, 'The Glasgow Cotton Spinners, 1837', in J. Butt and J. T. Ward (eds), *Scottish Themes* (Edinburgh, 1976), pp. 80–97.

49. Miller, *My Schools and Schoolmasters*, p. 158.

50. *NSA*, Vol. V, *Ayrshire*, pp. 854–5. See also N. Murray, *The Scottish Handloom Weavers, 1790–1850* (Edinburgh, 1978).

51. Fraser, 'Developments in Leisure', p. 240; and W. Kenefick, *'Rebellious and Contrary'. The Glasgow Dockers, 1853–1932* (East Linton, 2000), pp. 132 and 221.
52. Dunlop, *Drinking Usages*, p. 7.
53. I. Donnachie, *A History of the Brewing Industry in Scotland* (Edinburgh, 1998), p. 208.
54. NSA, Vol. I, *Edinburgh and the Lothians* (Edinburgh, 1845), pp. 586–7.
55. NSA, Vol. II, *Linlithgowshire (West Lothian) and Haddingtonshire (East Lothian)* (Edinburgh, 1845), pp. 315–16.
56. NSA, Vol. II, p. 201.
57. NSA, Vol. III, *Roxburgh, Peebles, Selkirk* (Edinburgh, 1845), p. 23.
58. NSA, Vol. III, pp. 187 and 217.
59. NSA, Vol. III, p. 351.
60. Harrison, *Drink and the Victorians*, pp. 153–5; and King, *Scotland Sober and Free*, p. 9.
61. I. Maver, 'Glasgow Town Council in the Nineteenth Century', in T. M. Devine (ed.), *Scottish Elites* (Edinburgh, 1994), pp. 105–6.
62. *Drink and the Victorians*, p. 202.
63. *Drink and the Victorians*, pp. 220 and 275.
64. M. Archibald, *A Sink of Atrocity. Crime in 19th Century Dundee* (Edinburgh, 2012), pp. 210–20.
65. Mitchell Library, Glasgow (ML), MP 24.320, Report by the Superintendent of Police on the working of the new Act for the better regulation of public houses in Glasgow, September 1855.
66. R. J. Morris, 'New Spaces for Scotland, 1800 to 1900', in T. Griffiths and G. Morton (eds), *A History of Everyday Life in Scotland, 1800 to 1900* (Edinburgh, 2010), pp. 238–9.
67. J. Fleming, *Looking Backwards for Seventy Years, 1921–1851* (Aberdeen, 1922), p. 27.
68. ML, MP 24.320, Report by Superintendent of Police, Glasgow, September 1855.
69. ML, MP 24.328, Report by Superintendent of Police on the working of the Public House Act in Glasgow, 1856.
70. ML, Report on the Workings of the Forbes McKenzie Act [Public Houses (Scotland) Act] by the Directors of the Scottish Licensed Victuallers' Association, Glasgow, May 1858.
71. A. Hopkin, *The Aberdeen Pub Companion* (Aberdeen, 1975), p. 9.
72. ML, Glasgow Dean of Guild Plans, 1/3283, Plan of Proposed Lavatory at 114 Trongate, 12 July 1894.
73. *Perthshire Advertiser*, 25 November 1933.
74. ML, MP 31.44, Report by Magistrates of Glasgow on visit to Liverpool regarding Licensing Acts, March 1902.
75. ML, MP 31.25, Report by Magistrates of Dundee on visit to Liverpool regarding Licensing Acts, July 1902.

76. *People's Palaces*, p. 70.
77. S, M'Alpine, *Glaiska Fair* (Glasgow, 1852?), pp. 5–6.
78. *Victualling Trades Review* (*VTR*), 15 August 1898.
79. A. Durie, 'Movement, Transport and Tourism', in Griffiths and Morton (eds), *A History of Everyday Life in Scotland, 1800 to 1900*, p. 157.
80. *NSA*, Vol. VIII, *Dumbarton, Stirling, Clackmannan*, p. 12–14.
81. *NSA*, Vol. VIII, pp. 76–7.
82. *NSA*, Vol. VIII, p. 101.
83. *Stirling Observer*, 30 April 1986, p. 13.
84. *NSA*, Vol. XIV, *Ross and Cromarty*, p. 35.
85. D. Walker, 'Inns, hotels and related building types', in G. Stell, J. Shaw and J. Stonier (eds), *Scottish Life and Society*, Vol. 3, *Scotland's Buildings* (East Linton, 2003), pp. 164–5 and 172.
86. A. Durie (ed.), *Travels in Scotland, 1788–1881* (Woodbridge, 2012), p. 179.
87. Walker, 'Inns, hotels', pp. 173–7.
88. *Dundee Advertiser*, 29 May 1889.
89. Perth Library, Perth and Kinross Archives (PKA), PE 17/Bundle 182, Perth Burgh Police Commissioners, 9 January 1890.
90. ML, AGN 2114, *North British Daily Mail*, 27 December 1870, 'The Dark Side of Glasgow'.
91. Anon, *Doings of a Notorious Glasgow Shebeener* (*c*.1870?).
92. *VTR*, 1 June 1893.
93. Archibald, *Sink of Atrocity*, pp. 219–21.
94. *VTR*, 1 March 1894.
95. *VTR*, 15 March 1894.
96. G. Bell, *Day and Night in the Wynds of Edinburgh* and *Blackfriars Wynd Analysed* (Wakefield, reprinted 1973); and J. F. McCaffrey (ed.), *Glasgow 1858, Shadow's Midnight Scenes and Social Photographs* (Glasgow, 1976). For Alexander Brown, see Morris, 'New Spaces for Scotland', pp. 235–8.
97. D. Phillips (ed.), *Chapters in the Life of a Dundee Factory Boy* (Dundee, 1980); A. Clark, *Reminiscences of a Police Officer in the Granite City* (Aberdeen, 1873). and *North British Daily Mail*, 27 December 1870.
98. Harrison, *Drink and the Victorians*, p. 180.
99. Bell, *Wynds of Edinburgh*, pp. vii, x, 7–27. See also R. J. Morris, 'Death, Chambers Street and Edinburgh Corporation', in Cooke, et al. (eds), *Modern Scottish History*, Vol. 4, pp. 139–46.
100. McCaffrey (ed.), *Midnight Scenes*, pp. 17–99.
101. S. Stevenson, *Thomas Annan, 1829–1887* (Edinburgh, 1987), p. 4; and A. V. Mosley, *Thomas Annan, Photographs of the Old Closes and Streets of Glasgow* (New York, 1977), p. v.
102. R. Rodger, *The Transformation of Edinburgh, Land, Property and Trust in the Nineteenth Century* (Cambridge, 2001), p. 421.

103. Harrison, *Drink and the Victorians*, p. 157; T. Guthrie, *Autobiography and Memoir* (London, 1877); and Smout, *Century of the Scottish People*, pp. 141 and 205.

104. G. Lewis, *Scotland: A Half Educated Nation* (Glasgow, 1834), p. 30; and D. J. Withrington, 'Education', in Cooke, et al. (eds), *Modern Scottish History*, Vol. 1, pp. 289–91.

105. W. Donaldson, *Popular Literature in Victorian Scotland* (Aberdeen, 1986), p. 97.

106. C. McCracken-Flesher, *The Doctor Dissected. A Cultural Autopsy of the Burke and Hare Murders* (Oxford, 2012), pp. 70–86.

107. D. Pae, *Lucy the Factory Girl or the Secrets of the Tontine Close* (Hastings, 2001 edition), p. xviii.

108. Pae Mss, J. G. Bertram to David Pae, 6 August 1858.

109. C. Harman, *Robert Louis Stevenson* (London, 2005), p. 55.

110. Bell, *Wynds of Edinburgh*, p. 16.

111. Archibald, *Sink of Atrocity*, p. 210.

112. D. Barrie, *The City of Dundee Illustrated* (Dundee, 1890), p. 228.

113. *NSA*, Vol. VII, *Renfrew and Argyle*, p. 699.

114. McCaffrey (ed.), *Midnight Scenes*, p. 113.

115. Pae, *Lucy the Factory Girl*, pp. 22–3.

116. Smout, *Century of the Scottish People*, p. 162.

117. W. Logan, *An Exposure of Female Prostitution in London, Leeds, Rochdale and especially in the City of Glasgow* (Glasgow, 1843), pp. 23–32.

118. Logan, *Female Prostitution*.

119. B. Dempsey, 'By the Law of This and Every Well-Governed Realm: Investigating Accusations of Sodomy in Nineteenth-Century Scotland', *The Juridical Review*, 2006, Part 2, pp. 103–30.

120. *North British Daily Mail*, 27 December 1870.

121. *Glasgow Herald*, 11 November 1890.

122. R. Kenna and A. Moody, *People's Palaces. Victorian and Edwardian Pubs of Scotland* (Edinburgh, 1983), p. 70.

123. King, *Scotland Sober and Free*, pp. 19–24.

124. *People's Palaces*, p. 69

125. A. Sherwell, *The Drink Peril in Scotland* (Edinburgh, 1903), pp. 14–15.

126. McCaffrey (ed), *Midnight Scenes*, p. 85.

127. E. King, 'Popular Culture in Glasgow', in R. A. Cage (ed.), *The Working Class in Glasgow, 1750–1914* (London, 1987), p. 159.

128. See P. Maloney, *Scotland and the Music Hall, 1850–1914* (Manchester, 2003).

129. *North British Daily Mail*, 27 December 1870.

130. *North British Daily Mail*, 27 December 1870.

131. W. Freer, *My Life and Memories* (Glasgow, 1929), p. 34.

132. *Sixty Years of Work, 1854–1914, Glasgow Abstainers' Union* (Glasgow, 1914), pp. 5–7.

133. Pae Mss, and A. J. Cooke, *From Popular Enlightenment to Lifelong Learning. A History of Adult Education in Scotland, 1707–2005* (Leicester, 2006), pp. 90–1.
134. C. A. Whatley (ed.), *The Diary of John Sturrock, Millwright, Dundee, 1864–65* (East Linton, 1996), p. 102.
135. J. H. Muir, *Glasgow in 1901* (Glasgow, 2001), pp. 176–7.
136. NRS, SC 37/42/20/604, Sheriff Court of Hamilton, Inventory of Robert Robin, of Castlehill, Hamilton, 23 August 1905.
137. NRS, SC 36/48/202/764, Sheriff Court of Glasgow, Inventory of Edward Taylor, Woodside Place, Glasgow, 9 January 1906.
138. J. Gorevan, *Glasgow Pubs and Publicans* (Stroud, 2002), p. 147.
139. King, 'Popular Culture in Glasgow', p. 152.
140. Burnett and Jarvie, 'Sport, Scotland and the Scots', p. 4.
141. Fraser, 'Developments in Leisure', p. 255.
142. B. Murray, *The Old Firm. Sectarianism, Sport and Society in Scotland* (Edinburgh, 1984), p. 36.
143. Smout, *Century of the Scottish People*, p. 153.
144. Murray, *The Old Firm*, pp. 13–15.
145. *Victualling Trades Review (VTR)*, 15 August 1898.
146. Murray, *The Old Firm*, pp. 18–19 and 25.
147. NRS, SC 37/42/25/155, Sheriff Court of Hamilton, Probate Inventory of John Herbert McLaughlin, wine and spirit merchant, 11 November 1909.
148. *National Guardian*, 3 October 1914.
149. Mitchell Library, Glasgow, TD 509/13/1, Sederunt Books of Trust of Lilias Smith, Greenock, Vol. 1, 1898–1905.
150. NRS, SC 36/51/168/447, Sheriff Court of Glasgow, Will of Thomas Reid, 4 June 1916.
151. T. Collins and W. Vamplew, *Mud, Sweat and Beers. A Cultural History of Sport and Alcohol* (Oxford, 2002), p. 13.
152. J. Kay and W. Vamplew, 'Horse-Racing', in Jarvie and Burnett (eds), *Sport, Scotland and the Scots*, p. 167.
153. *People's Palaces*, pp. 30–1.
154. N. Morgan and R. Trainor, 'The Dominant Classes,' in Fraser and Morris (eds), *People and Society in Scotland, Vol. II, 1830–1914*, p. 111.
155. *Scottish Wine, Spirit and Beer Trades Review (SWSBTR)*, 13 February 1888.
156. Collins and Vamplew, *Mud, Sweat and Beers*, pp. 22–3.
157. *VTR*, 13 July 1891.
158. NRS, SC 6/46/39/133, Sheriff Court of Ayrshire, Will of Archibald Lauder, 30 March 1912.
159. *People's Palaces*, p. 33.
160. NRS, Sheriff Courts of Ayr, Glasgow, Hamilton and Paisley, Wills and Probate Inventories; Mitchell Library, Glasgow, Sederunt Books of Trusts.

161. King-Clark (ed.) *The John Caldwell Letters from Canada, 1821–1837* (Paisley, 1991), p. 38.

162. Morgan and Trainor, 'The Dominant Classes', p. 110.

163. D. W. Gutzke, *Protecting the Pub. Brewers and Publicans against Temperance* (Woodbridge, 1989), p. 1; and R. Jenkins, *Gladstone* (London, 1996), p. 379.

164. Dundee City Archives, GD/DLT 4, A. Robb, Draft History of the Dundee Licensed Trade Association (formerly Dundee Wine, Spirit and Beer Trade Protection Association), 1863–1907 (*c*.1950).

165. M. Simmons, *The Scottish Licensed Trade Association, 1880–1980* (Edinburgh, 1981), pp. 2–3.

166. *People's Palaces*, p. 64.

167. Bell, *Day and Night in the Wynds of Edinburgh*, pp. 25–6.

168. McCaffrey (ed.), *Shadow's Midnight Scenes*, p. 63.

169. D Campbell, *Reminiscences and Reflections of an Octogenarian Highlander* (Inverness, 1910), p. 96

170. A. Durie (ed.), *Travels in Scotland, 1788–1881* (Woodbridge, 2012), pp. 167 and 176.

171. A. Geikie, *Scottish Reminiscences* (Glasgow, 1906), p. 305.

172. NRS, SC 58/42/44/551, Sheriff Court of Paisley, Will of Mathew Robin, 22 December 1876.

173. NRS, SC 37/42/20/604, Sheriff Court of Hamilton, Inventory of Robert Robin, 23 August 1905.

174. NRS, SC 36/48/123/288, Sheriff Court of Glasgow, Inventory of John Brown, 26 September 1888.

175. NRS, SC 36/48/139/666, Inventory of James Cush, 4 January 1893.

176. Geikie, *Reminiscences*, pp. 311–12.

177. *Glasgow Shebeener*, pp. 2–3. A 'rattler' was a cheap 'geggie' or music hall.

178. *SWSBTR*, 26 April 1887.

179. *SWSBTR*, 3 May 1887.

180. *Victualling Trades Review* (*VTR*), 12 December 1891.

181. *People's Palaces*, p. 59.

182. Gorevan, *Glasgow Pubs*, p. 110.

183. *People's Palaces*, p. 29.

184. *VTR*, February 1903.

185. Hopkin, *Aberdeen Pub Companion*, p. 7.

186. W. Carnie, *Reporting Reminiscences* (Aberdeen, 1902), pp. 321–2.

187. *NSA*, Vol. VII, *Renfrew and Argyle*, p. 689.

188. *NSA*, Vol. VI, *Lanarkshire*, p. 249. See also R. Duncan, *The Mine Workers* (Edinburgh, 2005); and A. B. Campbell, *The Lanarkshire Miners, 1775–1874* (Edinburgh, 1979).

189. *Shadow's Midnight Scenes*, p. 63.

190. *North British Daily Mail*, 30 June 1891

191. Barrie, *City of Dundee Illustrated*, p. 228.

192. Dundee City Libraries, D 32273, Register of Inebriates, Dundee, 1905.
193. E. Burns, *Ale in Stirling* (Stirling, 2004), p. 60.
194. *Glasgow Shebeener*, p. 3.
195. Fraser, 'Developments in Leisure', p. 240 and Kenefick, *Glasgow Dockers*, pp. 132 and 221.
196. *Dundee Courier*, 21 October 1960, Article on 'Pubs in the Blackscroft, c.1900'.
197. *VTR*, 12 December 1891.
198. ML, MP 24.328, Report by Glasgow Superintendent of Police, 1856.
199. PKA, PE 17/Bundle 182, Perth Police Commissioners, 9 January 1890.
200. Durie, 'Movement, Transport and Tourism', p. 151.
201. Geikie, *Reminiscences*, p. 310.
202. Y. Hillyard, *Raising the Bar* (Edinburgh, 2012), p. 29.
203. *People's Palaces*, p. 71.
204. *People's Palaces*, p. 71.
205. Glasgow University Archives, Scottish Brewing Archive, GDL 1/10/3, Glasgow Licensed Trade Defence Association, Annual Report, 1901.
206. *People's Palaces*, pp. 74–5.

5

'Serious Attacks on the Trade': The Two World Wars and the Interwar Period, 1914–45

INTRODUCTION

THE TWO WORLD WARS and the interwar years comprised a period of major discontinuity in British and Scottish history. The two world wars were marked by heavy loss of life in combat and, in the case of World War II, by civilian casualties, such as the German bombing of Clydebank in March 1941. Civilian casualties per head of population in World War II, however, were lower in Scotland than in England and Wales.[1] On the other side of the coin, both wars saw a boost for the Scottish economy, as demand for ships and armaments provided work for the Clydeside shipyards and the heavy industries of central Scotland. Around 250,000 Scots worked in war-related industries in the Clyde basin during World War I,[2] and the west of Scotland was transformed into 'a vast arsenal for the mass production of ships, shells, guns and other munitions'.[3] Both wars were 'total wars', and women were drafted into previously all-male occupations as the men left to join the armed forces. This led to a gradual improvement in the status of women, marked most obviously at the end of World War I by the Representation of the People Act of 1918 which extended the vote to all adult males over twenty-one and all women over the age of thirty.[4]

The two world wars saw an extension of state control into many aspects of life, from the building of large national munitions factories, nationalisation of parts of the drink trade and requisitioning of buildings, including hotels, for the armed forces, hospitals and other government use in World War I, to blackout regulations, food rationing, evacuation, billeting of troops and children, and further requisitioning in World War II. Both world wars were extremely expensive, and government debt to pay for them rose to record levels, particularly by the end of World War II when the country was practically bankrupt. During World War I, patriotic Scots bought larger numbers of war bonds proportionately than the rest of the United Kingdom.[5] John Scouller, for example, a wealthy Glasgow wine and spirit merchant, who owned three pubs in the centre of Glasgow, including the Horseshoe Bar, left an estate of £81,265 on his death in 1923, of which £17,735 (22 per cent) was held in war bonds.[6]

In many ways, the interwar period in Scotland represented two 'lost decades'. There was economic depression in Scotland at the end of World War I, followed by a world slump after the Wall Street Crash of 1929. For much of this period, Scotland experienced high levels of unemployment compared to England (though lower than Wales). In July 1933, unemployment stood at 33 per cent in Wales, 28 per cent in Scotland and 16 per cent in England and Wales combined,[7] and Scots emigrated in record numbers. Emigration had been a feature of Scottish society throughout the nineteenth century but peaked in the decade from 1921 to 1932, when 523,981 Scots emigrated – 446,212 (85 per cent) overseas, the rest to England and Wales.[8] At the same time, church adherence in Scotland reached record levels in 1925, when it made up 41.6 per cent of the total age population, to decline slowly thereafter.[9] In his remarkable *Scottish Journey*, published in 1935, the poet Edwin Muir summed up the feelings of quiet desperation in Scotland in this period, 'a silent clearance is going on in industrial Scotland, a clearance not of human beings, but of what they depend on for life'.[10]

THE SCOTTISH RESPONSE TO WORLD WAR I

There were widely differing responses to World War I in Scotland. The outbreak of war in 1914 was met with an outburst of patriotism. Scots volunteered in record numbers for the British army and, by the end of the first week of September 1914, Glasgow was able to claim that it had recruited more than 22,000 men. Cities such as Aberdeen, Dundee and Edinburgh vied with each other to recruit larger numbers of young men. By the time conscription was introduced in January 1916, about a third of a million Scots had enlisted voluntarily. At the end of the war, 690,235 Scots had served in the armed services: 585,171 in the army, 72,219 in the navy and 32,845 in the air force, amounting to about half of all Scottish men aged between eighteen and forty-five.[11]

On the other side of the coin, the Independent Labour Party, which was strong in Scotland, and other socialist organisations, such as John Maclean's Scottish Labour Party, adopted a largely pacifist and anti-war stance. In spite of this, membership of the ILP in Scotland grew during

World War I from three thousand to ten thousand, whereas it fell in England and Wales, being seen there as pro-German.[12] The Scottish section of the ILP had a strong temperance cast to its politics. As late as 1926, it was passing motions for 'the total prohibition of the manufacture and sale of intoxicating liquors'.[13] Trade unionists in the Clyde shipyards, coal mines, heavy industries and munitions factories also adopted a largely critical attitude to the war and to wartime reorganisation which they saw either as a capitalist conspiracy or an attempt to replace highly skilled and unionised men by cheaper and more compliant female labour. The engineering unions had agreed officially to ban all strikes during the war but a group of shop stewards linked to the Clyde Workers' Committee led a series of unofficial strikes. In October 1915, Glasgow women led a successful rent strike, involving 25,000 tenants, contrasting the behaviour of rack-renting landlords with the sacrifices of their sons and husbands in the trenches.[14]

THE SCOTTISH LICENSED TRADE AND WORLD WAR I

The reaction of the licensed trade in Scotland to the outbreak of World War I was one of unbridled patriotism. By the beginning of September 1914, the licensed trade had raised £3,266 for war relief funds: £1,029 from Glasgow, £781 from Leith and £574 from Greenock. A week later, the *National Guardian* reported that 'subscriptions continue to roll in unchecked', including a fund to relieve distress among Belgian refugees. Tennent's Wellpark Brewery in Glasgow had donated £500 to the Red Cross and subscriptions had been raised by the trade across Scotland, including Kilmarnock, Paisley, Hamilton, Dundee, Peterhead, Morayshire, Inverness, Dumfries and Ayrshire.[15]

The licensed trade further displayed its patriotism by encouraging staff to enlist for the armed forces. In Dundee, the licensed grocers were lobbied by the Lord Provost in September 1914 to encourage their assistants to enlist. It was agreed to do this by keeping their places open for them until they returned.[16] The Glasgow and District Licensed Trade Defence Association (GDLTDA) held 'a good Recruiting Rally' in Glasgow City Hall on 1 June 1915, in response to Kitchener's appeal for an additional 300,000 men for the war effort. All licence holders in the city and their employees were urged to attend, and Glasgow pubs were shut that day from 1.00 to 5.00 p.m. Two full pipe bands were laid on, and there was a bumper attendance, with four hundred men enlisted as a result. One cloud on the horizon was that the Defence of the Realm Act had appointed a Board of Control for the Liquor Trade and the

GDLTDA urged that there should be 'at least one member of the Retail Trade on the Board'.[17]

As male bar staff left to fight in the trenches, their replacement by women was fiercely resisted by the Glasgow magistrates. They placed an embargo on the employment of women in pubs but the president of the GDLTDA argued that 'the employment of women in public houses under proper conditions would be as great a success as the employment of women on the tramways had proved to be.' Women licensees formed a small minority of the GDLTDA's own membership: eighty-five (11 per cent) out of a total membership of 770.[18]

With so many men away fighting in the trenches, there was great concern by the Church of Scotland and others about female morality, as married women were left at home with a service allowance to spend, and both married and unmarried women entered employment to fill the gap left by men leaving for war service. There were reports that sexual immorality was rife, that women were drinking, smoking and swearing more, and that child abuse and neglect were increasing.[19] In Aberdeen, it was claimed that, with men away at the war, soldiers' wives were entering pubs in greater numbers and spending their service allowances on drink, 'having more money in their hands than usual, there were only too many ready to help them spend it in the wrong way'.[20]

The Dundee Society for the Prevention of Cruelty to Children reported on the drinking habits of the wives of Dundee servicemen. It estimated the number of women drinking in the city in 1915 as 275, of whom 175 (55 per cent) were soldiers' wives. This proportion rose over the next two years, though the overall numbers fell slightly, from 55 per cent in 1915, 66 per cent in 1916 and 71 per cent in 1917. In a city where wages were notoriously low, the report concluded that, 'in many cases the Service allowance to soldiers' wives was larger than the ordinary labouring man's wife was accustomed to receive from her husband . . . the result (of drinking) was neglect of the children, and abandonment of parental responsibility, and not infrequently unfaithfulness to the husband at the front'.[21]

Similar claims were made in Edinburgh where, during the second quarter of 1915, 181 children of serving soldiers were placed in shelters, 'owing to intemperance amongst women'. From the same city, the SNSPCC reported in 1917 that 'there is a determination amongst a large number of women to go their own way and live as they like in the absence of their husbands'. A real concern was that children were being left alone for long periods, often from an early hour in the evening to the early morning. A common practice is for women to lock children in and take the key away so that the Inspectors cannot get access to the children. The early part of the night is spent in public houses, picture houses and theatres and it is often not until the early hours of the morning that they return home.[22]

In January 1916, the *National Guardian* carried an article, 'The Trade and the War', which reported that there were ten thousand licence holders in Scotland and some twenty thousand men connected with the trade. So far, the licensed trade had supplied some three thousand volunteers for the war effort, of whom three hundred had died and a thousand been wounded. They had also supplied twelve ambulances to the Scottish Branch of the Red Cross. The article welcomed the appointment of Sir Douglas Haig as Commander-in-Chief of the British Army in France in rather lukewarm terms, 'a thorough sportsman and a fairly good shot'. Haig's family owned Cameronbridge Distillery in Fife and leased a sporting estate in the Cabrach.[23]

The licensed trade's patriotism was all the more pronounced because it viewed its temperance opponents as tainted with socialism, pacifism and anti-war leanings. At the beginning of the war, the *National Guardian* taunted their temperance opponents, the '"Holy Willies" who had been the "little Navy" and "peace at any price" men of yesterday but today pose as the only pure-souled patriots in the land'.[24] On the Home Front, drink was important to the war effort. The *Daily Record* in February 1915 carried a photograph of a pub near Fairfield shipyard on the Clyde with the bar lined up with 'half and halfs' (half pints of beer and a whisky chaser) waiting for the shipyard workers when they finished their shift.[25] In the same year, shipyard employers in Scotland called for total prohibition owing to absenteeism as a result of heavy drinking by shipyard workers.[26] In January 1916, the *Guardian* carried an article headed 'Discontent on the Clyde', criticising the 'crass minded and selfish workers' who were hampering the war effort. They also attacked Lloyd George, 'the great Welsh crusader' and temperance advocate, who had described drink 'as a worse enemy than Germany or Austria'. Another favourite target was Philip Snowden, Labour MP for Blackburn in Lancashire, whom Lloyd George had appointed to the Board of Liquor Control and whom the *National Guardian* dismissively described as 'a Socialist of extreme views upon social questions . . . an avowed prohibitionist and is a pacifist'.[27]

By February 1916, the *National Guardian* was concerned that the government planned to take over the grain distilleries to manufacture

essential ingredients for explosives. A month later, there was continuing
suspicion of Lloyd George who was now Minister of Munitions and had
boasted he was going to become 'the greatest distiller in the world'.[28]
The government had established the Central Control Board (Liquor
Traffic) in July 1915, under the Defence of the Realm Act (1915), and
placed restrictions on brewers in terms of raw materials, the gravity and
output of beer. Three areas of Britain were marked out as particularly
vital to the war effort: Enfield in Middlesex, where Lee-Enfield rifles
were manufactured; the Carlisle–Gretna area, where there were large
munitions factories; and the Invergordon–Cromarty area, where there
was an important naval base and dockyards.[29] As part of the war effort,
National Munitions plants were built by the Ministry of Munitions on
selected sites, one of the largest being Gretna, on the English border,
where a huge munitions factory was built, together with a 'temporary
township', to house thousands of workers who had to be fed and entertained. By 1916, there were ten thousand workers at Gretna, many of
them Irish, which placed great strain on accommodation and the local
pubs. It was a youthful workforce and, in 1916, 60 per cent of them
were under nineteen. At its height, H. M. Factory Gretna employed
thirty thousand workers, many of them young women, producing 1,100
tons of cordite a week in 1917. Drunkenness figures soared, from sev-
enty-two in Carlisle and six in Annan from January to June 1915, to
564 in Carlisle and 146 in Annan for the same period the following year.

Figure 5.1 The Blue Bell Inn, Annan, Dumfriesshire. Part of Gretna and District
State Management Scheme, 1917. © Anthony and Judith Cooke.

Between July and October 1916, the board took over local breweries around Carlisle and nationalised 120 licensed premises.[30] The board had the power to take over or close any public house which was prejudicial to the 'output of munitions, the transport of materials or the discipline of troops'.[31]

In Annan, two public houses, the Alexander and the Albert, were closed and two new ones, the Globe and Gracie's Banking Tavern, which were encouraged to serve food, were opened. A cinema and a bowling green were also provided for workers but the cinema was not popular with the Gretna labourers. Eventually, one nationalised brewery in Carlisle supplied all the beer to state pubs in Carlisle, Gretna and Invergordon on the Cromarty Firth, where another state-controlled drink scheme operated at the naval base and dockyards, scene of a naval mutiny in 1931.[32]

Elsewhere in Scotland, state control tightened as regards opening hours for pubs. In west-central Scotland, the opening hours for pubs were set from 12 noon to 2.30 p.m. and from 6.00 p.m. to 9.00 p.m. weekdays and 4.00 p.m. to 9.00 p.m. Saturdays. This increasing degree of government control was a potent recruiting agent for the licensed trade protection associations. The retail membership of the Glasgow Association rose from 770 in 1915 to 952 in 1916 in response to what Malcolm M'Intyre, the association's treasurer, called 'serious attacks on the trade'.[33]

There were similar concerns in other parts of the country. The *National Guardian* reported in December 1916 that, in Aberdeen, few public houses now opened before noon. In Haddon Street, Aberdeen, 'a section of the farmers and those who assembled on Fridays are in the habit of adjoining to a neighbouring house, there to discuss over a ginger ale or lemonade the business of the day'. Now 'they will be obliged to do without the shelter of the hostelry and the teetotal beverages' but their traditional market business would continue.[34]

Another concern of the licensed trade was the shortage of grain for distilling as a result of the war. In Glasgow, it was claimed that the use of methylated spirits to adulterate whisky (a long-established practice in Glasgow) had increased since wartime restrictions were imposed.[35] A Paisley magistrate reported that, out of five people charged with being drunk and incapable in December 1915, three claimed to have drunk meths. In 1916, restrictions were imposed on the sale of whisky in small amounts, and retail sales were confined to quart bottles, leading to 'clubbing' and heavy drinking involving men and women in Aberdeen and Dundee.[36] There were complaints from Dundee in December 1916 about 'the great scarcity of Whisky and the advance in Prices', and the executive of the Dundee Wine, Spirit and Beer Trade Protection Association resolved to fix prices at 6d per glass and 4/6d per bottle for Ordinary Whisky, 8d per glass and 5/6d per bottle for Proprietary Whisky.[37]

In the midst of their wartime difficulties, however, the licensed trade had two trump cards to play. As the cost of the war increased, the increased taxes on licences and drink provided a major income stream for the government. Even before the war, the income from spirit licences brought in considerable tax revenues. In the financial year 1912–13, there were 10,055 spirit licences in Scotland, providing an annual revenue of £253,589. This compared with Ireland, where a larger number of spirit licences (17,849) brought in a smaller revenue (£166,429). In England, 71,484 spirit licences generated a substantial annual revenue of £2,930,034.[38] Early on in the war, Lloyd George imposed a beer tax of 17 shillings 3d new barrelage duty, which was generally condemned by the Scottish licensed trade as too high, though it was welcomed by a Dundee licensee as it did not affect the heavily taxed whisky drinker.[39] The other trump card was the effect on morale of troops on leave or in training and on key workers such as munitions workers if pubs ran out of beer or whisky.

A hint of the future electoral troubles awaiting Winston Churchill, Liberal MP for Dundee, is given in a threatening letter sent to him by the Dundee District Lodge of Good Templars. They had reported to him on a conference demanding prohibition and asked if his failure to reply to their letter was 'another example of your studied neglect and insult of those who honoured you by finding at that time a safe seat for you in the House of Commons'.[40] This sort of clash between Churchill and his prohibitionist constituents, together with the widening of the franchise in 1918 to include all men over twenty-one and all women over thirty, helps to explain his heavy defeat by the Scottish Prohibition Party candidate, Edwin Scrymgeour, and the Labour candidate, E. D. Morel, at the 1922 election.[41]

THE END OF THE WAR AND THE LOCAL VETO CAMPAIGN

The end of the Great War brought important political and economic changes. The Scottish electorate almost tripled, from 779,000 in 1910 to 2,205,000 in 1918. There were difficulties, however, in getting all these new voters registered. Only 60 per cent of the electorate voted in 1918, compared to 75 per cent in 1922, when Labour made its electoral breakthrough to become the largest party in Scotland.[42] The prohibitionist movement believed that the new female electorate was likely to be much more receptive to the temperance message than men and could be their trump card in the forthcoming local veto polls and in other elections. An article on 'Will Scotland Go Dry?', published in 1919, warned members of the Dundee licensed trade that the Scottish Permissive Bill and Temperance Association had been working 'especially among the women, on whom they are counting for the majority of their votes'. The slogan of the prohibitionists was said to be 'Scotland First and England and Wales to follow'. The prohibitionists had powerful allies on both sides of the Atlantic. Their supporters, advertised to speak at their meetings, included Robert Munro, Secretary for Scotland, David Lloyd George, the American Reverend G. A. King, and another American, 'Pussyfoot' Johnson, who had 'slipped into Scotland' to campaign for temperance.[43]

World War I had seen a large increase in taxation on whisky to pay for the war effort. In July 1919 a poster was produced to denounce the high level of taxation on whisky, the drink of the working man in Scotland, compared to upper- and middle-class alcoholic drinks such as champagne, port and sherry. Headed 'What Workers Provide', the poster showed that champagne, priced at 20 to 30 shillings a bottle, paid only 7.5d duty per bottle and port and sherry, priced from 5 to 7 shillings a bottle, only 2.5d and 6d a bottle. This contrasted with whisky, priced at 10/6d a bottle, which paid a massive 5/10d a bottle duty. The duty on whisky had soared from 14/9d per gallon (4.55 litres) before the war to 50 shillings per gallon after, while that on beer had risen by 800 per cent from 7/9d per barrel (164 litres) pre-war to 70 shillings a barrel post-war.[44]

The end of the war brought major economic and social problems, as the shipbuilding and armaments industries began to run down, with knock-on effects on the production of coal, iron and steel, textiles and so on. It was against this background that employers launched a cost-cutting campaign, often focusing on wage reductions and changes in working conditions. These changes were resisted by workers across the country, from the 40 Hours Strike among Glasgow shipbuilding and engineering workers in 1919, the miners' strike in 1921, the bitter strike and lockout in the Dundee jute industry in 1923 and the General Strike of 1926.[45]

The Temperance (Scotland) Act of 1913 had made provision for local veto polls but its implementation was delayed because of the outbreak of World War I. The first polls took place in 1920, and the No

Licence Campaign was supported by the Independent Labour Party in its attempt to introduce 'dry' areas into Scotland.[46] The ILP was strongly pro-temperance and, as late as World War II, Cliff Hanley, a member of the Glasgow ILP, remembered that 'Even with wartime rationing, the ILP in Glasgow went through whole plantations of tea.'[47] As a recent historian has noted, 'teetotalism and prohibition were most strongly associated with the Labour Party, whose Members of Parliament were teetotallers almost to a man'.[48] Of the 584 polls which took place, 508 districts (87 per cent) voted for 'No Change', thirty-five for Limitation and forty-one for No Licence. There were 315 licences lost and burghs, such as Kirkintilloch, Kilsyth, Stromness and Wick, went 'dry'. The 'dry' vote in Kirkintilloch depended on the strength of the local temperance societies and the female vote and, it was claimed, 'the women's organisations in the town cast their strength at the ballot boxes, it was said, to the last skirt'.[49] In the Glasgow area, it was largely Protestant suburban residential areas, such as Cathcart, Pollockshields (a favourite residential area for Glasgow wine and spirit merchants!), Kelvinside and North Kelvin, which voted for No Licence and Limitation.[50] Given the strength of the temperance movement in Scotland and its powerful allies in local and central government, it was remarkable that the vast majority of wards polled voted to keep the status quo and rejected prohibition.

In 1923, the Scottish Prohibition Party MP for Dundee, Edwin Scrymgeour, tried to introduce a national Prohibition Act in Parliament, supported by the ILP Clydesider MPs, especially James Maxton. The bill, however, was soundly defeated in the Commons by 235 votes to fourteen.[51] The effects of prohibition on the few areas in Scotland that voted for it were similar to what happened during prohibition in the United States – drinking went 'underground'. In 'dry' Wick, in Caithness, it was claimed that more alcohol was consumed in 1933 than when it was 'wet' because of the growth of shebeens or unlicensed drinking places.[52] An apocryphal story from this period describes a visitor arriving at Wick railway station, where he asks a local, 'Where do I get a drink in Wick?' The local replies, 'See that big building over there? That's the police station. You won't get any drink there but you'll get a drink at every other house in Wick!'[53]

ECONOMIC DEPRESSION AND MIGRATION

Scotland between the wars was a depressed country economically, and many Scots followed the traditional solution to lack of opportunity at home – emigration. The 1920s and 1930s also saw the growth of the cinema as a leisure activity for large numbers of working-class Scots, a relatively cheap pastime that appealed to both sexes and to children.[54] The Carnegie investigation in the 1930s found that about 80 per cent of their sample of the young unemployed attended the cinema at least once a week, compared to 15 to 20 per cent who went cycling and only 6 per cent who used the public library.[55] Cinema numbers boomed and, on the eve of World War II, Glasgow had 104 cinemas, Dundee twenty-eight and Aberdeen nineteen.[56] Green's Playhouse in Dundee was the second largest cinema in Europe with the tallest advertising tower, at 90 feet (27.4 metres), and required a staff of almost fifty people to run it.[57] Aberdeen had the 2,000-seater Astoria cinema, opened in 1934, and the city boasted one cinema seat per seven inhabitants, more than double the ratio for London. In the 1930s, it was claimed that the social life of Aberdeen revolved around two polar institutions – the church and the cinema.[58]

Emigration and the growth of the cinema, combined with the economic depression and rising prices of spirits, reduced the attractions of the public house. The number of public houses in Scotland fell from 5,175 in 1913 to 4,328 in 1933, while the number of licensed grocers fell from 3,516 to 2,592 in the same period.[59] Increased taxation also affected whisky consumption in Scotland which saw a steep decline between 1910 and 1930 when adults were drinking on average less than a sixth of a pint (0.1 litre) of whisky per week.[60] The increase in duty on whisky in 1926, from 50 shillings to 72/6d per gallon (4.55 litres), yielded less revenue than under the lower rate. Revenues from spirit duties fell from £71 million in 1921 to £51 million in 1925. In the same period, the sales of wine rose from 11 million gallons (50,050,000 litres) in 1922 to 15.6 million (71 million litres) in 1925.[61] By 1930, Sir Alexander Walker, speaking for the Whisky Association, told a Royal Commission that drinking Scotch whisky was now 'almost entirely confined to those of middle age and the aged'.[62] Between 1928 and 1935, almost 50 per cent of Scotland's distilleries closed down.[63] During the interwar period, the number of pubs remained fairly constant in Scotland, at about one for every eight hundred people, but the consumption of spirits fell by about a fifth owing to increased taxation, and deaths due to alcohol and crimes of drunkenness both decreased.[64]

The economic depression and changes in leisure-time activities produced changes in drinking patterns. Because people had less money to spend, the long-established practice of adulterating whisky with methylated spirits flourished in the interwar period. In Glasgow, skilled trades in the Gorbals area, such as cabinetmaking, used meths in their

manufacturing processes and, when this was combined with the 'numerous shebeens and also illicit stills' in the area, adulteration of whisky
continued to be a major problem. In February 1928, it was claimed 'that
in the Docks area it is quite common to break cases of whisky'.[65] Trade
was so fragile, the Glasgow licensed trade even worried about 'displace-
ment of business through Greyhound Racing and the resuscitation soon
of Cycle Racing'.[66]

The licensed trade in Scotland continued to search for friends and
allies in its campaigns, not always with much success. One approach
was to try to smear the prohibitionist movement as unpatriotic and
subversive, given its strong links with the Independent Labour Party
and other socialist organisations in Scotland. In September 1926, the
National Guardian attacked the 'Pussyites' and the 'old women' of both
sexes in Kirkintilloch, which had gone 'dry'. It claimed that the British
Pussyite, 'plays so important a part in the Bolshevist plot to cause a
revolution amongst our workers'.[67] The following month, Dr Salter,
the Labour MP for Bermondsey West, gave a speech at a Lodge of
Good Templars. He claimed that fifty-six Labour MPs were 'definite
teetotallers' and many of them were Scottish. The *National Guardian*
complained that the trade had supported the Conservatives 'through
thick and thin' over the last few years but had seen precious little reward
for their efforts.[68]

In Perth, the licensed trade fought a losing campaign in 1929 against
the Temperance Alliance and the local kirk session to extend opening
hours by half an hour from 9.00 p.m. The lawyer representing the
licensed trade played the tourism card by arguing 'Perth has now become
definitely established as a summer resort and if refreshment facilities are
not provided we will find that the influx of visitors will fall away.' Both
the Temperance Alliance and Perth kirk session objected to the proposed
increase in opening hours, as did the Chief Constable. The lawyer for
the licensed trade countered that 'people were not to be made sober by
means of prohibition but by education and character', and pointed out
that the Local Options Act had been tried several times in Perthshire and
the people had voted against prohibition. In spite of these arguments, the
extension of opening hours was refused.[69] Ministers provided a bedrock
of support for the temperance movement. In Aberdeen, the Reverend
J. H. Wilken condemned the city's pubs in 1932 as, 'little Black Holes
of Calcutta' and claimed that, 'barmen were in an unhealthy occupation
and were dying off rapidly'. In the 1920s and 1930s, Aberdeen Town
Council was opposed to building pubs in new housing areas, and the
Hilton housing scheme had no pub as late as 1975.[70]

By the early 1930s, the licensed trade in Glasgow was concerned about the Scottish National Movement, 'and the danger to our trade should a Parliament be established in Edinburgh'.[71] The fear was that a Scottish Parliament was more likely to be dominated by prohibitionists than Westminster. In the same year, the president and secretary were sent to visit industrial cities in England to see how arrangements for early closing worked there. They reported back that, in Carlisle, Sheffield, Birmingham, Manchester and Liverpool, 'a reasonable time to clear the premises' was observed by the police.[72]

The following year, in April 1933, the problem of methylated spirit drinking in Glasgow raised its ugly head again when it was claimed that, 'some drysalters (chemists) open as early as 5 a.m. for the alleged purpose of selling Methylated Spirits'. By September, the Glasgow trade was campaigning for methylated spirits to be included in the category of poisons under the Dangerous Drugs Act. A new challenge appeared in December 1933 when it was reported that the Glasgow Licensing Court might require lavatory accommodation for women to be made compulsory in public houses, which raised predictable complaints from the trade about the likely expense of such a move.[73]

In spite of these challenges, the drinks industry, including the manufacturing and distribution side, was a substantial employer north and south of the border. Table 5.1 reveals significant differences in employment patterns between the drinks industry in England and Wales, and in Scotland in the early 1930s. The balance in drinks manufacturing was tilted heavily towards beer in England and Wales, where malting and brewing accounted for 86 per cent of the total drink-manufacturing workforce, and was more evenly balanced in Scotland, where malting and brewing made up 52 per cent of the manufacturing workforce and whisky distilling 45 per cent. In both countries, employment in drink distribution (wholesale dealing, hotels, public houses and so on), far outnumbered employment in drink manufacturing. In England and Wales, the distribution side employed 75 per cent of the total drinks industry workforce, compared to 70 per cent in Scotland. In both countries, there was a broadly similar gender balance in the workforce, with men making up 64 per cent of the total workforce in England and Wales, women 36 per cent, while, in Scotland, men accounted for 67 per cent of the workforce, women 33 per cent.

Figures for drunkenness in Glasgow in 1935 (Table 5.2) show that levels began to rise from Thursday night, which was often pay night, to record levels on Fridays and Saturdays, falling away to insignificance on Sundays when pubs were closed. Out of 6,466 cases of drunkenness in

Table 5.1 Employment in the drink trade, England and Wales, and Scotland, 1931.

	England and Wales	Scotland
Manufacturing		
Malting and beer brewers	74,387	6,565
Cider and perry	1,642	1
Distilling, rectifying	4,151	5,666
Bottling and 'other'	5,785	338
Total manufacturing	85,965	12,570
Distribution		
Dealing (wholesale)	21,918	2,873
Hotels, public houses, etc.	239,567	27,520
Total workforce in manufacturing/distribution	347,450	42,963
Males	224,299	28,995
Females	123,151	13,968

(Source: G. B. Wilson, *Alcohol and the Nation, 1800–1935*, London, 1940, p. 205)

Table 5.2 Figures for arrests for drunkenness in Glasgow, 1935.

	8 a.m.–8 p.m.	8 p.m.–8 a.m.	Total
Sunday	79	58	137
Monday	200	488	688
Tuesday	226	388	614
Wednesday	247	557	804
Thursday	295	729	1,024
Friday	416	1,110	1,526
Saturday	454	1,219	1,673
Total	1,917	4,549	6,466

(Source: G. B. Wilson, *Alcohol and the Nation, 1800–1935*, London, 1940, p. 293)

Glasgow in 1935, 3,928 cases (61 per cent of the total) took place from Thursday nights to Saturday evenings. This confirms the truth behind the old music hall song: 'When I get a couple of drinks on a Saturday, Glasgow belongs to me.'

In his journey through Scotland in 1935, Edwin Muir described his impressions of Edinburgh and Glasgow street crowds as filled with 'unsatisfied desire' and 'drenched in unsatisfied sex', from which the only refuge were the male-only pubs where 'men put into harbour and wrap themselves in the safe cloak of alcohol'.[74] Another Scottish exile, Lewis Grassic Gibbon (James Leslie Mitchell), set *A Scots Quair*, his trilogy of novels, in rural Kincardineshire. In *Cloud Howe* (1933), he described the dire impact of the world depression on the area, where 'the only creature that seemed to flourish as the harvest brought a dour end to the weather ... was Will Melvin that kept the Segget Arms, him and that sharp tongued besom his wife, the spinners would go down to the Arms and get drunk, instead of biding at home in their misery and cutting their throats, as decent folk would'.[75]

In the late 1930s Scottish pubs remained largely male-only spaces, a refuge from overcrowded homes and the pressures of work, family and children. Many pubs were closely linked either with the world of work, catering for coal miners, iron workers, shipyard workers, dockers, carters and so on, beginning or coming off their shifts during the week, or with the world of football on Saturday afternoons. One historian has described the Scottish pub in this period as 'a rite of passage for young men, who would there be initiated into the mysteries of male bonding. Manliness was associated with consumption, and holding one's drink was an essential part of male self-respect.' This was a world in which 'failure to buy a round would lead to social ostracism'.[76] This type of attitude is highlighted in the literature of the period. Neil Gunn's novel *The Silver Darlings*, published in 1941, is set at the end of the Napoleonic Wars in the herring fishing communities of the Highlands. Gunn describes a brawl at the Sloop Inn between fishermen in a general, almost timeless context: 'the bar was filled with seamen and voices and drink ... Finn at last got two whiskies from the landlord, who was a small forceful man, with a tubby body and a sharp commanding voice.' The fight breaks out when a fisherman called Roddie is teased by another man, 'Big Angus', over a navigation error. Only the landlord is unsurprised by Roddie's violent reaction, as he 'had long experience of the moment when, with a few drinks, a client in the pride of his manhood has the urge to sweep the seven seas'.[77]

Similar attitudes towards masculinity and its links with heavy drinking are found in the male characters in William McIlvanney's novel, *Docherty*, published in 1975 but set in the fictional Ayrshire industrial town of Graithnock, beginning in 1903 and continuing through World War I into the 1920s. In one of the early scenes in the novel, a drunken outsider with a Glasgow accent taunts a group of local Roman Catholic men standing on a street corner, with the inflammatory words 'the Pope's a mairrit man'. The man from the group who responds is 'Tadger Daly, father of ten', who headbutts the man and breaks his nose. As the injured man lies on the ground in a pool of blood, one of the onlookers makes the sardonic comment, 'That's whit ye call doin' penance, big man'.[78]

Drinking, pubs and entertainment venues, such as music halls and theatres, were also linked with female prostitution, as had been the case in the nineteenth century. Edwin Muir remarked on the 'invisible barrier' between Leith Walk and Princes Street in Edinburgh in the 1930s, between the middle- and working-class thoroughfares of the city, which was breached only by the prostitutes who 'are the sole class who rise superior to this inhibition' because they were 'tacitly outlawed by all society' and Princes Street was their main beat, though they generally lived in working-class areas.[79]

This subject has recently been revisited by Louise Settle who examined the social geography of prostitution in Edinburgh from 1900 to 1939. She found that, by the 1920s, there was a wide variety of entertainment venues, including pubs, in Edinburgh's East End (at the top of Leith Walk). Many of the new dance halls and cinemas, which opened in this period, were in this area, such as the Playhouse on Greenside Row and Fairley's dance hall on Leith Street. It was also close to Waverley Station and, as such, provided a first port of call for soldiers on leave during World War I and for sailors coming into the city centre from Leith docks. By the 1920s and 1930s, many prostitutes convicted of soliciting lived in this part of Edinburgh, though the largest number still lived in the Old Town. There was also a high concentration of pubs and shebeens – in 1911 there were no fewer than twenty-two pubs in the small triangle between Leith Street and York Place. The women often solicited outside cinemas, dance halls, restaurants and pubs. A police report in 1921 described how a prostitute, called Marjorie Milner, had accosted a naval petty officer outside the K. B. Hotel and had been found with another prostitute in a shebeen, at 3a Greenside Place, known as the 'dug out'. Seven years later, a witness described how he and another man had been solicited in the street by two prostitutes and, after a few drinks in a pub, they had gone back with them to a house to have sex.[80]

By 1937, the licensing court in Dundee was flexing its muscles over regulation of public houses under its control and applying stricter conditions to the issue of licences. It took legal opinion about imposing conditions for the issue of licences and was advised that premises were not to be deemed suitable for a public house 'unless provided with adequate water closets and urinals, sufficiently ventilated and in good order and condition'. A long series of conditions (ten in all) were imposed on the issue of licences, including one that no premises were to be accepted for licensing, 'if they have any back door or opening (except for goods) leading to or from any close, staircase, lane or back thoroughfare'.

Another stated that the doors of all sitting rooms and boxes (private drinking spaces) 'shall be wholly clear glass about 4 feet 6 inches [1.37 metres] from the floor'. There were to be no free drinks or gifts allowed, nor raffles or lotteries. Music was also disapproved of, 'the Court disapproves of pianos or other musical instruments being installed or played in licensed premises without their express approval'. There was to be zero tolerance of crime or prostitution being carried on in public houses, and publicans were not allowed to 'permit or suffer men or women of notoriously bad fame or girls or boys to assemble and meet therein', while they were not allowed to sell liquor to girls and boys under fourteen, or to anyone in a state of intoxication. They also could not permit 'any unlawful games'.[81] Magistrates in Glasgow also disapproved of games in pubs and, in April 1939, decided to ban them from all licensed premises. After lobbying by the trade, they agreed to allow dominoes and darts to be played.[82]

Towards the end of the 1930s, economic conditions began to improve. Car ownership, associated with the rising middle class, began to grow, and reached 147,000 in 1938, while motorcycle ownership, more of a working-class form of transport, reached 31,000 in the same year.[83] Surprisingly, in his classic thriller, *The Thirty-Nine Steps*, published as early as 1915, John Buchan has his hero, Richard Hannay, seek refuge in a fictional inn in the Galloway hills patronised only by 'motor cars full of fat women, who stop for lunch, and a fisherman or two in the spring and the shooting tenants in August'.[84] On the outskirts of Glasgow in 1935, Edwin Muir noticed that 'the petrol stations along the roadside steadily thicken' and that 'a little country tearoom' that he used to walk out to fifteen years earlier was 'now so obviously a place of call for motorists and not for walkers'.[85] Between 1935 and 1940, seventy new seven-day licences were granted in Scotland, and the *National Guardian* reported, 'Many hotels are becoming little more than Sunday public houses, often due to Sunday motor excursions'.[86]

Tourism, including the hotel trade, was increasingly dependent on the motor car. Neil Gunn claimed in 1937 that, in a coastal area of Caithness on the road to John o'Groats, where most of the people were personally known to him, there were only 'two families that benefit, to a certain extent, from the tourist traffic: the family that runs the hotel and the family that runs the garage'.[87] The period saw the growth of the roadhouse 'to provide smart restaurant, cocktail bar and leisure facilities for the motorised classes'. The best surviving example of the genre is the Maybury Roadhouse in Edinburgh, a classic art deco design by

Figure 5.2 The Hawes Inn, South Queensferry, West Lothian, 1926. © RCAHMS.

Paterson and Broom in 1936. Another art deco roadhouse is located in the Borders on the site of a much older inn, the Crook House, with an extraordinary art deco gentlemen's lavatory.[88] The Crook House is currently closed but plans to reopen under a community buyout arrangement.

As war began to loom on the horizon, the International Hotel Alliance held a conference in Edinburgh in October 1938 with 140 delegates from seventeen countries. They were welcomed by Arthur Towle, [London, Midland and Scottish Railway (L.M.S.)] Chairman of the Scottish Committee of the Hotels and Restaurants Association of Great Britain. The bulk of the delegates arrived by train from King's Cross, though the Canadian delegation came by boat on the Clyde. In his welcoming speech, the chairman remarked that 'we were more worried than in other countries by what were called the licensing laws ... fortunately for the visitors, they were not spending a Sunday in Scotland' [LAUGHTER)].[89]

Figure 5.3 Maybury Roadhouse, Edinburgh. A classic art deco building from 1936 built for the growing motor trade. Now a casino. © Anthony and Judith Cooke.

Figure 5.4 The Crook Inn, Tweedsmuir, Scottish Borders. A drovers' inn founded in 1604 but remodelled in 1936. Currently closed. © Anthony and Judith Cooke.

WORLD WAR II

The outbreak of World War II saw the extension of state power in areas such as conscription, rationing, evacuation of mothers and children, blackout regulations and so on. The scale and the speed of the changes were striking. In Scotland, 170,000 mothers and children were evacuated in three days, with transport and billeting laid on.[90] The large-scale

conscription of men into the armed forces led to a good many traditionally male-only jobs being filled by women, as had happened during
World War I. In April 1940, it was calculated that the number of male
bar staff called up for military service and those up to age twenty-
seven required to register for military service was 1,400. This led to a
rerun of the Great Glasgow Barmaid Controversy. Glasgow magistrates
were asked to lift the thirty-year ban on the employment of women
in Glasgow pubs because of the call-up of male bar staff for military
service. They agreed to consider this after consultation with the Shop
Assistants' Union which represented bar staff. In February 1940, the
National Guardian ran an article entitled 'Bailies and Barmaids', arguing
that the Labour council in Glasgow was guilty of prejudice towards the
working class because it opposed the employment of women in public
houses, where the working man drank, but not in lounges or hotel bars,
patronised by the middle and upper classes. By August, the magistrates
had relented and removed the ban on women working in bars, provided
they were aged twenty-five or over.[91]

In the licensed trade, there were shortages of malt for brewing and
distilling, and hotels were requisitioned for troops and the war effort.
In Edinburgh, the New Carlton Hotel on the North Bridge was requisitioned in September 1939 for men and officers of Scottish Command,
with catering run by the Women's Voluntary Service. Three hot meals a
day cost 2/5d. The New Carlton was a substantial hotel, built in 1900
with eighty-nine bedrooms, and was requisitioned in both world wars,
being released by the army in 1952. Because of the depression, however,
it had stood empty for much of the 1920s and 1930s.[92]

In Dundee, there was concern in September 1939 about the increase in
drunkenness since the outbreak of war because of the bounty money paid
to men on joining the army and the closure of 'all houses of entertainment'. Because of this, the government had decided that houses of entertainment were to be reopened. Other issues for the licensed trade were
the increase in excise duties, forcing them to increase retail prices for
drink, and whether licensed premises should close early because of the
blackout. By August 1940, a pint of Bass and Worthington cost 11d, a
half pint of Guinness 10d and of Barclay Perkins 11d. With the spiralling
costs of war, the licensed trade was increasingly becoming a government
cash cow. In April 1941, the Scottish Licensed Trade Defence Association
agreed to raise beer prices. The Dundee association complained that the
government regarded the trade firstly 'as a means of revenue and secondly as a necessary adjunct to war work. They are anxious that those
engaged in war work should have their liquor supplies.' They called on

the retail trade to delay price increases until they had had time to discuss it with the manufacturing and wholesale trade.[93]

In the middle of the war, with Britain threatened with invasion, Dundee magistrates were concerned about singing in public houses, and the local trade association was pleased to report that 'in the great majority of the Licensed Premises in Dundee, singing is discouraged and is the exception rather than the rule'. Of course, these could have been sectarian songs and, as such, likely to lead to fights and disorder. In January 1941, the Executive of the Dundee Licensed Trade Association discussed the 'singing and playing of musical instruments' in public houses. It was pointed out that these could hardly be banned, as some licence holders held functions on their premises.[94] This was in a long tradition of detailed church and municipal intervention in the drink trade and associated activities in Scotland that went back at least to the Reformation, as previously discussed in the Introduction.

Rationing and shortages of food and drink dominated a good deal of press reporting on the home front during World War II. In January 1942, the *National Guardian* carried the headline 'Lord Woolton Defines Café Meals. Eating Out in War-Time'. Shortages extended to screw-top stoppers for bottles, and the *Guardian* reported that the lack of whisky had given a fillip to sales of gin and rum. To conserve dwindling stocks of malt, the Ministry of Food had decided to lower the strength of beer by 5 per cent (average gravity).[95] Before World War II, Gillespie's stout had been a very popular drink in the west of Scotland. During the war, restrictions on malt production in Britain led to a decline in the production of Scottish-produced stout. No such restrictions were in force in the Irish Republic and so Guinness established a strong foothold in the west of Scotland, which it has held ever since.[96] In January 1942, a cut of 10 per cent in the production of malt whisky was announced by the Ministry of Food. The announcement was welcomed by the Speyside distillers, as they feared that no whisky production at all would be allowed. Not everyone seemed totally committed to the war effort, however. The Chief Constable of Stonehaven in Kincardineshire complained that Sunday trippers were still venturing out to seek liquor in the middle of 'the biggest war the world has ever seen'.[97]

As more women entered the employment market during the war, and female incomes rose, they began to assert themselves and challenge patriarchal attitudes in some unexpected areas, just as they had during World War I. In 1944, the licensed trade in Dundee was dragged unwillingly into a debate about 'lavatory accommodation in Public Houses in Dundee', particularly as regards provision for women, which suggests that women were going into public houses in increasing numbers. This is confirmed by a report in March 1944 from the Acting Chief Constable, which claimed that 'there is no doubt that the drinking of alcoholic beverages by females is increasing'. The licensed trade in Dundee was concerned about providing 'a service to the general public of both sexes', though they also worried about the cost implications, as their Glasgow counterparts had in 1933. There was a general lack of public lavatories, for men or women, in the centre of Dundee and 'it is believed that . . . there are only two ladies' lavatories available in Dundee'. The police were concerned about 'nuisances occurring in the streets of Dundee' by women relieving themselves in back closes, and the licensed trade tried to avoid responsibility by calling on the local authority to provide 'additional available accommodation for ladies'. A police report, dated 31 March 1944, confirmed that out of 203 licensed premises in Dundee, only thirty-eight (18 per cent) had separate women's toilets, in nineteen the toilets were used by both sexes, in sixty-nine (34 per cent) women were allowed the use of the toilet on men being excluded, and fifty-three (26 per cent) had no toilet accommodation for women. The report commented that the arrangement, whereby a waiter was posted at the door while the woman used the toilet, 'in my opinion savours of the dismal distant past and does not reflect to the credit of the licensing trade in Dundee'.[98] It was not until the Sex Discrimination Act of 1975 that many Scottish pubs were forced to install women's toilets.[99]

World War II had a more permanent effect on female employment than World War I had had, particularly as regards the employment of married women. From 1911 to 1931, the proportion of married women in the female workforce in Scotland stayed very low, rising from 5.3 per cent of the female workforce in 1911 to 8.5 per cent in 1931. The proportion of single women in the female workforce remained at over 90 per cent throughout this period. The years after World War II marked a watershed and, by 1951, the female workforce in Scotland contained 23.4 per cent of married women and continued to rise steadily thereafter.[100]

Though pubs were affected by a shortage of drink supplies during the war, there was more purchasing power around, with plenty of employment and overtime for men and women in the armaments industry (at places such as Gretna and the giant Nobel explosives factory at Ardeer in Ayrshire) and in coal mining, iron and steel manufacturing, heavy engineering and shipbuilding.

Because of wartime shortages of malt, drink supplies were precarious and pub opening hours shortened. Cliff Hanley, who came from a family of nine, remembered drinking at the Kirk Hoose pub in Shettleston, Glasgow during the war when his older brother and four brothers-in-law were home on leave from the Royal Navy, the Merchant Navy and the RAF. The pub shut at 9.30 p.m. and the barman began shouting last orders at 9.00 p.m. A pint of beer cost 8d.[101] At the James Watt Bar in Greenock, Renfrewshire, wartime opening hours in April 1941 were 10.00 a.m. to 2.00 p.m. and 5.00 p.m. to 9.00 p.m. These were to reduce to 11.30 a.m. to 1.30 p.m. and 5.30 p.m. to 9.00 p.m. to eke out drink supplies. At this time, the clientele of the bar appears to have been virtually all male, as no female had been served with liquor for some time and it was claimed that no female toilets needed to be provided.[102] Table 5.3 shows the impact of the Second World War on drink consumption at the James Watt Bar from 1940 to 1945.

Table 5.3 reveals that whisky consumption at the James Watt Bar fell dramatically during World War II owing to chronic shortages of malt and a consequent fall in whisky production. The consumption of draught beer rose though it was almost certainly weaker than pre-war, and a shortage of bottles meant that very little bottled beer was consumed. The high-volume sales of cheap Australian wine in 1940/41 are explained by the drinking habits of the west of Scotland where, during the interwar years, 'jake' and 'red biddy' had become popular in poorer areas, being lethal but different combinations of methylated spirits and cheap red wine. Another popular drinks combination in the west of Scotland was a glass of cheap red wine and half a pint of beer, the wine replacing the more expensive whisky which had previously formed the basis of 'a hauf an' a hauf pint'. The pubs which sold this potent combination were known as 'wine shops'.[103]

The takings from the bar business at the James Watt increased from £33,579 in 1944 to £35,973 in 1945, and the net profit for the year rose

Table 5.3 Consumption of drink during World War II at the James Watt Bar, Greenock, Renfrewshire, 1940–5.

Year	Whisky (gallons)	Draught beer (barrels)	Australian wine (gals)
1940/41	1,385	528	1,746
1941/42	1,077	717	299
1942/43	802	643	14
1943/44	705	670	12
1944/45	583	750	0

(Source: Mitchell Library, Glasgow, TD 509/13/8, Sederunt Book of Trustees of the late Mrs Lilias Smith, wine and spirit merchant, Greenock, Vol. VIII, 1945–1955)

to £1,631. This was in spite of severe shortages of bottles for beer and the disruption of supplies of imported beverages such as Australian wine. Whisky consumption in the James Watt Bar fell from 705 gallons (3,200 litres) in 1943/4 to 583 gallons (2,650 litres) in 1944/5, and the consumption of Australian wine from 12 gallons (55 litres) in 1943/4 to zero the following year. Only beer consumption showed an increase, from 670 barrels (110,000 litres) in 1943/4 to 759 (124,500) in 1944/5.[104]

Victory in Europe Day was celebrated all over the country. The 8 and 9 May were declared a National Holiday, and staff at the James Watt Bar were paid double wages for working, and all got extra holidays with full pay. The bar was so busy that 'three spare men' were employed to cope with the rush. Bar staff at this time consisted of a male manager, three shop assistants (two male, one female), a 'boy' and the three 'spare men'. William Reid, the shop manager, was paid £9/10 shillings a week, and the three shop assistants £4 a week each. Gratuities were paid to staff just before Greenock Fair time (11 to 23 June).[105]

The end of the war brought the dissolution of the coalition government, large-scale demobilisation of troops and the nation facing massive war debts. The 1945 General Election, with its heavy and unexpected defeat of the Conservatives under Winston Churchill, the wartime prime minister, brought further major changes, with the new Labour government having a large working majority for the first time and bringing in ambitious plans for nationalisation of the coal industry and railways, and extensive changes in health, education and social welfare, with the implementation of the Beveridge Report of 1942. This will be discussed in the next chapter.

NOTES

1. R. J. Finlay, *Modern Scotland, 1914–2000* (London, 2004), p. 186.
2. Finlay, *Modern Scotland*, p. 9.
3. T. M. Devine, *The Scottish Nation, 1700–2000* (London, 1999), p. 309; and C. H. Lee, 'The Scottish Economy and the First World War', in C. M. M. MacDonald and E. W. McFarlane (eds), *Scotland and the Great War* (East Linton, 1999), pp. 11–35.
4. Finlay, *Modern Scotland*, p. 55.
5. W. Kenefick, 'Scotland and the Great War', paper given at a conference 'Scotland and World War One', held at UHI (Perth Campus), 14 March 2014.
6. National Records of Scotland, Edinburgh (NRS), SC 36/51/199/25, Sheriff Court of Glasgow, Will of John Scouller, 8 August 1923.

7. E. Muir, *Scottish Journey* (1935) (Edinburgh, 1979 edition), p. 244.

8. W. Kenefick, 'Demography', in Cooke et al. (eds), *Modern Scottish History*, Vol. 2, *The Modernisation of Scotland, 1850 to the Present* (East Linton, 1998), p. 105.

9. C. Brown, 'Religion', in Cooke et al. (eds), *Modern Scottish History*, Vol. 2, *1850 to the Present*, p. 146

10. Muir, *Scottish Journey*, p. 2.

11. Finlay, *Modern Scotland*, pp. 6–7.

12. Kenefick, 'Scotland and the Great War'.

13. E. King, *Scotland Sober and Free. The Temperance Movement, 1829–1979* (Glasgow, 1979), p. 19.

14. I. McLean, *The Legend of Red Clydeside* (Edinburgh, 1983), pp. 17–85; and W. Kenefick and A. McIvor (eds), *Roots of Red Clydeside, 1910–1914* (Edinburgh, 1996).

15. *The National Guardian and Licensed Trade Journal* (*National Guardian*), 5 and 12 September 1914.

16. Dundee City Archives (DCA), GD MUS/5/3, Minute Book of the Dundee, Lochee and Broughty Ferry Licensed Grocers' Association, Vol. II, 1913–1931.

17. Glasgow University Archives (GUA), Scottish Brewing Archive (SBA), GDL 1/10/4, Glasgow and District Licensed Trade Defence Association (GDLTDA), 52nd Annual Report, 1915, pp. 12–13.

18. GDLTDA, 52nd Annual Report, 1915, p. 34. See also A. McIvor, 'Women and Gender Relations', in Cooke et al. (eds), *Modern Scottish History*, Vol. 2, *1850 to the Present* (East Linton, 1998), p. 175, which argued that 'the heightened participation of women during the 1914–18 war had little long-term effect, with few holding wartime jobs thereafter due to trade union opposition, legislation (the Restoration of Pre-War Practices Act) and a barrage of newspaper and magazine propaganda post war, which resuscitated the Victorian domestic ideal'.

19. Finlay, *Modern Scotland*, p. 30.

20. *Aberdeen Journal*, 25 November 1914, 'Drinking among Wives of Soldiers'.

21. *Evening Telegraph and Post*, 25 February 1918, 'The Dundee Liquor Problem. The Care of the Soldier's Wife'.

22. C. G. Brown, 'Piety, Gender and War in Scotland in the 1910s', in C. M. M. Macdonald and E. W. McFarland (eds), *Scotland and the Great War* (East Linton, 1999), p. 187–8.

23. *National Guardian*, 1 January 1916.

24. *National Guardian*, 5 September 1914.

25. Finlay, *Modern Scotland*, p. 11.

26. T. C. Smout, *A Century of the Scottish People* (London, 1986), p. 148.

27. *National Guardian*, 8 January 1916.

28. *National Guardian*, 19 February and 18 March 1916.
29. J. Dallas and C. McMaster, *The Beer Drinker's Companion* (Leith, 1993), p. 81.
30. I. Donnachie, 'World War One and the Drink Question: State Control of the Drink Trade', *Scottish Journal of Labour History*, Vol. 17, *1982*, pp. 19–26.
31. M. Simmons, *The Scottish Licensed Trade Association, 1880–1980* (Edinburgh, 1981), p. 40.
32. Donnachie, 'World War One and the Drink Question', pp. 23–4.
33. GUA, SBA, GDL 1/10/4, GDLTDA, 53rd Annual Report, 1916, pp. 60–8 and 73.
34. DCA, GD/DLT/1/4, Dundee Wine, Spirit and Beer Trade Protection Association (DWSBPTA), Minute Book, No. 5, 1910–1919.
35. GDLTDA, 53rd Annual Report, 1916, pp. 60–1.
36. Simmons, *Scottish Licensed Trade Association*, p. 39.
37. DCA, GD/DLT/1/4, DWSBPTA, Minute Book, No. 5, 1910–1919.
38. DWSBPTA, Minute Book, No. 5, 1910–1919.
39. *National Guardian*, 28 November 1914.
40. *National Guardian*, 30 December 1916.
41. W. M. Walker, *Juteopolis, Dundee and its Textile Workers, 1885–1923* (Edinburgh, 1979), pp. 439–85 and Smout, *Century of the Scottish People*, p. 147.
42. Finlay, *Modern Scotland*, p. 55.
43. DCA, GD/DLT, 1/4, DWSBPTA, Minute Book, No. 5, 1910–1919.
44. DCA, GD/DLT, 1/8, DWSBPTA, Minute Book, No. 9, 1956–66.
45. McLean, *Red Clydeside*, pp. 121–38; Walker, *Juteopolis*, pp. 486–528; and Finlay, *Modern Scotland*, pp. 67–72.
46. W. W. Knox, *Industrial Nation* (Edinburgh, 1999), p. 198.
47. C. Hanley, *Dancing in the Streets* (1958) (Edinburgh, 1983 edition), p. 99.
48. Finlay, *Modern Scotland*, p. 148.
49. T. Johnston, *Memories* (London, 1952), p. 30.
50. King, *Scotland Sober and Free*, p. 24.
51. Smout, *Century of the Scottish People*, p. 147.
52. Simmons, *Scottish Licensed Trade Association*, p. 54.
53. I am grateful to David Morrison, originally from Durness, now of Monikie, for this story.
54. T. Griffiths, *The Cinema and Cinema-going in Scotland, c.1896–1950* (Edinburgh, 2012).
55. Smout, *Century of the Scottish People*, p. 158.
56. Finlay, *Modern Scotland*, pp. 137–8.
57. C. McKean, *The Scottish Thirties* (Edinburgh, 1987), p. 67; and J. Searle and C. Muir, *The Big Picture. Cinemas of Dundee* (Dundee, 2012), p. 39.

58. I. Maver, 'Leisure and Social Change: The Twentieth Century', in W. H. Fraser and C. H. Lee (eds), *Aberdeen, 1800 to 2000, A New History* (East Linton, 2000), pp. 428–9.
59. NRS, SEP 4/4434, Monopolies Commission, Report on Supply of Beer, HMSO, 1969.
60. Smout, *Century of the Scottish People*, p. 134.
61. *National Guardian*, 2 January 1926.
62. Smout, *Century of the Scottish People*, p. 134.
63. Simmons, *The Scottish Licensed Trade Association*, p. 61.
64. Finlay, *Modern Scotland*, p. 148.
65. GUA, SBA, GDL 1/6/1, GDLTDA, Directors' Minutes, 15 February 1928.
66. GUA, SBA, GDL 1/6/1, Directors' Minutes, 29 March 1928.
67. *National Guardian*, 11 September 1926.
68. *National Guardian*, 16 October 1926.
69. *Perthshire Advertiser*, 10 April 1929.
70. A. Hopkin, *The Aberdeen Pub Companion* (Aberdeen, 1975), p. 10.
71. GUA, SBA, GDL 1/6/1, GDLTDA, Directors' Minutes, 4 October 1932.
72. Directors' Minutes, 1 November 1932.
73. Directors' Minutes, 5 April, 5 September and 5 December 1933.
74. Muir, *Scottish Journey*, pp. 18–19.
75. L G Gibbon, *Cloud Howe* (London, 1973), p. 204.
76. Finlay, *Modern Scotland*, p. 148.
77. N. M. Gunn, *The Silver Darlings* (London, 1941), pp. 357–9.
78. W. McIlvanney, *Docherty* (Edinburgh, 1983 edition), pp. 47–8.
79. Muir, *Scottish Journey*, p. 12.
80. L. Settle, 'The Social Geography of Prostitution in Edinburgh, 1900–1939', *Journal of Scottish Historical Studies*, Vol. 33, No. 2, 2013, pp. 246–7.
81. DCA, GD/DLT 1/6, Minute Book of the Dundee Wine, Spirit and Beer Trade Protection Association, 1929–1944.
82. *National Guardian*, 3 February 1940.
83. Finlay, *Modern Scotland*, p. 143.
84. J. Buchan, *The Thirty-Nine Steps* (London, 1999), p. 141.
85. Muir, *Scottish Journey*, p. 98.
86. *National Guardian*, 27 January 1940.
87. N. M. Gunn, 'Gentlemen – The Tourist! The New Highland Tour', in Cooke, et al. (eds), *Modern Scottish History, 1707 to the Present*, Vol. 5: *Major Documents*, p. 297.
88. D. Walker, 'Inns, hotels and related building types', in G. Stell, J. Shaw and S. Stonier (eds), *Scottish Life and Society. Vol. 3, Scotland's Buildings* (East Linton, 2003), p. 184.
89. *Scotsman*, 17 October 1938.
90. Johnston, *Memories*, p. 136.
91. *National Guardian*, 3 and 10 February and 24 August 1940.

92. *Edinburgh Evening News*, 14 September 1939; and *Evening Dispatch*, 13 March 1952.
93. DCA, GD/DLT 1/6, Minute Book, 1929–1944.
94. DCA, GD/DLT 1/6, Minute Book, 1929–1944.
95. *National Guardian*, 3 January 1942.
96. Interview with Willie Mutch, Windsor Bar, Dundee, 18 September 2014.
97. *National Guardian*, 10 and 24 January 1942.
98. DCA, GD/DLT 1/6, Minute Book, 1929–1944.
99. Finlay, *Modern Scotland*, p. 281.
100. McIvor, 'Women and Gender Relations', p. 175.
101. Hanley, *Dancing in the Streets*, pp. 175–6.
102. Mitchell Library, Glasgow (ML), TD 509/13/8, Sederunt Books of Trustees of Lilias Smith, wine and spirit merchant, Greenock (died 1898), who owned the James Watt Bar, 30 East Hamilton Street, Greenock, Vol. VIII, 1945–1955.
103. J. House, 'Leisure Interests', in J. Cunnison and J. B. S. Gilfillan (eds), *Third Statistical Account of Scotland, Glasgow* (Edinburgh 1958), p. 623.
104. ML, TD 509/13/8, Sederunt Book, Vol. VIII, 1945–1955.
105. ML, TD 509/13/8, Sederunt Book, Vol. VIII, 1945–1955.

6

'A Place of Rules and Rituals':
Austerity and Regulation, Liberalisation and Change, 1945 to the Present

INTRODUCTION

THE ELECTION OF A majority Labour government at Westminster in 1945 ushered in an era of rapid social and political change, as returning servicemen and servicewomen voted for a change of government from the wartime coalition to a Labour Party that had campaigned on a platform of radical change. The heavy defeat of the Conservatives under Winston Churchill, the wartime leader of the country, had been unexpected, and the new Labour government set in train an ambitious programme which involved the nationalisation of key parts of the economy, such as railways, coal mining, electricity supply and so on, and reforms in health, education and social security, based on the Beveridge Report of 1942. From 1945 to 1951, the Labour government continued to intervene in many areas of British life that were previously unregulated, including the licensed trade, partly as a result of ideological conviction, partly as a continuation of wartime regulation.

Rationing, which had been introduced in wartime, continued through the 1940s and was ended only by the new Conservative government at Westminster in the early 1950s. The 1950s saw high employment and a modest increase in levels of affluence. The Scottish economy began a long drawn-out change from one dominated by employment in manufacturing industry to a service-based economy. The share of the service sector in employment in Scotland rose from 24 per cent in 1951 to 33 per cent in 1971, 66 per cent in 1991 and 70 per cent in 2000. This was linked to a rise in female, often part-time, employment and, by the mid 1990s, there were more women than men in the Scottish workforce, though many of them worked part-time.[1] The proportion of married women in the female workforce rose dramatically from only 23.4 per cent in 1951 to 60.45 per cent by 1991.[2] These changes in society, together with legislative changes, such as drink-driving laws and the smoking ban, had a profound effect on Scottish drinking places, and the stand-up, men-only pub faced a real challenge to its survival by the early years of the twenty-first century.

POST-WAR AUSTERITY AND REGULATION

At the end of World War II, there is considerable evidence that returning ex-servicemen were impatient with the limitations of the society they had left to defend. Bob Crampsey, who grew up as a schoolboy in Mount Florida in Glasgow during World War II, remembered that, after the War,

> the country had changed its attitude to certain fundamental things. It was much less Sabbatarian than before. The opening of municipal golf courses and bowling greens to cater for wartime munitions workers had dealt a severe blow to that and the returning ex-Servicemen who had experienced Christmas abroad would have no truck with the cold ignoring of the feast which had marked the 1930s.[3]

Because the country was heavily in debt to the United States, exports of whisky were prioritised over domestic consumption. Shortages of barley threatened whisky production and, when more barley was released, the Ministry of Food decreed that, of the additional whisky produced, 75 per cent would go for export and only 25 per cent to the home market. Further state control was proposed for the licensed trade in the new towns that were being established on both sides of the border. The Licensing Act of 1949 extended state ownership of pubs to Scottish new towns such as Cumbernauld, East Kilbride, Glenrothes, Irvine and Livingston.[4] In an era of high public spending, however, the licensed trade had a trump card to play, in the amount of revenue it generated for the Treasury. Though post-war employment was high compared to the interwar depression, wages were often modest and, in 1949, Aberdeen publicans complained about lean times and the high cost of drink, owing to increased taxation, 'last year a man would come in and have two pints. Now he swithers about having one or even half a pint.'[5]

There were also large shifts in population, as the urban slums were cleared and people moved to new towns and council-owned housing estates on the edges of towns and cities, often with few social facilities, such as pubs, cafes, sports facilities, churches, cinemas, bingo halls or even many shops. From the early 1950s to the mid 1970s, some 25,000 to 40,000 new homes were built every year in Scotland, the majority of them in the public sector. This was unusual in a European context – in Belgium, for example, only about 1 per cent of the housing stock was in the public sector. The long tradition of local-authority regulation in Scotland meant that pubs were not given permission to operate on council-owned land which encouraged the custom of people having to travel into the city centre for a drink.[6] There were no fewer than sixty six pubs on the Gallowgate in the East End of Glasgow in the 1950s and, it was claimed, 'Many of the people who lived round the Gallowgate are now living in newly built Glasgow suburbs which have no pubs at all. At present the majority of men who have "flitted" to a new suburb and who like a drink travel to their former neighbourhoods and use the pubs with which they are familiar.'[7]

Hotels which had been requisitioned during wartime for the Ministry of Defence or for troops were slowly returned to private ownership after the war. In Edinburgh, the New Carlton Hotel on North Bridge, which had been requisitioned as canteens for men and officers of Scottish Command and run by the Women's Voluntary Service, was vacated in March 1952. Built in 1900, with eighty-nine bedrooms, the hotel had been requisitioned in both world wars, and had stood idle for most of the 1920s and 1930s because of the depression. It October 1952, it was sold to Trust Houses Limited and renovated at a cost of £40,000.[8]

World War II had seen the consumption of whisky in Scotland fall dramatically owing to the shortage of malt for distilling and a rise in the consumption of beer but old patterns began to reassert themselves. At the James Watt Bar in Greenock, figures for 1951 and 1952 show that the largest spending by the business was on whisky, followed by beer and then wine. In 1951, the bar purchased spirits to the value of £12,309, beer valued at £8,609 and wine valued at £2,628. The following year saw very similar amounts of spirits and beer purchased but a fall in the value of wine purchased to £1,838. By 1954, whisky and beer sales were falling and wine sales rising. Spirit purchases were valued at £10,650, beer at £7,864 and wine at £3,527. The wartime staff of the bar consisted of a male manager and three shop assistants, of whom one was female. By 1952, the staff comprised the male manager and two female staff, and, three years later, there were five staff, a male manager, three female staff and one male.[9]

The 1950s was a time of austerity. In 1953 the Scots spent 18.4 per cent less than the United Kingdom average on drink and relatively little on eating out, owing to strict licensing laws and a dearth of restaurants. Stringent licensing laws were responsible for a dramatic decline in the number of licensed outlets in Scotland – from one pub for every 424

Scots in 1900 to one per 806 in 1955. In the same period, drunkenness convictions declined tenfold to 2.6 for every 1,000 population.[10]

In September 1959, the Secretary of State for Scotland set up a committee of inquiry under Lord Guest into Scottish Licensing Laws. It focused on four specific areas: the sale and supply of alcohol on Sundays; week-day licensing hours; the constitution of licensing courts; and courts of appeal and the arrangements for granting certificates in 'areas of housing development and redevelopment'. The Guest committee produced two reports: the first in 1960, which dealt with the first two areas, and was largely implemented in the Licensing (Scotland) Act of 1962, with the significant exception of Sunday opening for pubs; and the second in 1963 which did not recommend any radical changes in the thitd and fourth areas. The committee recommended that Sunday opening should be permitted for hotels, public houses and licensed restaurants but no legislation followed for pub opening. Under the 1962 Act, permitted hours in Scotland were fixed at 11.00 a.m. to 2.30 p.m. and 5.00 p.m. to 10.00 p.m. on week days and, on Sundays, when pubs were closed, hotels were allowed to open from 12.30 to 2.30 p.m. and from 6.30 to 10.00 p.m.[11]

Local authorities were permitted to set their own opening hours for pubs, and some curious anomalies resulted. Paul Waterson's father got the tenancy of his first pub, the Mosside Inn, Paisley in about 1960. The pub, now demolished, was near where Glasgow Airport is nowadays and lay in the county of Renfrewshire, just over the boundary from Paisley. In Paul's words, it turned out to be a 'goldmine', as pubs in Paisley at that time shut at 9.00 p.m., those over the county border at 9.30 p.m. This half hour difference turned out to be the financial making of Paul's father, as large numbers of people travelled 'by car, bus, taxi or whatever', to drink for that last half hour.[12]

The Guest committee's proposals for seven-day opening were greeted unenthusiastically by the licensed trade in Dundee, 'because of economic and staffing difficulties'. They proposed instead that seven-day opening should be optional. They also wished to repeal the Temperance (Scotland) Act of 1913 and to end the State Management Areas of Carlisle, Gretna and Cromarty that had been set up by Lloyd George during World War I. This finally happened in 1971, when Parliament abolished the two state management districts in Scotland – in the Cromarty Firth and Gretna.[13]

By 1965, the trade was campaigning unapologetically for Sunday opening under the banner of provision for tourism. The Scottish Tourist Board claimed that £100 million was spent every year in Scotland by tourists who expressed 'surprise and disappointment' that pubs were closed on Sundays.[14] Four years later, the Monopolies Commission reported that there was growing pressure on the government by 'tourist and consumer organisations' to relax the licensing laws on both sides of the border. The Monopolies Commission's Britain-wide report on the supply of beer was published in April 1969. It recommended that the licensed trade should be opened up, and ruled that the tied-house system in England and Wales, where 86 per cent of public houses were brewery owned, 'operated against the public interest'. The system in Scotland was quite different, however. Here, only 27 per cent of licensed hotels and public houses were brewery owned and most were operated by a single licensee.[15]

TRAVEL AND TOURISM

One of the main pressures for the liberalisation of Scotland's licensing laws in this period was the rise of tourism in Scotland and its growing importance as an employer and export earner. Tourism started from a low base after World War II as a result of post-war rationing, shortages of whisky, which often went for export, and second-rate facilities in the form of hotels and restaurants. By 1956, there were 380,000 overseas visitors to Scotland and about a million from other parts of the United Kingdom. In addition, some 1.3 million Scots spent their annual holiday in Scotland, a total of about 2,680,000 visitors to Scotland, generating an annual income of approximately £50 million.[16] About half of these tourists visited Edinburgh which had been opened up to a national and international market by the Edinburgh Festival, founded in 1947, shortly after the end of World War II. Hotel provision in Edinburgh, however, had not kept pace with this growing and more sophisticated market. Bill Nicholson, director of the Scottish Board, complained in 1963 that, 'Edinburgh is one of the major cities in the world where no modern hotel construction has been carried out in the past 30 years.'[17] This was confirmed by Egon Ronay's 1965 *Guide to Hotels and Restaurants* which rated standards of hospitality in Edinburgh as 'stagnant'. It listed six hotels in the capital, none of them higher than 'second grade', and twelve restaurants.[18]

Not only was hotel accommodation in Edinburgh inadequate, it was also very expensive for the mediocre facilities on offer. The *Edinburgh Evening News* carried a story in March 1965 that 'top-class' American tourists were willing to pay up to £4 to £5 a night for hotel accommodation but criticised the widespread assumption that the definition of a 'top-class hotel' in Scotland was a bathroom in every bedroom.[19] A few weeks later, the Scottish Tourist Board claimed that average prices in Edinburgh were £2 a night for a room with a bath and 25 to 30 shillings for one without.[20] The reasons behind all this soul-searching became clear in a story in the *Scotsman* in 1967 which revealed that tourist numbers in Edinburgh had fallen in the early 1960s, from 822,000 in 1961 to 743,000 in 1965. Even the Edinburgh Festival was not immune to this trend, as numbers attending the festival had declined from 99,000 in 1961 to 89,000 in 1965.[21]

Some modest improvements in hotel accommodation were starting to be made. In 1966, Scottish and Newcastle Breweries spent £100,000 modernising the Barnton Hotel on Queensferry Road, built in 1895. Even after modernisation, not all rooms had bathrooms which was seen as a basic requirement for North American visitors.[22] Criticism of the mediocre level of hotel accommodation in Edinburgh continued. In 1969, Lord Geddes, Chairman of the British Travel Association, complained about the poor quality of hotels in the capital. In 1969, only nine hundred hotel rooms in Edinburgh had baths, fewer than in one London hotel. Tourism was booming in Britain as a whole which had had one million overseas tourists in 1969 and was likely to exceed two million by 1975 with earnings of £850 million.[23]

Change came slowly in the early 1970s, as living standards continued to rise, until the OPEC (Organization of Petroleum Exporting Countries) oil crisis of the mid 1970s. Significantly, the 'first major hotel to be built in Edinburgh this century' was the Esso Motor Hotel opened on Queensferry Road in 1970, part of a British chain of Esso Motor Hotels. This hotel had 120 bedrooms, all en suite, and was designed to cater for the 'new' tourist and business visitors who came by car and were looking for hotels with easy access to major road links and ample free car parking.[24] It was symbolic of a new era that the owner was a multinational oil company. Tourism was becoming increasingly important to the Scottish economy and, in 1972, tourism earnings in Scotland were £275 million of which 20 per cent was in foreign currency.[25]

In the centre of Edinburgh, the eighteenth-century George Hotel saw an ambitious extension programme in 1972 funded by its owners, the Grand Metropolitan Hotel group, which more than doubled the number of bedrooms from eighty-four to two hundred. In an era just before the Sex Discrimination Act of 1975, the hotel boasted a 'men only' bar downstairs which fell victim to the new Act and closed down in January 1976.[26] In an era when petrol was still cheap, however, the future seemed to belong more to out-of-town developments, such as the Edinburgh Post House Hotel, opened in 1973 3 miles from the city centre, which had 208 en suite bedrooms and parking for 158 cars, mostly under cover. The hotel, owned by the Trust House Forte chain, had a rugby-themed Cross Bar, as it was situated close to Murrayfield rugby ground.[27]

Under the Thatcher government, elected in 1979, the privatisation of state-owned assets was in full swing by the early 1980s. As part of this programme of privatisation, the former railway hotels in Scotland, including the flagship Caledonian and the North British in Edinburgh and the Gleneagles in Perthshire, previously owned by British Transport Hotels, an arm of the nationalised British Rail, were sold in 1981 to a private limited company, Gleneagles Hotels Ltd.[28]

By the late twentieth century, tourism in Scotland had been boosted by the release of a number of blockbuster Hollywood films, such as *Braveheart* (1995), which offered a highly romanticised view of Scottish history but helped to popularise the image of the country abroad. In 1998 the United States Senate passed a resolution designating 6 April as Tartan Day, recognising the important contribution Scottish Americans had made to the development of the United States. The number of Americans describing themselves as Scottish Americans jumped from 4 million in 1990 to 15 million in 2000. Similar developments were taking place in New Zealand, Australia and Canada.[29]

The growth of golf as an international tourist attraction created a demand for upmarket hotels placed close to golf courses, and led to the development of expensive package holidays for golfers not only from North America but also from Japan and China where golf was a high-status game played by the economic and political elite. The American tycoon Donald Trump entered the arena by creating a controversial links golf course at Menie outside Aberdeen in an area of special scientific interest, and, in 2014, he took over the five-star Turnberry Hotel in Ayrshire which catered for wealthy golfers attracted by a links course that had housed the Open Championship.

SPORT AND THE SCOTTISH PUB

Because of the temperance legacy in Scotland and consequent strict local-authority regulation, many Scottish licensees were nervous or ambivalent about allowing games to be played inside their pubs. In the late 1950s, Jack House observed, 'there are strict rules in Glasgow against singing, music and any other games other than dominoes or draughts'. He added, 'however, this does not make Glasgow pubs "mere drinking dens" and the amount of social activity in pubs used by working class men is considerable'.[30] By contrast, in Aberdeen, darts was a popular game in pubs. The Aberdeen Darts Association, founded in 1937, had nearly 1,400 members in seventy-nine pubs by 1973–74.[31]

As well as being associated with upmarket sports, such as golf, Scottish pubs and hotels also catered for mass sports, such as football. In the 1950s, Jack House commented, 'football is the principal subject of conversation in any Glasgow pub, so footballers' pubs are generally popular'.[32] This was true all over the country. At Newhaven, on the edge of Edinburgh, for example, in 1969, the Peacock Hotel was owned by Tommy Younger, former Hibernian, Liverpool and Scotland goalkeeper in the 1950s. The lounge bar, the Goalmouth, was decorated with Hibs memorabilia, and (a sign of rising levels of affluence and social aspiration), dinner dances were held every Friday and Saturday night, with a table d'hôte menu from 19/6d in a bid to attract couples.[33] Not all pubs welcomed football supporters, or away supporters from particular clubs, particularly the Old Firm. Dundee licensees complained of rowdyism by Celtic supporters in 1961 when they caused trouble in city centre pubs after matches at Dens Park, home of Dundee FC. It was agreed that extra police should be on duty when Rangers or Celtic visited the city.[34]

Supporters of the Old Firm presented particular problems when it came to football violence. Though violence by football supporters on and off the terraces was often blamed on heavy drinking, it reflected deep-seated sectarian divisions in Glasgow and the west of Scotland. In 1977 the McElhone Report into spectator violence in Scottish football called for a ban on alcohol at matches. This was despite a report by Strathclyde Police which found no significant difference in the number of arrests between days when matches were played and when they were not. In other words, young men on different sides of the sectarian divide would fight each other whether or not there was a football match being played.

The Scottish Criminal Justice Act of 1980 outlawed the sale or possession of alcohol at football grounds, and made it illegal to be drunk inside a football ground or while trying to enter a ground. It also banned possession of alcohol on public vehicles going to or from a match and, later, in any vehicle which could carry more than nine people. This draconian piece of legislation had a class dimension to it because it applied only to football grounds in Scotland, not to rugby matches where there was also heavy alcohol consumption. By 1984, a Department of the Environment Report was claiming that the ban on alcohol was responsible for a 'marked decline' in football violence in Scotland, and this led to England introducing similar legislation with the Sporting Events (Control of Alcohol) Act of 1985.[35] This was a period when the Thatcher

Figure 6.1 Interior, The Blue Blazer, Spittal Street, Edinburgh, Calcutta Cup Day, 2012. © Stephen Hole.

government was at its height, with an agenda to stamp out football hooliganism by a variety of means, including an ill-fated identity card scheme for football supporters.

There was continuing controversy whether alcohol and pubs were key factors behind football violence or whether it would take place with or without alcohol consumption. A case study of a clash between Hibs casuals and Dunfermline casuals (the Carnegie Soccer Service) in September 1990, in the Well public house in Dunfermline, was divided as to whether those fighting were more under the influence of alcohol or of drugs. Similarly, the Chief Superintendent of Grampian Police described Aberdeen casuals as 'stone cold sober just plain bloody evil'.[36]

William McIlvanney sets his 1989 story, 'Tig', in 'The Narrow Place' a one-room bar on the edge of the fictional Ayrshire town of Graithnock which comes alive only on Tuesday and Thursday nights when the neighbouring local dog track is open and generates most of the pub's income, 'if there had been no dogs, there would have been no "Narrow Place"'. The central character is the animal-loving Mickey Andrews:

> The Narrow Place was, more than any other place, where Mickey found his social fulfilment. Every Tuesday and Thursday night it was packed. As far

as takings went, Big Fergie could afford to forget the rest of the week. Men and greyhounds crammed themselves in, in apparent defiance of the physical possibilities. The talk was all of dogs and who was trying and who wasn't and how best to prepare a dog for a race.

When Mickey is barred from the pub, the centre of his universe, he exacts an ingenious, if slightly comic, revenge.[37]

'A PLACE OF RULES AND RITUALS': THE CONTEMPORARY PUB IN LITERATURE AND THE MEDIA

The rise of a more 'realistic' school of literature, often set in working-class communities in the central belt of Scotland, portrayed the decline of industrial communities and the effects of this on families and individuals. The 'New Realism' often used pubs in urban areas as a setting for key meetings between characters, sometimes for confrontations, violent or otherwise. William McIlvanney's novel *Laidlaw*, published in 1977, has a maverick Glasgow policeman, the eponymous Laidlaw, as its central character. When investigating the murder of a teenage girl, the daughter of a criminal, Laidlaw and his colleague meet their contacts and informants from the criminal underworld in a variety of Glasgow pubs. A pub in the East End of Glasgow (the Gay Laddie) is described as, 'a shrine to the Thirties, when the Depression had spawned the razor-slashers and brought King Billy of Bridgeton to prominence. The dominant fixture was wood, from the long, stained bar to the tables spread around the place. Here, Formica hadn't been invented.' McIlvanney invokes the concept of unreconstructed masculinity as part and parcel of pub culture, 'This room was the resort of men who hadn't much beyond a sense of themselves and weren't inclined to have that sense diminished'. In an ironic twist, however, Harry Rayburn, the owner of Poppies, another East End bar, who plays a key role in the plot, is gay.[38]

In McIlvanney's short story, 'Mick's Day', the central character is the unemployed fifty-seven-year-old Mick Haggerty, an Irish Protestant living in the fictional Ayrshire town of Graithnock. His childless marriage has broken up and the local pub is central to his life:

The pub is the focal point of his life. It is companionship, unofficial social work department and cabaret. Everybody knows him. If he is struggling, there are quite a few people prepared to stand him a drink ... In the pub, too, both the owners and the customers have been known to help Mick out. He may get a pub meal for free. Someone may give him a winter anorak. He may get the offer of a few hours gardening. It's that kind of pub, a talking shop rich in anecdotes where most of the people who go are well known to one another.[39]

Similar themes are explored by Ian Rankin in his Inspector Rebus novels. Detective Inspector John Rebus (a rebus is a puzzle in which words are represented by combinations of letters and pictures) is a workaholic Edinburgh policeman who has difficulty in conforming to police authority and procedures. He seeks out criminals and informants in Edinburgh's numerous bars and meets his work colleagues there. His pub of choice, where he goes to unwind, near St Leonard's police station, is the Ox (the Oxford Bar). Even when Rebus is trying to give up alcohol, he seeks out the pub, 'Even on the wagon, he'd stayed a regular, drinking cola and mugs of coffee. A pub like the Ox was about so much more than just the hooch. It was therapy and refuge, entertainment and art.'[40] Another Edinburgh pub is described as a place where 'old men sat with their half pint glasses, staring emptily towards the front door. Were they wondering what was outside? Or were they just scared that whatever was out there would one day force itself in.'[41]

In *Resurrection Men*, Rebus has to visit Glasgow in the course of an investigation. On entering a Glasgow city-centre pub (the real-life Horseshoe Bar), he immediately feels both at home and in foreign territory:

> They ended up in the Horseshoe Bar. It was central and crowded with people who took their drinking seriously, the kind of place where no one looked askance at a tea-stained shirt, so long as the wearer had about him the price of his drink. Rebus knew immediately that it would be a place of rules and rituals, a place where the regulars knew from the moment they walked through the door that their drink of preference was already being poured for them. It had gone twelve and the fixed price lunch of soup, pie and beans, and ice cream was doing a roaring trade. Rebus noticed that a drink was included in the price.[42]

Ian Rankin's Edinburgh pubs are peopled by a varied cast, including 'respectable' Edinburgh lawyers and businessmen, police and professional criminals. Sometimes, it is hard to tell the different groups apart. Like the pubs, shebeens and 'first-class' brothels of Victorian Glasgow, Rankin's Edinburgh pubs are where low life intersects with high life – the (male) New Town meets the council estate. In *Set in Darkness*, Rebus enters the Royal Oak pub late at night and encounters an old adversary, an Edinburgh gangster called Maurice Cafferty. In a typical Rankin touch, Cafferty is singing a Burns song:

One of the barmaids took Rebus's order; a half of Eighty and a whisky. There was no conversation in the bar, respectful silence and even a tear in one patriot's eye as she sat on her stool with her brandy and coke raised to her lips . . . When the song finished, there was applause, a few whistles and cheers. Cafferty bowed his head, lifted his whisky glass and toasted the room.[43]

Few writers have described Scottish pubs and their customers better than Ian Rankin.

Irvine Welsh's 1993 novel *Trainspotting* is set in Leith and the less touristic parts of Edinburgh. Pubs and betting shops play a prominent role in the lives of its central characters, who take drugs as well as alcohol, and indulge in petty crime to pay for their habit. In one scene, entitled 'Her Man', a man punches his female companion in a pub, while the other customers look on with indifference, dismissing it as a 'lovers' tiff'. When Tommy, one of the central characters, intervenes to stop the assault, the woman turns on him with the words, 'That's ma man! That's ma fackin' man yir talking tae!', and claws at his face with her nails. Another scene is set in the Percy and shows how the clientele of urban pubs can change unpredictably on a day-to-day basis, 'normally the Percy's a family-type pub, but it's mobbed oot the day wi' these Orange cats fi the wild west, who're through here for their annual march and rally at the Links'. The Glasgow Orangemen begin to chant racist and sectarian abuse and a fight breaks out.[44]

In Welsh's *Porno*, published in 2002, 'Sick Boy' returns to Leith from London and becomes the landlord of a local pub, the Port Sunshine. The pub and its customers are described in an unflattering light, 'the bar itself is shambolic enough: old red floor tiles, formica-topped tables, nicotine-tanned tables, but it's the punters that get me. It's like a crowd of zombies in a George A. Romero movie, decaying away under the harsh strip lighting, which magnifies the multitude of sins.'[45]

The urban pub played a prominent role in a number of BBC Scotland comedy series, similar to that played by pubs in long-running English television soap series such as the Rover's Return in *Coronation Street* or the Queen Vic in *East Enders*. Here the pub functioned as the public space where characters met, argued, did business deals, fell out, fought or fell in love. The classic BBC Scotland comedy series, *Rab C. Nesbitt*, set in Govan, began with a pilot episode in 1988, then started with a first series in 1990, running on an annual basis until 1999. Since then, there have been Christmas and New Year specials, the last of which was on 2 January 2014. The series centres on the unemployed Rab C. Nesbitt, alcoholic and 'street philosopher', his long-suffering wife Mary and their children and friends. The first pub to feature in the series was the Two Ways Inn which was replaced by The Giblet, staffed by a variety of bar staff, both male and female. At one point in the series, Rab gives up alcohol, joins the temperance movement and becomes a Christian.[46]

In the BBC Scotland comedy series, *Still Game*, begun in 2002 and running for six series until 2007, the central characters were two pensioners, Jack and Victor, living in the fictional Craiglang, a Glasgow housing scheme. One of their main meeting places was the Clansman, a pub presided over by the barman, Boaby, superbly played by Gavin Mitchell. For the first three series of the show, a real-life pub, the Gimlet in Ruchill, was used but had to be abandoned when the landlord demolished the pub. Interior scenes were filmed in the Red Hoose, Dunipace.[47]

MUSIC IN THE PUB

A variety of music has been played in Scottish pubs over the centuries, often in the face of disapproval or opposition by the authorities, dating as far back as the Reformation when the town council in Presbyterian Dundee in the early 1560s placed a curfew on, 'dancing, drinking, playing or sic vain exercise' after 9.00 p.m., 'under the pain of the breking of the minstrels' instruments'.[48] Jazz, which originated in the bars and brothels of New Orleans, dispersed worldwide during the 1920s and particularly at the end of World War II, spread by American troops. In Scotland, traditional jazz was popular from the 1950s onwards and was frequently played in pubs and bars. The link between jazz and licensed premises has continued down to the present day. The Glasgow Jazz Festival, held every year in June is a large-scale event, operating in thirty-eight venues in June 2014. Of these, twenty-eight (73 per cent) were bars or clubs.[49] The smaller-scale Aberdeen Jazz Festival, held in March, meets in only six venues, of which three (50 per cent) are bars or clubs. The Edinburgh Jazz and Blues Festival, held in July alongside the Edinburgh Festival, is less dependent on pubs and bars as venues, with 140 gigs at thirteen venues, of which only three are bars or clubs.[50]

Scottish folk music underwent a revival in the 1950s, with the work of the School of Scottish Studies, founded in 1951, and the song collecting of Hamish Henderson and Norman Buchan. Sandy Bell's in Forrest Road, Edinburgh was a favourite haunt of Hamish Henderson, the father of the folk revival. Charlie Woolley, the landlord remembered, 'one morning the pub cleaner found a pair o' false teeth sittin' in a yoghourt carton on top o' the bar. A wee while later, the phone rings. It's Hamish. "Did I leave ma teeth there last night?"[51]

Folk music has traditionally been played on licensed premises, and pubs, such as the Scotia Bar, the Clutha and the Victoria Bar in Glasgow, were venues where performers like Billy Connolly cut their teeth. When Connolly and Tam Harvey formed the Humblebums, they used to drink in the Scotia Bar, 'a wild place in Stockwell Street that is still thriving'. Folk music was becoming more popular in Scotland and 'bars and lounges throughout the country became transformed into folk venues once a week'. The Humblebums travelled out of Glasgow and began to play in smaller pub venues on the east coast, such as the Windmill Bar in Arbroath, working up from a circuit of small towns and villages in Angus and Fife to larger venues.[52]

Ingirid Jolly, born in Orkney in 1946, learned to play guitar with the local Strathspey and Reel Society. She got married at twenty-one and remembered that the emerging folk scene on Orkney at that time centred on pubs:

> It was mainly traditional singing at that time. You find I think that at most of the concerts here at that time there was quite a lot of singing going on, and a few musical turns as weel. And maybe noo it's almost the opposite way aboot, that there's more music and less singing. But at that time there was a very small folk club that was going on for a short time in the Ayre Hotel here . . . But then I became more and more involved in local music. I think it really stemmed from the fact that I met up wi' a man here called Hugh Inkster who played the fiddle. I was playing the guitar along with the local Strathspey and Reel Society . . . If you go and play in a pub, for instance, lots of young folk who you would not imagine would enjoy it, come and say they really do like it.[53]

Nowadays folk music, often rebranded as Celtic music, can be big business. Celtic Connections, a three-week festival held in Glasgow in the tourist-dead months of January and February combines speech, music and dance from Scotland, Ireland, Brittany and North America. It is largely held in concert halls, contemporary arts centres, museums and libraries but the occasional concert is held in pub or hotel venues such as Oran Mor or the Holiday Inn to remind people of its origins.[54]

Rock music in Scottish pubs began to develop in the early 1960s. Paul Waterson recalled how his father bought the Burns Cottage pub near the Paisley Road toll on the edge of Glasgow in 1963. His father put a stage in a room that could hold 150 people and had a live resident band playing cabaret music, which required a music licence from the Glasgow magistrates. The Beatles exploded on to the British music scene that year and the whole nature of popular music in Britain changed. The Waterson family bought the Burns Howff pub in West Regent Street in the city centre. This became one of the first 'young people's pubs' in Glasgow where young women felt at home. It had closed-circuit television, on which you could watch the band playing upstairs, and a themed bar.[55]

Pubs were often where rock and pop bands would cut their teeth before a record deal or recording contract launched their careers into larger venues. Of course, the majority of bands never made it beyond this. In the 1960s David Bowie appeared on his first UK solo tour at the Moncrieffe Suite in the Salutation Hotel, Perth.[56] In the early 1980s, 'the first ever Primal Scream gig was at the Bungalow Bar in Paisley', while the Proclaimers from Auchtermuchty in Fife moved to the capital and began to play gigs in pubs such as Nicky Tams in Edinburgh.[57]

CRIME AND THE SCOTTISH PUB

Because of the strong temperance legacy in Scotland, there was great concern among urban local authorities about regulating the number and the opening hours of licensed premises in an attempt to reduce crimes of drunkenness. These attempts appear to have met with some success. Table 6.1 compares crimes of drunkenness with the number of licensed premises in six British cities in 1950 – three in Scotland and three in England. Contrary to popular mythology, Glasgow did not top the table for crimes of drunkenness per head of population at this time. Birmingham, with a slightly smaller population, had more licensed premises and a much higher level of crimes of drunkenness per head of population. Liverpool, with a smaller population than Glasgow, had more licensed premises per head of population and a higher rate of crimes of drunkenness. Glasgow had fewer licensed premises per head of population than either Dundee or Edinburgh which both had lower rates of crimes of drunkenness per head of population than either Birmingham or Liverpool. Of course, one has to remember that these figures were compiled by the Chief Constable of Glasgow and that Scotland and England had different legal definition of 'crimes of drunkenness'.

James Patrick's *A Glasgow Gang Observed* was based on undercover fieldwork carried out in 1966–67. The author made contact with a gang called the Young Team, based in Maryhill, and observed them over a

Table 6.1 Number of licensed premises and crimes of drunkenness figures in six British cities, 1950.

City	Population	Crimes of drunkenness per 1,000 population	Total licensed premises	Number of inhabitants per licensed house
Bristol	403,840	0.009	993	443
Birmingham	1,002,603	4.77	1,722	582
Glasgow	1,110,000	2.6	1,355	819
Liverpool	802,000	3.6	1,340	598
Edinburgh	439,010	2.4	807	544
Dundee	180,000	2.3	306	590

(Source: J. A. Mack, 'Crime', in J. Cunnison and J. B. S. Gilfillan (eds), *Third Statistical Account of Scotland, Glasgow* (Glasgow, 1958), p. 638, quoting the *Report of the Chief Constable of Glasgow*, 1950)

number of months. Pubs were central to Glasgow gang life and the gangs usually met up in them to plan the night ahead. The Young Team generally assembled around 5.00 p.m., just after opening time, in a pub in Maryhill which had 'dart boards, a TV set, dominoes, and from the gantry, a photograph of Benny Lynch, the famous Glasgow flyweight champion . . . This was no sawdust pub, but a well-appointed working-man's pub.' The gang were all underage and looked it, 'of the seven boys sitting round the table, only one looked old enough to be legally admitted' but they were served everywhere they went. Many of the gang had jobs and subsidised those who had just come out of approved school and had little money. After meeting up in Maryhill, the gang usually moved on to a city-centre pub or a dance hall.[58]

Scottish pubs offered attractive targets for both opportunistic and professional criminals, particularly in poorer areas, as they held more money in their tills than most other shops or houses in the area. Neil McCallum was born in Parkhead, in the East End of Glasgow, in 1955. In 1967, at the tender age of twelve, he broke into the pub his grandfather managed by stealing the keys on a Sunday morning when the pubs were closed and taking £600 out of the safe. He was sent to approved school for this for three years and, when he came out, he specialised in breaking into pubs, partly because he was a heavy drinker:

> My favourite target had become pubs. I could eye up a building and work out a way into it without setting any alarms off, and empty the stock. I wasn't selling the stock – I was drinking it with my pals. I remember my father saying to me, 'I'm glad you got prison, because you'd have been dead within another three months.'[59]

While some novelists have portrayed the dark side of Scottish pubs to great effect, the underside of Scottish pub life is often hidden behind police and crime reports or in newspaper stories. The Angel in Leith had its licence suspended by the Licensing Board for three months in November 1980 after thirty-two incidents of disorder in less than two years. On 21 June 1980, fifteen policemen were sent to the hotel on six occasions. The owners and licensees were husband and wife, Derek and June Aitchison. The hotel at 2 Tower Place had sixty bedrooms, a function room and a bar.[60]

Louise Settle has shown that there were close associations between pubs and hotels and female prostitution in Edinburgh in the period between the wars.[61] By the late twentieth century, a survey of 1,109 female sex workers in Glasgow showed that only seventy-three (7 per cent) were 'known alcohol users', a figure dwarfed by the number of drug users – 625 (56 per cent) were injecting drug users, 333 (30 per cent) were oral drug users. The individual case histories in this study reveal that pubs and alcohol use could sometimes act as a 'halfway house' before the women began to take drugs. Fiona had 'a good and happy childhood' but started to go 'off the rails' when she began truanting from school and 'started to drink alcohol at week ends' before developing a drug habit. Shirley had a baby when she was sixteen but proved too young to look after it properly. The first time she had sex for money 'I got really drunk. I couldn't believe it. I made £65 the first night.'[62]

Sometimes, disorder and criminal behaviour in pubs was linked to football violence by fans of a particular club. Baird's Bar, on the Gallowgate in Glasgow, was, 'one of Scotland's best known football pubs', a haven for Celtic supporters. In February 2013, it was shut down by the Licensing Board after the pub had been reported to it three times in eighteen months for causing problems. The final chapter came after a serious incident in September 2012, on the day of Scotland's opening World Cup qualifying match against Serbia, when a man was attacked by other pub customers at the pool table. The police reported that there had been a fifteen-minute delay between the fight breaking out and an ambulance being called, while there was no attempt to call the police. When the police arrived, they found that bar staff had engaged in an 'almost forensic clean-up of the area', similar to a previous incident reported to the board in October 2011. The bar had a record of arrests and complaints involving drug consumption and drug dealing, such as the arrest of a customer in possession of cocaine, and the discovery of polythene wraps, associated with drug dealing, in the toilets during a routine visit.[63]

'BELOW THE RADAR': GAY PUBS IN SCOTLAND

Gay pubs belong to the 'hidden history' of Scotland. Homosexuality and lesbianism are largely 'invisible' in Scotland until the second half of the twentieth century.[64] Whereas the trial of Oscar Wilde in 1895 provided a good deal of detail about homosexual life in late nineteenth-century London, nothing in such detail survives for Scotland. What information exists is contained in the reports of sodomy trials in Scotland, as discussed in Chapter 4. The breakthrough came with the social changes brought about by World War II, though they came more slowly in Scotland than in England, and one historian has argued that, as recently as the late 1960s, 'the Scottish gay community was driven so far underground that no one knew about it'.[65] Scottish attitudes towards homosexuality were more intolerant than in England, and the Sexual Offences Act passed in 1967, legalising homosexual acts for men over twenty-one, did not apply to Scotland and was vigorously opposed in the Cabinet by Willie Ross, then Secretary of State for Scotland.[66]

Though the Sexual Offences Act applied only to England and Wales, in 1971 the Solicitor General of Scotland let it be known that there would be no prosecutions of consenting sexual activity in private between males over twenty-one. Brian Dempsey has argued that, 'the early gay and lesbian movement in Scotland arrived late, compared to, for example, England and the US'. In England, the Homosexual Law Reform Society was formed in the late 1950s to campaign for reform of the law on homosexual acts, following the Wolfenden Report of 1957. Similarly, the Minorities Research Group was formed in the early 1960s to campaign on lesbian issues. Neither of these organisations had much presence in Scotland, and the establishment of an (all male) Scottish Minorities Group had to wait until 1969.[67]

Footsteps and Witnesses, published in 1993, a collection of gay and lesbian biographies, reveals how gay people in Scotland had to lead hidden lives before the legalisation of homosexual acts, and how certain pubs functioned as 'underground' or illicit meeting places for homosexual men and lesbian women.[68] The oldest person interviewed was the poet and academic Edwin Morgan, born in the West End of Glasgow in 1920, who served in the Royal Army Medical Corps during World War II. When Muir returned to Glasgow after the war, he discovered:

> there were certain pubs that you could go to that would attract gay people
> but wouldn't want to be known as gay pubs. The best known one was one in
> West Nile Street, not very far from the city centre, called the Royal. Some of

the hotels had either a bar or a lounge. The Central Hotel at Central Station was a place that people would often go to. They might meet in a pub and go to the Central Hotel for a coffee afterwards . . . A place like the Royal would be mixed in the sense of not everyone who was there was gay but it was predominantly gay. There were lots of married men there and that was surprising to me to begin with.[69]

This shows the importance of certain city-centre pubs as anonymous and illicit meeting places for gay men at a time when homosexual acts between consenting adults were still illegal. It also reveals the geography of gay pubs at this time – often near railway stations or entertainment venues, similar to the social geography of female prostitution in Edinburgh in the 1920s and 1930s outlined in Louise Settle's recent study.[70] At this time, the gay scene in Scotland was largely confined to a small number of pubs in the centres of Edinburgh and Glasgow, though others did exist in the provinces. James Mitchell, born in Bridgeton in 1927, remembered that 'the first gay pub I heard about was the Strand in Hope Street (Glasgow) . . . There was also Guys on the corner of Hope Street and the Royal Restaurant. The Royal was quite a good pub. There was a little bar off the street and you used to go through to the back which was men only.'[71]

Similarly, in Edinburgh, there was a small number of pubs where gay men could meet. Alan Alexander, born in 1937 into a middle class Communist family in Edinburgh, became a lecturer at Edinburgh College of Art. He used to go to Paddy's Bar in Rose Street, Edinburgh with his mother and her friend, where the bar was run by a woman, Alice Crossan. Gradually, he became aware of gay people drinking there. Along Rose Street, there was a number of gay-friendly pubs, including Robertsons and also the Kenilworth and the Abercromby Hotel which had a mixed clientele, both straight and gay. Another gay-friendly venue was the Imperial Hotel on Leith Walk, which was 'full of hookers'. Fairleys was 'a huge, huge bar on different levels, very popular with sailors'.[72] Alistair Ross was born in Edinburgh in 1938, the son of a policeman. When he was twenty-one, in 1959, he went into Paddys' Bar on Rose Street which he described as a 'gay pub'. At this time, Ross claimed that the only other gay venue in Edinburgh was the Caravel, attached to the North British Hotel, next to the railway station.[73]

Lesbian women in Scotland had similar memories of certain carefully selected pubs as places to meet other women. Lena Wright, born in 1940, came from a working-class mining community in Kelty, Fife. She did many jobs after a spell in the Women's Royal Air Corps and worked as a taxi driver for ten years. She used to go to a gay-friendly pub, the Victoria Arms, in Kirkcaldy. Mary, born in Stirling in 1942, never knew her mother and father and was brought up in care. She discovered lesbian-friendly pubs in Glasgow from a letter to an agony aunt, Anna Raeburn. The pubs included the Duke of Wellington, the Vintners, the Waterloo and the Strand in Hope Street.[74]

It was difficult to be accepted as gay if one grew up in a working-class community in the Scottish provinces. John Scott was born in 1946 in Selkirk, the son of a mill worker. At eighteen, when he was working in a bank, he discovered Paddy's Bar in Rose Street, Edinburgh. He would catch the bus from Selkirk into Edinburgh and start off at the Cafe Royal which was a gay-friendly pub. This story offers some insight into why gay pubs were often situated near railway or bus stations in city centres. Brian McCrossan, born in 1949 in Carluke, Lanarkshire into a strongly Roman Catholic family, worked in Samuels the jewellers and discovered the gay bars in Glasgow. When he moved to Aberdeen in the course of his work, he came across 'one bar down by the docks which was very working class and men from ships from all different countries would drink there, but at the same time, it was a very open gay bar'.[75] The 'underground' history of gay pubs in Scotland would make a fascinating study.

The geography of gay pubs in Scotland continues along similar lines to the present day. Pete Irvine's *Scotland the Best* includes a short section on gay bars and clubs in Scotland in its 2011 edition. Of the twelve gay bars and clubs listed in Edinburgh, one is on Rose Street North, but ten (83 per cent) are situated in what the guide calls 'the East End Pink Triangle', the area at the top of Leith Walk near the Playhouse Theatre and around Broughton Street.[76] This is the area close to Waverley Station, near theatres, pubs and cinemas, and on the way up from Leith Docks into Edinburgh, identified by Louise Settle in her article on female prostitution in the interwar period in Edinburgh.[77] In Glasgow, gay bars and clubs congregate in the Merchant City which houses six (54 per cent) out of the eleven listed, or near Central Station, the location of five (45 per cent) of the eleven listed. The oldest gay bar in Scotland is the Waterloo on Argyle Street, Glasgow. Similarly in Dundee, three out of four gay pubs and bars described in *Scotland the Best* are situated in or near the Seagate, close to the old dockland area and now near the bus station[78] while, in Aberdeen, Brian McCrossan remembered 'a very open gay bar' in the 1970s, a working-class pub near the docks, popular with seamen.[79]

LIBERALISATION AND THE CLAYSON REPORT

It was against a background of growing concern about alcohol abuse and the links between alcohol and football violence, on the one hand, and of lobbying from tourist interests and consumer organisations for liberalisation of the licensing laws on the other, that the government set up a Departmental Committee on Scottish Licensing Law, chaired by Dr Christopher Clayson. Its primary purpose was seen as a general enquiry into the liquor-licensing law in Scotland, with the underlying theme of controlling alcohol misuse which was significantly worse in Scotland than in England and Wales. Hospital admissions for alcoholism were seven times higher for men in Scotland in proportion to the population than in England and Wales and five times higher for women. Death rates from cirrhosis of the liver were 1.5 times greater in Scotland than in England and Wales and from alcoholism six times higher for Scottish men and twice as high for Scottish women. Motoring offences involving alcohol were about three times higher in Scotland per head of population than in England and Wales.[80]

During the 1960s, there were major changes in society that affected the sale and purchase of alcohol in Scotland. There was a large increase in off-sales of alcohol, and the Clayson committee wished to encourage changes in attitudes by encouraging the sale of food in licensed premises. The number of off-sales certificates in Scotland had risen from 2,409 in 1953 to 3,872 in 1972, while the number of registered clubs, where alcohol could be consumed, generally at lower prices than in pubs, more than doubled from 990 in 1953 to 2,148 in 1972. Spending per head on alcohol was higher in Scotland than in England and Wales, whereas in 1955 it had been lower, at 89 per cent of the UK level. In 1970–71, the average weekly spend on wine and spirits was 70 pence per head in Scotland, compared to 44 pence in Britain as a whole.[81]

In an interesting aside, the report claimed that, in Scotland, '"men only" activities such as football match attendance, have shown a diminishing trend', although 'regular pub going is predominantly a male activity and a youthful one'. A 1970 survey by the Office of Population Censuses and Surveys (OPCS) found that 63 per cent of Scottish men visited a pub at least once a month, compared with only 18 per cent of women, and, in the eighteen to twenty-four age group, about 75 per cent visited a pub at least once a month, falling to 16 per cent of the over sixty-fives.[82]

Only a minority (48 per cent) of those sampled in the OPCS survey of 545 adults aged eighteen and over favoured Sunday opening by pubs in Scotland and half (50 per cent) were against. The Guest committee reports of 1960 and 1963 had recommended Sunday opening for hotels, public houses and licensed restaurants but no legislation had followed. The same committee had noted the abuse of Sunday-opening legislation through the increase in travel on Sundays by coach and car to drink in hotels in neighbouring districts as 'bona fide' travellers, as permitted by the law. Clayson recommended Sunday opening for public houses in Scotland, from 12.30 p.m. to 11.00 p.m., to be standardised for all hotels, public houses and restaurants. This was partly in response to 'gross overcrowding' in Scottish hotel bars on Sundays and the development of hotels 'which are in effect seven day public houses'.[83] This is confirmed by a Glasgow licensee, who claimed that the Stakis chain of hotels in Glasgow and the west of Scotland used to make most of their money on Sundays, when pubs were closed.[84]

Clayson also recommended the abolition of the Temperance (Scotland) Act of 1913 which provided for local veto polls to be held to ban or limit the sale of alcohol in specified areas of Scotland. Glasgow Corporation had prohibited the sale of alcohol on council property since 1890, so that the expansion of council housing on large estates on the edge of the city since the end of World War II resulted in large residential areas with no licensed premises. This meant that established residential areas close to new council estates were reluctant to allow new (or, in some

Figure 6.2 The Shand Bar, Menzieshill, Dundee. A typical 1960s pub in a Dundee housing scheme. Currently closed. © Anthony and Judith Cooke.

cases, any) licences to be granted, as they feared it would lead to an influx of council-house tenants to drink in their area. This explains why many successful prohibitionist polls at this time were in Glasgow and its immediate environs, in places such as Cathcart, Pollockshields, Kelvinside and North Kelvin. Even though Glasgow Corporation had reversed its policy on licences on council property in 1967, few pubs had been built in housing estates since then. As late as 1972, seventeen areas of Scotland were still 'dry' (one burgh, eight wards of burghs and eight parishes) and fifteen had limiting resolutions (two burghs, ten wards of burghs and three parishes). The committee concluded on a pessimistic note that 'the Scottish public house retains its old and not very attractive image as a place where men go for the purpose of drinking with other men'.[85]

LICENSEES

In many communities the licensee was a figure of considerable authority and, on occasion, traditional masculine drinking behaviour could be tempered by an assertive female licensee. Jean Stevenson ran the Bull Inn in Paisley with an iron rod:

> Men coming in at 5 o'clock on pay day were allowed only one drink. They were then sent home to hand over the housekeeping and have a meal before returning for their night's drinking. Miss Stevenson, while looking after the wives' interests, would not, however, allow any women into the premises.[86]

Betty Smart, born in 1937 in Kirkintilloch, got a job in Woodilee Hospital as a trainee nurse, then worked as a bus conductress for five years. In the 1960s, after she got married, she 'started working in a pub, then I bought my own pub' which she remembered with affection, closely linked as it was with the worlds of entertainment and sport, in her case Celtic Football Club:

> to me, going back years ago, the public house is where you get all the laughter and the banter. You met a lot of stars that came into your pub. Billy Connolly used to come into my sister-in-law's pub and I had Danny McGrain and Jock Stein; these people came into my pub and we became friends and they helped me with my charity work. To me that was a great life, the pub work. Great for meeting people from all walks of life.[87]

Life Behind Bars. Confessions of a Pub Landlady, published in 2011, consists of humorous anecdotes by two Edinburgh landladies, Kate McGregor and Linda Tweedie who, between them, have spent

over thirty years in the licensed trade. It is fairly unrevealing about the
writers themselves but shows that pubs still function as public spaces
where people can behave or misbehave as they choose. One anecdote
concerns a 'respectable' couple who meet once a week on the same night
in the same Edinburgh pub for many years. Eventually, the man's wife
turns up out of the blue and the cosy arrangement comes to an abrupt
end. The book also reveals the changing nature of Scottish pubs in terms
of the social and sporting activities carried on there. The writers claim
that team games, such as skittles, dominoes and darts, in pubs 'are very
much in decline' and have been replaced by pool and video game nights.
The book also reveals the continuing links between Edinburgh pubs and
horse racing.[88]

Between September 2013 and September 2014, I interviewed seven
licensees across Scotland plus Colin Wilkinson, the Secretary of the
Scottish Licensed Trade Association, Edinburgh. The licensees, six men
and one woman, were based in Angus, Dundee, Glasgow (3), Leith
and Stirling. Most of them had spent many years in the business and
had seen many changes, including the decline of the heavy manufacturing industry that had provided much of the male clientele for bars in
Glasgow and the west of Scotland. Jim Clancy of the Lauriston Bar
in Glasgow remembered running the Braemar Bar on Garscube Road,
Maryhill as a brewery tenant between 1974 and 1979, 'when there
were lots of factories, foundries, bottling plants, building firms in that
area'.[89] Willie Mutch, who co-owns eight pubs in the east of Scotland,
grew up in Coatbridge, Lanarkshire where his parents ran a pub. At that
time, in the 1960s, it was a 'men-only' pub, 'a spit-and-sawdust place'
without a women's toilet, and the customers were overwhelmingly men
working in heavy industry and the iron and steel industry. Coatbridge
was known as 'Ironburgh', and about 150,000 people were employed
in iron and steel and heavy engineering in the North Lanarkshire area.
Willie himself, on leaving school aged fifteen, was apprenticed for six
years in a local brass foundry which closed down long ago.[90] In these
ways, the Scottish pub has reflected the de-industrialisation of Scotland
and the disappearance of large numbers of full-time, male, manual jobs,
both skilled and unskilled.[91]

Of the seven licensees I interviewed, five had relatives in the licensed
trade – a father, mother or brother and only two had no family connections with the trade, though one was heavily influenced by her father
into entering the business in Scotland. The oldest person I interviewed
is Jim Clancy of the Lauriston Bar, Glasgow, whose father came over
from the Enniskillen/Sligo area of Ireland in the 1940s to work at the

Dixon Foundry at Parkhead. Jim's father had a serious accident at work, bought a pub with his compensation money and, by 1965, owned the Rising Sun pub in Lauriston. Jim began his working life in the pub trade after leaving school at sixteen or seventeen, his first pub being in the East End of Glasgow, which was 'frantic' on days when Celtic were playing at home at Parkhead.[92]

Another long-serving licensee I interviewed is Willie Mutch who grew up in Coatbridge, Lanarkshire. His father and mother ran a pub in Coatbridge and another in Airdrie, and Willie helped out in the Coatbridge pub from the age of ten. On leaving school, Willie was apprenticed in a brass foundry but left after his apprenticeship finished and went into the licensed trade. His father died of cirrhosis of the liver in 1979 aged only forty-six, when Willie was twenty-eight, so he has been teetotal ever since, and his widowed mother moved over to Newport, Fife to run the Brig o' Tay pub.[93]

Jonathan Stewart's father was a retail pharmacist in Dundee's West End but his brother, Jeff, bought the Three Barrels, Dundee after leaving the merchant navy with eyesight problems. Jeff bought the pub with a 'soft' brewery loan from Scottish and Newcastle Breweries at low interest rates (6 to 7 per cent) in return for which he had to sell the brewery's products exclusively. Jonathan, who trained as a hairdresser, helped out in his brother's pub and found he enjoyed it, getting his first pub, the Ladywell Tavern in Dundee, in 1974 at the age of twenty, again with a 'soft' loan from Scottish and Newcastle Breweries.[94] Alistair Don, of the Doublet Bar, Glasgow had a father, Alex Don, who was a sales representative for Dunn and Moores, Glasgow wholesalers and bottlers, and also ran the Doublet and a number of other Glasgow pubs. Alistair began a dentistry course at Glasgow University but dropped out after a year to become the assistant buyer for Watlings, the civil engineering group. When his father died in 1974, he went into the family business, as he was the only son, and has remained there ever since.[95] Paul Waterson, who owns the Golden Lion Hotel in Stirling, had a father who worked all his life in the trade, and the family owned and ran pubs in Glasgow until the mid 1990s, then hotels in East Kilbride and finally the Golden Lion.[96]

Two licensees who had no previous family connection with the trade are Marshal Bain, of the Queen Charlotte Rooms in Leith, and Petra Wetzel of West on Glasgow Green. Marshall Bain was born in Leith but worked abroad for ten years as a musician, piano player and singer, ending up as an entertainment manager running clubs in Portugal. He returned to Leith twenty years ago, when property prices were quite

Figure 6.3 Jonathan and Jonathan Iain Stewart, Speedwell Bar (Mennie's), Perth Road, Dundee, 2014. © Anthony and Judith Cooke.

low, and bought his current premises which had an existing licence, with a loan from Belhaven Brewery on condition he took a set amount of their beer.[97] Petra Wetzel, the only woman I interviewed, is much younger than the other interviewees. She grew up in a rural area of Bavaria and came to study at Glasgow University. When her father came to visit her in 1994, he was unimpressed by the quality of lager on sale in Glasgow and asked her if there was any decent German-style lager available. When she said no, he suggested 'why don't you make your own'. She eventually created a German lager brewery and pub (West) in the former Templeton's Carpet Factory on Glasgow Green, opening in 2006. She employs ninety people, sixty full-time, and has just opened another pub, the revamped Halt Bar on Woodlands Road, now rebranded as 'West on the Corner'.[98]

I asked the licensees what changes they had seen. Willie Mutch remembered that, in Coatbridge in the 1960s, as well as beer and whisky, Buckfast Tonic Wine was a favourite drink, and his father used to order eighteen cases of Buckfast a week for the pub. Apart from its high alcohol content, Buckfast had a high caffeine content and would get you feeling 'high' quickly. Another popular drink was a cheap wine called Eldorado (otherwise known as LD) which got you drunk quickly.[99] Marshall Bain, of the Queen Charlotte Rooms, Leith, has seen a dramatic decline in beer sales over twenty years but a large increase in spirit sales, such as vodka, gin and Jack Daniels, mainly to women. Wine sales grew from 5 per cent of alcohol sales in 1994 to around 30 per cent today. Marshall also sells a lot of tea, coffee and soft drinks, and the customer spend is around 50 per cent food, 50 per cent drink, because he caters for christenings, weddings, birthdays, funerals, family occasions, Rotary functions and so on. The customer base is around half women, half men.[100]

When I asked licensees about real ale, Jonathan Stewart, who was a pioneer of the movement in Dundee, was an early enthusiast. As a young tenant at the Ladywell Tavern in 1974, his customers included councillors and party workers from the Labour and Conservative offices in the same tenement block, plus clergymen from different denominations (Church of Scotland, Episcopalian and Roman Catholic) who met in a back room in the mornings. The clergymen persuaded Jonathan to start serving real ale which they said was as different from keg as Stilton cheese from processed cheddar. Initially, he had difficulty persuading Scottish and Newcastle to supply him with cask-conditioned beer but, eventually, they did and he switched from selling McEwen's 80 shilling keg to the cask-conditioned variety. At that time, the breweries disliked cask-conditioned beer which did not last as long as keg and had to be well kept by experienced staff who knew what they were doing.[101]

Another enthusiast for real ale was Alistair Don at the Doublet Bar in Glasgow, who starting serving it in 1974, when McEwen's brought out cask-conditioned 80 shilling ale. In 1974, he sold three 18-gallon (82-litre) measures a week of real ale or 54 gallons (246 litres) a week. Nowadays the consumption is lower, four 9-gallon (41-litre) measures or about 36 gallons (164 litres) of real ale a week.[102] Jim Clancy at the Lauriston Bar in Glasgow is a recent convert to real ale which brings in a different type of customer, customers who are 'prepared to travel to get a decent pint'. The Lauriston is helped in this by being close to the underground, as there is a recognised circular route for real-ale drinkers in Glasgow, based on underground stations.[103]

Modern pubs still function as public spaces for social, cultural and sporting activities. When I was interviewing Alistair Don at the Doublet in Glasgow, a female pole-dancing class (average age sixty plus) came in for a lunchtime drink after their class across the road had finished. The clientele at the Doublet is a mix of students, who are accommodated in an upstairs room with a jukebox, teachers, lawyers, actors, journalists and Partick Thistle supporters. The pub has a well-supported (and difficult) quiz night on Tuesdays. There is no Sky television, the Doublet is 'a pub for conversation and a social centre'. Alistair is a Director of Breast Cancer 2000 (his first wife died of breast cancer) and the pub raised £4,500 for this charity simply from the charity bottle on the bar.[104] Another Glasgow pub, the Lauriston Bar, has live music once a week, run on a 'drop-in' basis, and a samba group meets there.[105] The Central Bar in Arbroath caters for a varied clientele, including a number of former Royal Marines from the nearby Condor base. The Central has two football teams, that play in the Sunday League, and supports darts and dominoes teams.[106] West on Glasgow Green has comedy nights aimed at a younger clientele.[107]

BAR STAFF

At the end of World War II, the new Labour government was keen to continue to intervene in areas of everyday life, including wages and the supply of drink and foodstuffs, drawing on the experience of wartime regulation. A Wages Board was set up by the Ministry of Labour, and orders were issued for Scotland in January 1947. The 'normal' working week was fixed at forty-eight hours – five days of nine hours and three hours on Saturdays. The minimum wage for men aged twenty-one or over was £4/5s and for those under twenty-one £2/7s. Gender inequality in the workplace was built into the system. Barmaids over twenty-one earned £3/17s a week and those under twenty-one £2/7s. There was provision for overtime and for holidays from six to twelve days, depending on length of service.[108]

The late 1950s was an era of high employment and rising wages, when the Macmillan government won the 1959 General Election on the slogan 'You've never had it so good'. Growing prosperity led to a general rise in wages, and the rising costs of staffing and the recruitment and retention of bar staff were matters of growing concern to the licensed trade in Scotland. There were eighty-nine objections when the Ministry of Labour proposed raising wages in February 1959. Towards the end of the year, the Dundee association lobbied to lower the age of working in a bar from eighteen to sixteen, as the present limit 'discourages the entry of young people because they are forced to take up other occupations at an earlier age'. This preoccupation with staffing shortages continued, and the Edinburgh association complained in May 1961 about 'the great shortage of employees', and attempted to amend the 1959 Act to allow boys of sixteen to be employed in public houses.

The Licensing (Scotland) Act of 1962 did not allow pubs to open on Sundays but seven-day licensed hotels were permitted to sell alcohol on Sundays from 12.30 p.m. to 2.30 p.m. Weekday opening hours for pubs were fixed at 11.00 a.m. to 2.30 p.m. and 5.00 to 10.00 p.m.[109]

As wages and living standards rose in the early 1970s, it was reported in 1975 that 'Barmen are through the £30 barrier'. A £7.45 increase in weekly pay had been agreed between Scottish and Newcastle managed public houses and the Transport and General Workers' Union, to be implemented on 3 February 1975. The minimum rates for full-time staff working a forty-hour week were fixed at £32.50 for a head barman/cellarman and £31.88 for a head barmaid. First- and second-year barmen and barmaids were to receive less and 'other staff' least of all. Staff received eighteen days of annual holiday in 1975, plus two more days in 1976. There was to be equal pay from 29 December 1975. A pay award had been made to five hundred managers of licensed premises owned by Tennent Caledonian breweries.[110]

In his 1989 short story, 'At the Bar', William McIlvanney describes a confrontation in an Ayrshire bar between two men, one of them just out of prison, from the point of view of the barman. The barman is alive to small signals from his clientele, even those unknown to him who have just come in off the street. The story begins when the 'big man with the ill-fitting suit' enters the bar and orders a pint of heavy. While pouring his pint, the barman sums him up, 'His pallor suggested a plant kept out of the light. Prison, the barman thought.' When violence suddenly explodes between the 'big man' and another customer, we are told, 'Not unused to fast violence, the barman was stunned.' He reacts by barring the customer who started the row.[111]

Willie Mutch co-owns eight bars in the east of Scotland, six in Angus, one in Dundee and one in Denny, Stirlingshire. Each of his pubs employs about six people, nearly all women and nearly all part-time, and his six managers are all women, 'because they can handle men much better'. Most of his managers have worked for him for fifteen to twenty years. The benefits system dictates how many hours people can work – for example, you can work sixteen hours a week and be better off than if you work for twenty-one hours because you can retain your housing benefit and working tax credits.[112] Paul Waterson of the Golden Lion in Stirling thinks that bar staff are taking more pride in their work these days, thanks to compulsory training courses. Every pub is now required to have a number of staff holding a personal licence and some forty thousand people hold one, of whom thirty-thousand are still active in the trade. Paul thinks this has led to more people seeing their job as a trade, rather than a stopgap.[113] Petra Wetzel of West on Glasgow Green employs about ninety people, of whom about sixty are full-time, most of them front-of-house staff. The balance between male and female staff is about fifty–fifty, and West runs an in-house training programme for staff. Security training for staff is carried out by outside commercial training firms who specialise in this area.[114]

CUSTOMERS

At the Annual General Meeting of the Scottish Licensed Trade Association in Glasgow in 1949, the Lord Provost of Glasgow compared Scottish pubs unfavourably to those in England which had 'bowling greens and lounges into which a man could bring his wife and children'.[115] This desire for change became a feature of the post-war period as living standards began to rise and the status of women slowly improved. In the early 1950s, there was a shift in consumption from draught to bottled beer, and from whisky, which was heavily taxed and relatively expensive, to strong beer. Rising levels of prosperity led to increasing consumption of wine and the improvement of pub premises, with better toilets, more comfortable seating and furnishings and food being served to attract female customers, couples and families. In Glasgow, a number of pubs began to develop lounges for both sexes, with drinks at slightly higher prices than in the all-male stand-up bars, and boasting 'chromium, concealed lighting and imitation leather in scarlet or bright blue'.[116] This was linked to social changes that offered a threat to the survival of traditional men-only pubs, such as rising levels of comfort in the home, the spread of television (the number of television-licence holders rose from 62,400 in 1952 to 1,253,000 in 1965) and floodlit football matches in the evenings.[117]

Not all Scottish drinking places were stand-up, men-only bars for the working class. Journalists were a notoriously thirsty group who worked odd hours and patronised pubs close to their workplaces. Cliff Hanley remembered working as a journalist at *The Record* in Glasgow, when he and his colleagues drank regularly at the Corn Exchange, 'a beautifully old fashioned pub' on Gordon Street. The pub had a 'Gentlemen's Lounge' with the drinks served by 'good-natured waitresses of middle age or at least mature years'. The journalists were joined by an ever-changing group of 'travel agents and airline people', and certain unwritten and unspoken rules and rituals were observed, such as always standing a round, however many people were in the group on a particular day: 'the group at the bar would start with two members, and snowball into seven, or eight, or twelve, and every man satisfied that if he had been given a drink, he couldn't leave without standing a drink'.[118]

Twentieth-century accounts of Scottish pubs reveal them to be places that were often dominated by customers drawn from one particular occupation and where unwritten and unspoken rules and rituals were important to observe. Matthew Sanderson was born in the mining village of New Cumnock, Ayrshire in 1924 and became a miner at the age of fourteen. He remembered the local bars being packed out on Friday and Saturday nights, in the period after World War II, when there was full employment in the pits:

> The likes of a Friday nicht, we'll say roughly half the village are no' teetotal, so you'd go down to some of the local bars and they'd be stowed to the door on a Friday and a Saturday. I'm no' talking noo about alcoholics – mostly beer drinkers. And there's always be some liked their feet against the counter. I don't think you get that nowadays but there used to be a sawdust trough in them working areas. That was because, like I was, a lot of chesty old miners and it was a bit for them to spit into, this sawdust trough, which run alongside the bottom of the bar. And there'd be a separate room set aside for men who liked to play cards – I don't know what games they played. I was never involved in the card playing. And another big room that was known as the singers' room – a big round table in it. But if you went in there, it was expected that you would sing. And it was the same song every week because everyone had their own favourite song that they was able to sing every week with gusto, ken, it was their song. You'd have been looked at if you tried to have sung somebody else's song.[119]

Heavy drinking was linked with high levels of employment, long working hours, often involving overtime, and male manual labour which dominated the Scottish economy until the deindustrialisation of the 1980s. Ronnie Macdonald, born in Airdrie in 1946, worked in the offshore oil industry. In 1977 he was working at Kishorn, building an oil rig for the North Sea, a highly paid job attracting 'thousands of construction workers'. There was little to do apart from working and drinking:

> Drink. That's all there was to do at Kishorn. We had two bars. One in particular, the legendary Wellie Bar, where people knocking off after a twelve hour shift just went in with their oilskins on, and they drunk until closing time and went to their beds and grabbed a few hours sleep and were back up in the morning and back at work. The money that passed across that bar must have made it the richest licensed premises in the history of Scotland. It wasn't very good for safety standards though, but it's a free country and the guys were earning the money and it's up to them how they wish to spend it.[120]

By contrast, some Edinburgh pubs were exclusive middle-class enclaves, with different occupational groups keeping themselves rigidly apart, and the socially undesirable kept out by a dress code and high prices. In the sumptuously decorated Cafe Royal, in West Register Street, off Princes Street, Tom Shields noticed in the mid 1970s, 'On Fridays after five you can see the lawyers, journalists, accountants and other trades and professions sitting in apartheid-like sections. An interesting sight for observers of pub life and social customs.' There were 'police pubs' in most Scottish towns and cities, such as the Oxford Bar on Young Street in Edinburgh, and Chrystal Bell & Co. in the Gallowgate, Glasgow, 'a favourite spot with officers and staff from the nearby police headquarters'. Other urban pubs served as gathering places for migrant groups from particular areas. The Park Bar, on Argyll Street, Glasgow, near Kelvingrove Park, was a place where, in the 1970s, 'the majority of its customers are Highlanders and almost every night there is a lively sing-song in the lounge'.[121]

Scottish writers recorded social change as it affected pub life, including the rise of the lounge bar and increasing numbers of women using pubs, usually accompanied by men. In James Kelman's *The Bus Conductor Hines* (1984), Hines and his wife Sandra join some of his workmates, their wives and girlfriends in the lounge bar of a pub for a (gender-segregated) night out. Men and women sit at separate tables to drink, and the drinks they choose are different – a pint of heavy for Hines and a Martini and lemonade for his wife. Each man puts £5 into the kitty. There is entertainment laid on in the lounge bar, 'two entertainers in red trousers, tartan waistcoats and red bow ties, singing a song and accompanying themselves on accordion and rhythm guitar'. The pub closes at 10.30 p.m. and, as closing time approaches, the man in charge of the kitty advises everyone 'to order doubles in case they couldn't get one later'.'[122]

Today, many licensees still feel a duty of care towards their custom-ers. The Windsor Bar in Albert Street, Dundee is a pub mainly patron-ised by pensioners. The pub is the main point of social contact for many of its customers, a lot of whom live alone. They are creatures of habit who come in at the same time every day, sit or stand in the same place, and order the same drinks. If one fails to turn up one day, they will send someone around to his house (they are usually men) to see if they are unwell. If someone has too much to drink, they will make sure they get home safely. They also have a 'Christmas Do' for pensioners each year. Willie Mutch's wife even looked after a customer's dog when he went into hospital.[123] The staff of the Lauriston Bar in Glasgow have similar attitudes towards their customers. Jim Clancy told me that he had created a no-smoking area at the back of the pub, away from the street and passers-by, as customers faced being hassled by passers-by for a cigarette or a light if they were smoking outside on Bridge Street which is a main thoroughfare into the centre of Glasgow. Similarly, they encourage customers to call a taxi from inside the pub, rather than try to flag one down on the street.[124]

CONCENTRATION OF OWNERSHIP IN THE DRINKS TRADE AND THE CAMRA RESPONSE

By the mid 1980s, many smaller breweries in Scotland had closed or been taken over by larger ones. This mirrored the situation in the rest of Britain where concentration of ownership was producing a semi-monopolistic position in the supply to pubs of beer and other alcoholic drinks. The Belhaven Brewery Company, Dunbar complained in 1992 about the lack of choice in the Scottish beer market which was domi-nated by Scottish Brewers (Scottish and Newcastle), with a 45 per cent share of the market, and Tennent Caledonian (Bass plc) with a 40 per cent share. Tetley/Carlsberg (Allied Lyons) had 9 per cent of the market and other breweries 6 per cent. Belhaven owned sixty-two public houses in Scotland and produced about 55,000 barrels (9 million litres) of beer annually, with 99 per cent sold in Scotland. Their sales were 18 per cent tied trade and 82 per cent free trade.[125]

It was to challenge this type of monopoly and the increasingly limited choice of beer in pubs that CAMRA (the Campaign for Real Ale) was set up in 1972, following an article in the *Guardian* by Richard Boston. The first annual meeting took place in 1972, and three of the four founding members were journalists which ensured that the organisation got good press coverage.[126] By October 1973, Britain-wide member-ship of CAMRA was four thousand but the organisation was run from Salford and there were no CAMRA branches in Scotland.[127] In Scotland, CAMRA started with an advert in *What's Brewing* in 1974 proposing a Scottish chapter. In October 1974, fifty people turned up at the Golf Inn, Bishopton, Renfrewshire and the Glasgow and West of Scotland branch of CAMRA was formed.[128]

By 1980, *What's Brewing* had grown into a colour magazine which carried a full-page advertisement for McEwan's cask-conditioned ale from the Fountain Brewery, Edinburgh, and an article on Edinburgh pubs entitled 'It's Heavy Going'. At that time, the real-ale pubs in Edinburgh were: the Royal Arches in the Netherbow; the Royal Mile

Tavern on the High Street; Coppers on Cockburn Street; the Black Bull in the Grassmarket; the Tap o' Lauriston in Lauriston Place; Bennets Bar in Tollcross; the Cafe Royal; the Station Bar at Abbeyhill; the Southsider near the Old College; Greenmantle and Greyfriars Bobby Bar; the St Vincent next to St Stephen's Church; and the Raeburn in Stockbridge. Out of fifty-nine guides to real ale on sale across the United Kingdom, only four were Scottish: Edinburgh and the Lothians; Glasgow; Grampian and Tayside; and Fife. There were 162 CAMRA branches across Britain but only eight were in Scotland – Aberdeen, Ayrshire, Dumfries, Edinburgh, Forth Valley, Glasgow, Midlothian, Tayside, and Fife.[129]

In Scotland, CAMRA began to take off as a grass-roots movement in the early 1980s and, in 1982, the West of Scotland Beer Guide listed nearly two hundred pubs which served real ale compared to a mere twenty six years earlier.[130] The Good Beer Guide for 1984 hailed the change in Scotland from a 'beer desert' to 'one of the better areas for ale' in only ten years. In Edinburgh and Glasgow there were now over 180 real-ale outlets in each city and only Manchester and London offered a wider choice. The guide singled out Belhaven 80 shilling ale from Dunbar, East Lothian as 'the best of the breed'.[131]

Eight years later, the Herald surveyed real-ale pubs in Glasgow, including: Tennent's Bar, Byres Road (1992 CAMRA pub of the year) which had twelve real ales on tap; the Blythswood, Hope Street; the Bon Accord, North Street; the Victoria Bar, Briggait; Bert's Bar, St Enoch Square; and Stirling Castle Bar in Dumbarton Road. In 1992, CAMRA had 35,000 members in the United Kingdom compared to only four thousand in 1973.[132]

By 2014, real ale was an established feature of many Scottish pubs, though by no means all. Some of the licensees I interviewed thought that the future for pubs was craft beer which was becoming more prominent and attracting younger people into the trade. Paul Waterson of the Golden Lion Hotel in Stirling, Chief Executive of the Scottish Licensed Trade Association, had been a judge at the recent Scottish Craft Beer Awards ceremony and had been impressed by the commitment, dedication and knowledge shown by the young people in the industry. Many of them had reopened pubs which had closed down in unpromising areas and 'were making a go of it' with new attitudes and new products. He saw it as a Scottish-wide movement with the six finalists drawn from Inverness, Aberdeen, Dundee, Edinburgh and Glasgow.[133]

Despite the best efforts of CAMRA, most beer drinkers in Scotland continue to drink mass-produced beers, such as Tennent's lager or

McEwen's Heavy, or foreign beers, such as Heineken (Dutch), Beck's (German) or Stella Artois (Belgian). Like much of the rest of the Scottish economy, Scottish breweries and distilleries have become increasingly centralised, with control moving out of Scotland to London or to overseas-based multinationals. Tennent's in Glasgow was an early example of this trend, with control moving to Carrington United Breweries in England as early as 1963 and to Bass Charrington four years later. In 2000 the company was bought by the giant Belgian brewer Interbrew and sold to C&C Group of Ireland in 2008. Scottish and Newcastle breweries stayed independent much longer but were eventually bought by the Dutch-based Heineken group in 2008 for £7.8 billion, ending 250 years of independent brewing history.[134]

In distilling, the Scottish-based Distillers Company was bought in a controversial and hostile takeover by Guinness in 1986. Guinness merged with Grand Metropolitan in 1997 to form Diageo, a London-based multinational with leading brands, such as Smirnoff vodka, Johnny Walker whisky and Guinness. The Johnny Walker plant in Kilmarnock was closed down in March 2012 although, in June of that year, Diageo announced a £1 billion investment in Scotch whisky production over five years.[135]

THE NICHOLSON COMMITTEE 2003

The Nicholson Committee was set up with the remit to 'review all aspects of liquor licensing law and practice in Scotland, with particular reference to the implications for health and public order'. It noted that 'many of the problems associated with that [overindulgence in alcohol] are deeply engrained in the Scottish psyche'. Training for licensees and staff was seen as one of the 'seven guiding principles' of the review. A major recommendation was the concept of a 'personal licence', which individuals would apply for and would be granted, subject to 'approved qualifications', to run for ten years. Anyone applying for a licence would have to specify a 'designated personal licence holder' who would be responsible for day-to-day management.[136]

The changes that had taken place since the 1976 Act included: firstly, the emergence of the 'superpub' – much larger than the traditional pub; secondly, the increase in the number of off-sales licences; thirdly, the large number of entertainment licences; and finally the widespread grant of regular extensions to permitted hours. The committee had particular concerns about the adverse effects of heavy alcohol consumption on people's health and behaviour, particularly those of young people.

Deaths from excessive alcohol consumption in Scotland had more than doubled in ten years, from 13.4 per thousand in 1990 to 31.2 per thousand in 2000. Similarly, acute hospital admissions linked to alcohol had increased fivefold between 1980 and 2000, from 120 per 100,000 in 1980 to 649 in 2000. Men were twice as likely as women to require treatment, and, in 2000, acute intoxication leading to hospital admission was highest among the fifteen to nineteen age group.[137]

Binge drinking related partly to 'happy hours' in pubs, which involved women as well as men, usually under thirty. Underage drinking was also common, and a survey of Edinburgh teenagers revealed that 51 per cent had drunk alcohol when they were thirteen, rising to 84 per cent by the time they were fifteen. The commonest source of alcohol for underage drinkers was the small licensed grocer or local corner shop. There were strong links between alcohol consumption and crime and public order. Alcohol was a factor in 40 per cent of recorded incidents of domestic violence and featured in 40 per cent of violent crimes, 78 per cent of assaults and 88 per cent of criminal-damage cases. Similarly, 19 per cent of all violent incidents occurred in or around pubs or clubs. The commonest perpetrators of violence were young males aged sixteen to twenty-four.[138]

There was a positive side to the alcohol and hospitality industry in Scotland which employed 200,000 people and contributed £2.4 billion in exports. In 1999/2000 the total tax revenue from excise duty and VAT on alcoholic drinks in the United Kingdom was £11.5 billion, 4.4 per cent of total government tax revenue. Some promising initiatives in the industry included deals between two licensing boards in Scotland (South Ayrshire and Perth and Kinross) and local late-night club operators to grant late night licences provided the promoters did not lower prices. This might, however, turn out to be a breach of competition law in both Britain and the European Union.[139]

The rise in the consumption of beer in off-sales had taken place at the expense of sales in licensed premises. In 1970 the consumption of beer in licensed premises was 93 litres per head, compared to 9 litres per head in off-sales. By 1998 the consumption figures were 64 litres per head in licensed premises and 31 litres in off-sales. Another major change was the normalisation of late-night extensions. Clayson had recommended more flexibility in opening hours in special circumstances, such as in holiday resorts in the summer. By 2001, 90 per cent of all licensed premises in Scotland had one or more regular extensions in opening hours, extending drinking time into late night or early mornings.[140]

INDIVIDUALISM, THE CHANGING WORKPLACE AND THE SCOTTISH PUB

In common with other northern European countries, Scotland was becoming a more individualistic society by the early twenty-first century, at least as far as housing arrangements went. Scotland shared a 'northern' pattern of household with Denmark, the Netherlands, England and Wales, France, Belgium and Luxembourg. The pattern was one of young people leaving home early to set up on their own, aside from expensive property 'hotspots', such as London where many young people stayed with their parents because they could not afford high rents or expensive mortgages. This contrasted with the 'southern' pattern of 'more traditional, family-orientated and predominantly Catholic countries', such as Italy, Spain, Portugal, Ireland and Greece. When this was combined with high divorce rates and an ageing population, it was no surprise that, by 2001, the typical Scottish household was no longer the nuclear family which now accounted for only 20 per cent of all households, compared to 34 per cent in 1981, but the single-person household, which made up 33 per cent of Scottish households, compared to 22 per cent twenty years earlier.[141] There was also a major shift in employment patterns from an economy dominated by manufacturing industry, employing mainly men in full-time jobs, to one dominated by service industries, often employing women on a part-time basis. The share of the service sector in employment in Scotland rose steadily from 24 per cent in 1951, to 33 per cent in 1971, 66 per cent in 1991 and 70 per cent by 2000.[142]

These changes all had an impact on the nature of the Scottish pub. Increasing numbers of women began to use pubs and hotels, often as part of a mixed work group, sometimes in all female groups, and, as households became increasingly affluent and owner-occupancy increased, people began to entertain more at home in mixed groups, rather than in single-sex, largely male groups in pubs. Off-sales of alcohol from off-licences or supermarkets grew steadily as a proportion of alcohol consumed at the expense of sales from licensed premises. This was partly because pubs were becoming increasingly expensive places to buy a drink compared to cut-price supermarket offers on beer, wine and spirits. Supermarkets were now responsible for some 70 per cent of sales of alcohol, pubs a diminishing 30 per cent.[143]

Table 6.2 demonstrates that, while the number of public houses in Scotland showed a modest increase from 4,080 in 1945 to 5,084 in 2001, the number of outlets for off-sales rocketed from 2,188 in 1945 to 6,336 in 2001. Similarly, the number of hotels in Scotland increased from

Table 6.2 Liquor licences in force in Scotland, number by type of premises in 1915, 1945, 1965, 1980, 1997 and 2001.

Type of premises	Number of licenses					
	1915	1945	1965	1980	1997	2001
Public house	5,088	4,080	4,213	4,472	5,267	5,084
Hotel	1,569	1,506	2,265	2,959	2,612	2,455
Restricted hotel	–	–	149	438	542	475
Off-sale	3,412	2,188	3,385	4,899	6,386	6,336
Restaurant	–	–	175	921	1,507	1,473
Refreshment	–	–	–	34	380	499
Entertainment	–	–	–	169	889	840
Total	10,069	7,774	10,187	13,892	17,583	17,162

(Source: The Nicholson Committee on Liquor Licensing Law, Edinburgh, 2003)

2,188 in 1945 to 2,455 in 2001, while licensed restaurants increased rapidly from 175 in 1965 to 1,473 in 2001 and licensed entertainment venues also increased from 169 in 1980 to 840 in 2001.

Despite all these changes, it could still be claimed by the early twenty-first century that, in Scotland, 'the backbone of leisure was the consumption of alcohol'. In 1995, Scottish men drank 20.1 units of alcohol a week compared to 18.3 in England. Scottish women drank less – 6.3 units a week compared to 7 units in England. Alcohol-related deaths rose in the last quarter of the twentieth century and the early years of the twenty-first. Some 641 deaths were alcohol related in 1979, falling to 633 in 1993, but then rising steeply to 832 in 1995, 1,292 in 2000 and 1,546 in 2006.[144] This was partly related to the rise in the number of retail outlets with liquor licences in Scotland, as shown in Table 6.2, from a total of 13,892 in 1980 to 17,162 in 2001.

Another major change was the rise of the 'superpub', much larger than the traditional pub, which meant that fewer pubs could sell larger amounts of alcohol. The prime example was the J. D. Wetherspoon's chain, set up by Tim Martin, a New Zealander, in 1979, beginning with a number of small pubs in West London. According to its website, the chain 'champions cask ale, low prices, long opening hours and no music'. In the early 1990s, Wetherspoon's began a process of selling off their smaller, less profitable outlets and replacing them with much larger outlets. They often chose large historic and redundant nineteenth-century buildings in town centres, such as banks, to convert into pubs. The chain arrived in Scotland in February 1999, opening the Standing Order in Edinburgh and the Counting House in Glasgow in the same month. By 2014, they had sixty-four pubs in Scotland, from Wick in the north (the Alexander Bain) to Dumfries in the south (the Robert the Bruce), plus three landside bars at Aberdeen, Edinburgh and Glasgow airports. The only one in the West Highlands is the Corryvreckan in Oban and there are none in the islands. The chain has 930 pubs in Britain, 128 (14 per cent) in Greater London and sixty-four in Scotland (7 per cent). Wetherspoon's pioneered the smoking ban, beginning in selected outlets in 2005 and introducing a complete ban in 2006. This predated the Health and Social Care (Scotland) Act of 2005 and the Health Act (2006) in England and Wales. It is a profitable company; half-year figures for March 2013 show revenue up 10 per cent at £626.4 million but profits down by 2 per cent to £52.1 million.[145]

While Wetherspoon's pursued the cut-price drinks route, other pubs went in the opposite direction, going upmarket by turning into gastropubs or becoming a 'destination pub' with expensive fixtures and fittings and regular artistic events to attract customers. Pete Irvine's *Scotland the Best* lists eleven gastropubs in Edinburgh, four of them in Leith, and six in Glasgow. Oran Mor in Glasgow was the brainchild of Colin Beattie who invested heavily, converting a nineteenth-century church in Glasgow's West End into a gastrodining and arts pub. He commissioned the artist Alasdair Gray to paint the murals on the ceiling and introduced the long-running format of 'A Pie, a Pint and a Play' at lunchtimes, presenting specially commissioned short plays, sometimes with the playwright present.[146] At West, on Glasgow Green, Petra Wetzel has created a venue where customers are encouraged to bring their families and their dogs, the emphasis being on quality in beer and food.[147] Other gastropubs are located in rural areas, such as the Sorn Inn in rural Ayrshire.

Despite all the social, economic and cultural changes over the centuries, Scottish pubs and drinking places still remain places of rules and rituals where people gather to mark rites of passage in life. Nowadays Scottish stag and hen parties tend to be expensive and highly organised affairs that are as likely to involve pubs and drinking places in Dublin, Prague or Riga as in Dundee, Paisley or Rothesay. Nonetheless, Scottish towns and cities still fill up on Friday and Saturday nights with single-sex groups dressed up to celebrate a forthcoming wedding. Similar rituals go on in rural areas. In April 2014, *The Herald* carried a story about a young farmer, from Guardbridge near St Andrews, Fife, who had been a victim of the farming tradition of 'blackening' on his stag night. A participant explained, 'us farmers catch the farmer that's due to get married, strip him naked, put a potato sack nappy on him, take him to the local pub, tie him up outside, feed him loads of alcohol. Then we take him back to his farm to blacken him, which is when we cover him in black waste oil from our tractors, old milk from the dairy farm, wheat ears to make it itchy and cover him in cow slurry.'[148]

Another ritual that has greatly expanded in numbers over the years is the student pub crawl at the beginning of the university year, a 'coming-of-age' rite of passage that nowadays involves equal numbers of young men and women. The Scottish pub still tends to be the place of choice to celebrate 'pay off' nights when someone leaves the workplace, and is often the starting venue for workplace Christmas celebrations. It also still features in life rituals, such as 'wetting the baby's head' after a birth, marriages and funerals.

NOTES

1. D. McCrone, *Understanding Scotland. The Sociology of a Nation*, 2nd edition (London, 2001), pp. 74–6.
2. A. McIvor, 'Women and Gender Relations', in Cooke, et al. (eds), *Modern Scottish History, 1707 to the Present*, Vol. 2: *The Modernisation of Scotland, 1850 to the Present* (East Linton, 2003), p. 175.
3. B. Crampsey, *The Young Civilian. A Glasgow Wartime Boyhood* (Edinburgh, 1987), p. 139.
4. See D. Cowling. *An Essay for Today. The Scottish New Towns, 1947 to 1997* (Edinburgh, 1997).
5. M. Simmons, *The Scottish Licensed Trade Association, 1880–1980* (Edinburgh, 1981), pp. 71–8.
6. R. Finlay, *Modern Scotland, 1914–2000* (London, 2004), pp. 220 and 224–56.
7. J. House, 'Leisure Interests', in J. Cunison and J. B. S. Gilfillan (eds), *The Third Statistical Account of Scotland, Glasgow* (Glasgow, 1958), p. 624.
8. *Evening Dispatch*, 13 March 1952 and *Scotsman*, 14 October 1952.
9. Mitchell Library, Glasgow, TD 509/13/8, Sederunt Books of Trustees of Mrs Lilias Smith, wine and spirit merchant, Greenock (died 1898), Vol. VIII, 1945–1955.
10. C. Harvie, *No Gods and Precious Few Heroes. Twentieth Century Scotland* (Edinburgh, 1998 edition), pp. 73 and 118.
11. Report of the Departmental Committee on Scottish Licensing Law (Clayson Committee) (Edinburgh, 1973), pp. xv and 97–8.
12. Interview with Paul Waterson, Golden Lion Hotel, Stirling, 30 September 2014.
13. Clayson Committee, p. xvii.
14. Dundee City Archives (DCA), Dundee Wine, Spirit and Beer Trade protection Association (DWSBTPA), GD/DLT/1/8, Minute Book No. 9, 1959–1966, 102nd Annual Report, pp. 6–7.

15. Clayson Committee, p. xvi.
16. D. R. Ritchie, A. Imrie and J. R. James, 'The Traveller and the Inn' in D. Keir (ed.), *The Third Statistical Account of Scotland, Edinburgh* (Glasgow, 1966), p. 673.
17. *Evening Dispatch*, 5 October 1963.
18. *Evening News*, 30 August 1965.
19. *Edinburgh Evening News*, 16 March 1965.
20. *Evening News and Dispatch*, 31 May 1965.
21. *Scotsman*, 16 January 1967.
22. *Scotsman*, 19 May 1966.
23. *Evening News*, 25 October 1969
24. *Scotsman*, 23 and 26 May 1970.
25. Simmons, *SLTA*, pp. 106–7.
26. *Scotsman*, 26 September 1972 and 9 January 1976.
27. *Scotsman*, 5 March 1973.
28. *Scotsman*, 14 December 1981.
29. Finlay, *Modern Scotland*, p. 382.
30. House, 'Leisure Interests', p. 624.
31. A. Hopkins, *The Aberdeen Pub Companion* (Aberdeen, 1975), p. 11.
32. House, 'Leisure Interests', p. 625.
33. *Evening News*, 18 December 1969.
34. DCA, GD/DLT/1/8, DWSPBTPA, Minute Book, No. 9, 1959–1966.
35. T. Collins and W. Vamplew, *Mud, Sweat and Beers. A Cultural History of Sport and Alcohol* (Oxford, 2002), pp. 83–4.
36. R. Giulianotti, 'Taking liberties: Hibs casuals and Scottish law', in R. Giulianotti, N. Bonney and M. Hepworth (eds), *Football, Violence and Social Identity* (London, 1994), pp. 229–61.
37. W. McIlvanney, 'Tig', in W. McIlvanney, *Walking Wounded* (London, 1990 edition), pp. 101–8.
38. W. McIlvanney, *Laidlaw* (London, 1977), p. 94.
39. W. McIlvanney, 'Mick's Day', in McIlvanney, *Walking Wounded*, pp. 95–100.
40. I. Rankin, *The Hanging Garden* (London, 1998), p. 134.
41. Quoted in J. Bruce-Gardyne and J. Skinner, *Rebus's Favourite. The Deuchars Guide to Edinburgh Pubs* (London, 2007), p. 22.
42. I. Rankin, *Resurrection Men* (London, 2001), pp. 241–2.
43. Quoted in Bruce-Gardyne and Skinner, *Rebus's Favourite*, p. 27.
44. I. Welsh, *Trainspotting* (London, 2004 edition), pp. 59–60 and 126–8.
45. I. Welsh, *Porno* (London, 2013 edition), p. 46.
46. *The Daily Telegraph*, 15 January 2010, and *The Sun*, 19 January 2010.
47. *Daily Record*, 4 August 2006, and *Evening Times*, 16 September 2008.
48. A. Maxwell, *The History of Old Dundee* (Dundee, 1884), p. 80.
49. See www.jazzfest.co.uk for Glasgow Jazz Festival.

50. See www.aberdeenjazzfestival.com and www.edinburghjazzfestival.com for Aberdeen and Edinburgh Jazz Festivals.

51. A. Foster, *The Literary Traveller in Edinburgh* (Edinburgh, 2005), p. 53.

52. P. Stephenson, *Billy* (London, 2001), pp. 110–12.

53. C. Bell (ed.), *Scotland's Century. An Autobiography of the Nation* (Glasgow, 1999), pp. 232–3.

54. See J. McMillan, 'The Performing Arts', in G. Hassan and C. Warhurst (eds), *Anatomy of the New Scotland. Power, Influence and Change* (Edinburgh, 2002), p. 211.

55. Interview with Paul Waterson, 30 September 2014.

56. Leaflet on The History of the Salutation Hotel, Perth from 1699.

57. B. Hogg, *The History of Scottish Rock and Pop* (Enfield, 1993), pp. 87, 237, 273 and 322.

58. J. Patrick, *A Glasgow Gang Observed*, London, 1973), p. 34.

59. Bell, *Scotland's Century*, p. 279.

60. *Evening News,* 11 November 1980.

61. L. Settle, 'The Social Geography of Prostitution in Edinburgh, 1900–1939', *JSHS*, Vol. 33. No. 2, 2013, pp. 234–59.

62. A. Stewart, *Where is She Tonight? Women, Street Prostitution and Homelessness in Glasgow* (Glasgow, 2000), pp. 16, 31 and 33.

63. *The Herald*, 9 February 2013.

64. I should like to acknowledge the assistance I received in writing this section from Brian Dempsey and Richard Dunphy, both of Dundee University, who both gave me extremely helpful advice, particularly in suggesting reading material.

65. Finlay, *Modern Scotland*, p. 293.

66. R. Jenkins, *A Life at the Centre* (London, 1992 edition), p. 208.

67. B. Dempsey, *Thon Wey. Aspects of Scottish lesbian and gay activism, 1968 to 1992* (undated paper, 1992?, publisher unnamed).

68. B. Cant (ed.), *Footsteps and Witnesses. Lesbian and Gay Lifestories from Scotland* (Edinburgh, 1993).

69. Cant (ed.), *Footsteps and Witnesses*, p. 19.

70. L. Settle, 'The Social Geography of Prostitution in Edinburgh, 1900–1939, *Journal of Scottish Historical Studies*, Vol. 33, No. 2, 2013, pp. 234–59.

71. Cant (ed.), p. 35.

72. Cant (ed.), pp. 50–1.

73. Cant (ed.), p. 58.

74. Cant (ed.), pp. 67 and 83.

75. Cant (ed.), pp. 95 and 104–5.

76. P. Irvine, *Scotland the Best* (London, 2011), pp. 196–7.

77. Settle, 'Social Geography of Prostitution', pp. 234–59.

78. Irvine, *Scotland the Best*, pp. 197–8.

79. Cant (ed.), p. 104.

80. Clayson Committee, p. 5.
81. Clayson Committee, pp. 10 and 27–34, and Harvie, *No Gods and Precious Few Heroes*, p. 156.
82. Clayson Committee, p. 38.
83. Clayson Committee, pp. 97–113.
84. Interview with Jim Clancy, Lauriston Bar, Glasgow, 28 January 2014.
85. Clayson Committee, pp. 34 and 158–64.
86. T. Shields, *Great Scottish Pubs* (Alexandria, 1975?), not paginated.
87. Bell (ed.), *Scotland's Century*, p. 187.
88. K. McGregor and L. Tweedie, *Life Behind Bars. Confessions of a Pub Landlady* (Edinburgh, 2011).
89. Interview with Jim Clancy, 28 January 2014.
90. Interview with Willie Mutch, Windsor Bar, Albert Street, Dundee, 18 September 2014.
91. See P. L. Payne, 'Industrialisation and Industrial Decline', in Cooke, et al., *Modern Scottish History 1707 to the Present*, Vol. 2, *1850 to the Present* (East Linton, 1998), pp. 73–94.
92. Interview with Jim Clancy, 28 January 2014.
93. Interview with Willie Mutch, 18 September 2014
94. Interview with Jonathan Stewart, Mennie's Bar, Dundee, 4 and 13 September 2013.
95. Interview with Alistair Don, Doublet Bar, Glasgow, 10 December 2013.
96. Interview with Paul Waterson, Golden Lion Hotel, Stirling, 30 September 2014.
97. Interview with Marshall Bain, Queen Charlotte Rooms, Leith, 27 November 2013.
98. Interview with Petra Wetzel, West, Glasgow Green, 18 August 2014.
99. Interview with Willie Mutch, 18 September 2014.
100. Interview with Marshall Bain, 27 November 2013.
101. Interview with Jonathan Stewart.
102. Interview with Alistair Don, Doublet Bar, Glasgow.
103. Interview with Jim Clancy.
104. Interview with Alistair Don.
105. Interview with Jim Clancy.
106. Interview with Willie Mutch.
107. Interview with Petra Wetzel.
108. M. Simmons, *The Scottish Licensed Trade Association* (SLTA), *1880–1980* (Edinburgh, 1981), p. 70.
109. Dundee City Archives (DCA), GD/DLT/1/8, DWSBTPA, Minute Book, No. 9, 1959–1966.
110. *National Guardian*, 4 January 1975.
111. W. McIlvanney, 'At the Bar', in McIlvanney, *Walking Wounded*, pp. 73–6.
112. Interview with Willie Mutch.

113. Interview with Paul Waterson.
114. Interview with Petra Wetzel.
115. Simmons, *SLTA*, p. 76.
116. J. House, 'Leisure Interests', in J. Cunnison and J. B. S. Gilfillan (eds), *The Third Statistical Account of Scotland, Glasgow* (Glasgow, 1958), pp. 622–3.
117. R J Finlay, *Modern Scotland, 1914–2000* (London, 2004), p. 239
118. C. Hanley, *Dancing in the Streets* (1958) (Edinburgh, 1983 edition), pp. 258–9.
119. C. Bell (ed.), *Scotland's Century. An Autobiography of the Nation* (Glasgow, 1999), p. 71.
120. Bell (ed.), *Scotland's Century*, p. 225.
121. Shields, *Great Scottish Pubs*.
122. J. Kelman, *The Bus Conductor Hines* (London, 1985 edition), pp. 47–52.
123. Interview with Willie Mutch.
124. Interview with Jim Clancy.
125. National Records of Scotland, Edinburgh, NRS, SEP 4, 4995, Monopolies and Mergers Commission, 1986 onwards, letter from Belhaven Brewery Company, Dunbar to the Clerk of the Agricultural Committee, Millbank, London, 29 December 1992.
126. Glasgow University Archives (GUA), Scottish Brewing Archive (SBA), CAM 12/1/1-7, *The Herald*, 19 June 1992, p. 8 (Advertising Feature to celebrate 20 years of CAMRA)
127. GUA, SBA, CAM 12/4/1/4, *What's Brewing*, October 1973.
128. GUA, SBA, CAM, 12/1/1-7, *The Herald*, 19 June 1992, p. 8.
129. GUA, SBA, CAM 12/4/1/4, *What's Brewing*, Summer 1980, pp. 41–2 and 48–9.
130. GUA, SBA, CAM 12/1/2, *Daily Record*, 19 August 1982.
131. GUA, SBA, CAM 12/1/5, *Scottish Licensed Trade News*, 8 December 1983.
132. GUA, SBA, CAM 12/1/3, *The Herald*, 19 June 1992.
133. Interview with Paul Waterson, 30 September 2014.
134. *Independent*, 26 January 2008.
135. K. Cunningham, *Business as Usual. The Miquel Way* (Durham, 2012).
136. *The Nicholson Committee, Review of Liquor Licensing Law in Scotland* (Edinburgh, 2003), pp. 1–3.
137. *Nicholson Committee*, pp. 35–7.
138. *Nicholson Committee*, pp. 37–9.
139. *Nicholson Committee*, pp. 42 and 128.
140. *Nicholson Committee*, pp. 27–8.
141. L. Paterson, F. Beckhofer and D. McCrone, *Living in Scotland. Social and Economic Change since 1980* (Edinburgh, 2004), pp. 31–2.
142. McCrone, *Understanding Scotland*, p. 74.
143. Interviews with Jonathan Stewart and with Colin Wilkinson, Secretary, Scottish Licensed Trade Association, Edinburgh, 6 November 2013. Colin

claimed that the top five supermarkets were responsible for 75 per cent of drink sales in Scotland.

144. C. Brown, 'Charting Everyday Experience', in L. Abrams and C. Brown (eds), *A History of Everyday Life in Twentieth-Century Scotland* (Edinburgh, 2010), pp. 40–1.
145. See the Wetherspoon's website at www.ucl.ac.uk/-ccaajpa/pubs-spoons
146. Irvine, *Scotland the Best*, 2011, pp. 43–4, 98 and 138.
147. Interview with Petra Wetzel, 18 August 2014.
148. *The Herald*, 26 April 2014.

Conclusion

HISTORIANS HAVE BEEN SLOW to recognise the importance of Scottish drinking places in the social, economic and cultural life of the country. Scottish pubs and their many variants were closely bound up with issues of national identity which has often been defined in opposition to 'the other', those who do not share the cultural, linguistic, religious or ethnic backgrounds of the host country. They were often the places where Scots first encountered 'the other' in the form of English, French or German visitors to the country, and where visitors encountered Scots for the first time. Sometimes, 'the other' simply described encounters between land dwellers and seafarers, as in the scene in Robert Louis Stevenson's *Kidnapped*, where Davy Balfour, who has never seen the sea in his life, is taken to the Hawes Inn at South Queensferry by his rascally uncle Ebenezer, then lured aboard the brig *Covenant* by Captain Hoseason, drugged and kidnapped for a life of servitude in the Carolinas.[1] This fictional scenario must have had many real-life equivalents, when young men were plied with drink in dockside or harbour pubs and then press-ganged for the navy, or when indentured servants or petty criminals were transported to the colonies. A less emotionally charged encounter takes place in Walter Scott's *Guy Mannering* between the English Colonel Mannering and the Edinburgh lawyer Counsellor Paulus Pleydell whom Mannering tracks down to an Edinburgh tavern where he finds him 'in his hebdomadal carousals' playing 'the ancient and now forgotten pastime of High Jinks' with his drinking companions.[2]

Real-life encounters between different cultures could be particularly fraught in the Scottish Highlands where an aristocratic French visitor, the Duc de la Rochefoucald, was horrified in 1786 to find that, at an inn near Fort Augustus, 'the whole family (running the inn) has scabies', so the travellers couldn't face the home-made oatcakes on offer but ate eggs instead. At another inn, at Bonawe on Loch Etive, the landlady had been in Britain for only twelve years and scandalised them with a frank account of her colourful life history. She redeemed herself, however, by serving up, 'an entire pig and the best port wine I've ever drunk'.[3] Even Lowland Scots could feel they were in a foreign country when travelling in the Highlands. James Hogg, the Ettrick Shepherd, described a visit in 1803 to an inn at Inverslich where there was only one bedroom for visitors. This was invaded during the night by 'a whole band of Highlanders, both male and female, who entered my room and fell to drinking whisky with great freedom'. Hogg described them as a 'party of vagabonds' and managed to foil an attempt by one of the men to pickpocket his waistcoat in the dark.[4]

Some of the inns and taverns north of the Highland line were run by Englishmen or women, often with a background in the armed forces, or by Scots former soldiers and sailors who had experienced the Empire at first hand during the many overseas wars of the eighteenth century. In the first category, we find the 'forward, vulgar, handsome woman from Portsmouth' (a major naval base) who was running the Grant Arms at Grantown on Spey in Inverness-shire when Robert Southey and Thomas Telford visited in 1819.[5] The remarkable Mrs M'Kenzie, who ran the Horns Inn at Tomintoul, Banffshire in the 1790s, falls into the second category. She had travelled extensively with her husband, a soldier in the Royal Highlanders, to Germany, France, Holland, England, Ireland, America and the West Indies,[6] making her just as much a child of Empire as the better documented Johnstones of Dumfriesshire, a gentry family described in Emma Rothschild's book, *The Inner Life of Empires*.[7]

The Scottish sense of 'the other' included immigrants, particularly those of a different religion. In the nineteenth century the arrival of Irish migrants, many of them Roman Catholic, in the west of Scotland, and to urban centres, such as Edinburgh and Dundee, was thought to threaten the Scottish Calvinistic sense of identity and 'respectability'. The Irish migrants were stereotyped as having lower levels of education and hygiene than the native Scots, as undercutting the Scots as regards wages and being overly addicted to whisky. The manager of the Blantyre cotton mills in Lanarkshire, where the workforce was mainly composed of Ulster Protestants, claimed in 1835 that 'in a small community like this, the Irish do not associate much with the Scotch; they spend their evenings and Sundays together and in all cases whisky is consumed'.[8] In the Ayrshire weaving parish of Maybole, the Reverend George Gray fulminated in 1837 about the 'drunken and filthy' habits of the Irish weavers.[9] From Greenock in Renfrewshire, a stronghold of the early temperance movement, the Reverend Patrick McFarlan launched an attack in 1840 on 'intemperance and licentiousness' which he blamed on 'the immigration from other quarters, of families unaccustomed in their infancy to the habits of a well-educated Scottish population [which] has tended not a bit to lower the standard by which they are wont to regulate their conduct'.[10] In other words, the immigrant Irish were accused of dragging the native Scots down to their own low standards of behaviour.

In Victorian Scotland, 'the other' often included the urban poor who were the subject of much horrified and prurient interest by middle-class observers, particularly as regards their drinking behaviour and sexual morality. This explains the number of sensationalist exposés in the Victorian Scottish press and in temperance tracts about conditions in the slums of Aberdeen, Dundee, Edinburgh and, above all, in Glasgow. In Edinburgh, the evangelical Dr George Bell described living conditions in the inner-city slums around Blackfriars Wynd, claiming 'the Scots are the most drunken people on the face of the earth' and complaining that 'the dram shops open before sunrise and they remain open until an hour short of midnight'. Bell was virulently anti-Irish and compared the 'base, abject, apathetic Irish beggar' to the 'virtuous and industrious Lowland Scotch mechanic'.[11]

Similar concerns and anxieties were expressed by Alexander Brown, an evangelical Glasgow journalist, who published a sensationalist exposure of the Glasgow slums in 1858 under the title *Shadow's Midnight Scenes*. On entering the Bridgegate in Glasgow on a Sunday night, Brown immediately echoed the theme of 'otherness' when he commented, 'the impression at once felt is that of intrusion. No nautical explorer ever fell among savages who looked with greater wonder at his approach.'[12] Another evangelical writer, David Barrie, condemned a 'very badly conducted public house' in a 'low lying neighbourhood' of Dundee, where 'wretched men and women and very young children in dirt and rags poured in and out to the great disgust of many of the neighbours'.[13]

The response of the local authorities to these revelations was to restrict the numbers of licensed premises, regulate their opening hours, and intervene in great detail as regards the internal layout of pubs and even the number of entrances and exits they had. This attempt to control drinking behaviour, linked to lobbying by the temperance movement, was part of a concerted attempt to regulate street behaviour, particularly on Sundays, when displays of public drunkenness were frequent in mid century and female prostitution was rife. The Forbes McKenzie Act of 1853, which fixed licensing hours and introduced Sunday closing for pubs, was a watershed in the battle for control of the streets, though much drinking went underground.

The temperance campaign continued into the first half of the twentieth century as the movement, with powerful allies in the Liberal and Labour parties, lobbied to restrict or ban the licensed trade altogether. During World War I, this led to the nationalisation of the licensed trade around Gretna because of the local munitions industry and, in Invergordon, a major naval base. This was followed by the Local Veto Campaign of the 1920s and a high degree of state regulation during World War II which carried on for some time afterwards.

After World War II, changes in Scottish public houses and licensed premises reflected wider changes in society, as living standards rose and women became more independent economically and socially. Pubs and licensed premises responded to this by improvements in levels of comfort, by the increasingly important provision of food, sometimes to a very high standard, and introducing child-friendly facilities. Other changes have been in response to the growth of the student market and 'youth culture', such as the emergence of large 'superpubs', of cut-price chains, such as Wetherspoon's, and the provision of live or recorded music in pubs and licensed clubs.

As a result of legislation and social and economic changes, Scotland has seen greatly extended opening hours for licensed premises and the normalisation of the late-night extension. Another major change has been the enormous growth in off-sales of alcohol, particularly from supermarkets, so that the bulk of alcohol drinking today takes place in the home rather than in the pub. All these changes provide challenges to the licensed trade which are being met by a new generation of licensees, committed to different ways of producing and selling alcohol than the traditional male drinker's pub.

NOTES

1. R. L. B. Stevenson, *Kidnapped* (London, 1994), pp. 39–43.
2. W. Scott, *Guy Mannering or the Astrologer* (Edinburgh, 1886), pp. 252–3.
3. N. Scarfe (ed.), *To the Highlands in 1786* (Woodbridge, 2001), pp. 166–7 and 184–9.
4. J. Hogg, *A Tour in the Highlands in 1803* (Paisley, 1888), pp. 54–5.
5. R. Southey, *Journal of a Tour in Scotland in 1819* (London, 1929), pp. 98–9.
6. *OSA*, Vol. XVI, *Banffshire, Moray and Nairnshire*, pp. 279–80.
7. E. Rothschild, *The Inner Life of Empires* (Princeton, 2001).

8. *Parliamentary Papers*, 1836, Vol. XXXIV, Appendix G, *Report on the State of the Irish Poor in Great Britain*, 1835, p. 108.
9. *New Statistical Account (NSA)*, Vol. V, *Ayr and Bute* (Edinburgh, 1845), p. 368.
10. *NSA*, Vol. VII, *Renfrew and Argyle* (Edinburgh, 1845), p. 429.
11. G. Bell, *Day and Night in the Wynds of Edinburgh, 1849* (Wakefield, 1973 edition), pp. 7, 25 and 29.
12. J. F. McCaffrey (ed.), *Glasgow 1858, Shadow's Midnight Scenes and Social Photographs* (Glasgow, 1976), pp. 17–18.
13. D. Barrie, *The City of Dundee Illustrated* (Dundee, 1890), p. 228.

Appendix 1
An Author's Dozen (plus three)

A PERSONAL SELECTION

THIS IS A PERSONAL and highly selective choice of Scottish pubs, some historic, some personal favourites. It is intended merely to give a flavour of the variety of pubs to be found in Scotland. Many fine pubs have been left out for reasons of space. Edinburgh and Glasgow, in particular, have a wide range of interesting pubs which could not all be included. For historians, the Guildford Arms is close to Register House, Edinburgh which houses the National Records of Scotland, and the Lismore Bar in Partick is within walking distance of Glasgow University Archives where the Scottish Brewing Archive is housed. My apologies to readers if I have left out their favourites.

Aberdeen: Prince of Wales, 7–11 St Nicholas Lane, Aberdeen AB10 1HF. Tucked away in a lane off Union Street in the shadow of the Kirk of St Nicholas. A fine mid-Victorian pub (1850) with real ales.

Dumfries: The Globe Inn, 56 High Street, Dumfries DG1 2JA. A seventeenth-century (1610) howff where Robert Burns drank during his time as an excise man in Dumfries. The atmospheric wood-panelled private rooms to the left of the entrance contain Burns's favourite chair and verses he scratched on the window (Figure 1.1).

Dundee: The Phoenix Bar, Nethergate, Dundee DD1 4DH. A Victorian tenement pub built in 1856 but with a greatly altered interior. Well-kept beer and a selection of the landlord's art collection displayed on the walls, some with pub connections, such as Peter Howson's faces of Glasgow drinkers.

Dundee: The Speedwell Bar (Mennies), 165–167, Perth Road, Dundee DD2 1AS. Unspoilt Edwardian interior (built 1903). Wide choice of real ales and 160 single malts (Figure 6.3).

Edinburgh: Bennet's Bar, 8 Leven Street, Tollcross, Edinburgh EH3 9LG. A wonderful theatrical pub next to the King's Theatre, with an Edwardian interior, refitted in 1906. Good beer and a choice of 120 single malt whiskies.

Edinburgh: The Guildford Arms, 1 West Register Street, Edinburgh EH2 2AA. Across the road from Waverley Station. Owned by the Stewart family since 1898. Good food and a wide range of real ales.

Edinburgh: The Oxford Bar, 8 Young Street, Edinburgh EH2 4JB. A very plain pub, built in 1811 as a shop. Immortalised by Ian Rankin in his Rebus novels as the 'Ox'.

Gairloch, Wester Ross: The Old Inn, IV21 2BD. Beautifully situated by the river and old bridge, with resident ducks. Real ales and malt whiskies, meals with an emphasis on seafood.

Glasgow: Horseshoe Bar, 17–19 Drury Street, Glasgow G2 5AE. Tucked away in a back street near Central Station. The longest continuous [104 feet (32 metres), horseshoe-shaped] bar in Britain. Rangers FC memorabilia round the walls (cover illustration).

Glasgow: Lauriston Bar, Bridge Street, Glasgow G5 9HU. On the other side of the Clyde from Central Station. A friendly bar run by the Clancy family on the Southside. A setting for 'Young Adam', a film about Alexander Trocchi, the Glasgow-born beat poet. The walls are lined with football and show-business photographs and memorabilia. Close to underground station.

Glasgow: Lismore Bar, 206 Dumbarton Road, Glasgow G11 6UN. Neighbourhood bar in Partick catering for a varied clientele, including students and some of Glasgow's Highland community. The gents' toilet features caustic comments on the landowners who carried out the Highland Clearances.

Mauchline, Ayrshire: Poosie Nansie's Inn, 21 Loudoun Street, KA5 5BA. An amazing survival, the setting for Burns's poem, *The Jolly Beggars*. Ask to see the room on the right of the main entrance which has been kept much as it was in Burns's day, with period furniture and fittings (Figure 2.4).

Pitlochry, Perthshire: The Moulin Hotel, Moulin PH16 5EH. An old coaching inn dating back to 1695, but greatly altered and expanded, in a beautiful situation, near the start of the path to Ben Vrackie. Open fires, decent food and excellent beer from its own brewery.

Rosemarkie, Inverness-shire: The Plough, 48 High Street, Rosemarkie IV10 8UF. Small village pub rebuilt in 1907 on an older site (lintel dated 1691 over fireplace).

Skye: The Stein Inn, Waternish, Skye IV55 8GA. Housed in a row of old cottages. Its waterside setting is typical of many pubs and hotels in the Highlands and Islands (Figures 3.3 and 3.4).

More comprehensive lists of Scottish pubs are given in:

Y. Hillyard, *Raising the Bar, An Introduction to Scotland's Historic Pubs*, Historic Scotland, Edinburgh, 2012.

P. Irvine, *Scotland the Best*, HarperCollins, London, 2011.

R. Protz (ed.), *Good Beer Guide, 2014*, CAMRA, St Albans, 2013.

M. Slaughter (ed.), *Scotland's True Heritage Pubs*, CAMRA, St Albans, 2007.

Appendix 2
Which is the Oldest Pub in Scotland?

D AVID WALKER, FORMER Chief Inspector for Historic Scotland, who spent a lifetime studying and recording historic buildings, came to the conclusion that 'no surviving building in Scotland, proven to have been built as an inn, is older than the seventeenth century', though earlier origins are claimed for a number of sites, including Tarbert, Loch Lomond, Dunbartonshire, which has a recorded history dating back to the sixteenth century.[1] The problem is that, though some Scottish pubs claim to have been founded from the twelfth to the sixteenth centuries, they have usually been rebuilt on the site of an earlier building or housed in an older building that was not built as an inn or a pub. In Edinburgh, the White Hart Inn at 34 Grassmarket is one of the oldest surviving inns in the capital, dating back to 1516, though only the cellars survive from this time, the present building dating from 1740.[2]

Some of the oldest inn and pub buildings in Scotland are situated in historic burghs, away from the pressures of redevelopment to be found in cities and larger urban centres. In Haddington, East Lothian, the former Bluebell Inn is a three-storeyed building, with a corbelled stair tower at the front, which dates from the late sixteenth or early seventeenth centuries. In the royal burgh of Falkland in Fife, the Stag Inn is dated 1630, while the Falkland Arms, another old inn, has an inscription dated 1607, from when it was a house.[3] Falkland is the likely home of Kind Kittock, the Fife alewife or 'Guddame', the central character of William Dunbar's poem *The Ballad of Kind Kittock*, so it seems an appropriate place to find early inns.[4] In another royal burgh, Linlithgow in West Lothian, the Four Marys pub on the High Street opposite Linlithgow Palace is housed in a building dating back to about 1500, though it began life as a house and was a chemist's shop in the nineteenth century.[5]

At Laurencekirk in Kincardineshire, the Boar's Head, now the Gardenstone Arms, has a date stone of 1638 but was rebuilt by Lord Gardenstone between 1770 and 1778 as part of a planned village. In Moffat, Dumfriesshire, the oldest inn is the Black Bull, opposite the parish church. It is a low, two-storeyed building, very different in appearance from the two mid Georgian inns in the burgh. The Whitehorse Inn in Edinburgh's Canongate has a date stone of 1623 though the inn was restored in 1889 and drastically rebuilt in 1962.[6]

Two of the oldest surviving inns or taverns in the country are in the border town of Dumfries, on the main road north between England and Glasgow. The Globe Inn, 56 High Street dates from 1610 and has survived thanks to its associations with Robert Burns who worked as an excise man in Dumfries from 1791 until his death in 1796. The 'howff', or room where Burns drank, with its wood-panelled walls and original furniture, is a remarkable and atmospheric survival and well worth a visit[7] (Figure 1.1). Another Dumfries pub, the Hole I' the Wa', 156 High Street, situated in a close off the High Street, dates back to 1620.

Another remarkable survival is Poosie Nansie's Inn in Mauchline, Ayrshire. This was the beggars' lodging house that inspired Burns to write his poem, *The Jolly Beggars*. The present-day pub contains an unremarkable public bar, with television switched on to the racing and the bar covered in racing papers. On the other side of the main entrance, however, is a room which has been preserved largely as it was in Burns's time, with period furniture and Burns memorabilia (Figure 2.4). Surprisingly, Poosie Nansie's is not included in either *Scotland's True Heritage Pubs* or *Raising the Bar* though, culturally and historically, it is a good deal more significant than many of those that are included.[8] Across the road from Poosie Nansie's, but no longer a pub, is the Whitefoord Arms, where the innkeeper was Johnnie Doo' or Johnnie Pigeon, immortalised in Burns's satirical obituary.[9] Mauchline also boasts an early ale house, Nanse Tinnock's Tavern or the Sma' Inn, across the road from the Burns House where Burns started his official married life with Jean Armour. It is open to the public as part of the Burns House Museum but houses a collection of Mauchline Ware and curling stones rather than anything associated with its original function.[10]

The Crook Inn, at Tweedsmuir in the Scottish Borders, began life as a drover's inn in 1604. The inn is currently closed, awaiting restoration by the community-owned Tweedsmuir Community Company which raised £160,000 for its purchase. Willie Wastle's Bar in the inn is a late nineteenth-century recreation, further altered in the 1936 renovation. It is named after Burns's visit to the Crook Inn when he was inspired to write the poem 'Willie Wastle's Wife' after she rejected his advances. The inn was a hiding place for local Covenanters in the seventeenth century and was visited by Sir Walter Scott and John Buchan among others. It was converted to a house in 1913 but reopened as an inn in

1936 when it was heavily restored and extended in the art deco style, including some remarkable art deco lavatories[11] (Figure 5.4).

NOTES

1. D. Walker, 'Inns, hotels and related building types', in G. Stell, J. Shaw and S. Stonier (eds), *Scottish Life and Society. A Compendium of Scottish Ethnology*, Vol. 3, *Scotland's Buildings* (East Linton, 2003), p. 127.
2. A. Foster, *The Literary Traveller in Edinburgh* (Edinburgh, 2005), p. 57.
3. Walker, 'Inns, hotels', p. 127.
4. T. and W. MacQueen (eds), *A Choice of Scottish Verse, 1470–1570* (London, 1972), pp. 134–5.
5. R. Protz (ed.), *The Good Beer Guide, 2014* (St Albans, 2013), p. 634.
6. Walker, 'Inns, hotels', pp. 127 and 135–6; and R. J. Morris, 'Whitehorse Close: Philanthropy, Scottish Historical Imagination and the Re-Building of Edinburgh in the later Nineteenth Century', *Journal of Scottish Historical Studies*, Vol. 33, No. 1, 2013, pp. 101–28.
7. M. Slaughter, *Scotland's True Heritage Pubs* (St Albans, 2007), pp. 28–9.
8. Slaughter, *Scotland's True Heritage Pubs*; and Y. Hillyard, *Raising the Bar* (Edinburgh, 2012).
9. *The Works and Correspondence of Robert Burns* (Glasgow, no date), p. 138.
10. See the leaflet *Robert Burns Blue Plaque Guide* (Burns House Museum, Mauchline)
11. Slaughter, *Scotland's True Heritage Pubs*, pp. 80–1; and Crook Inn websites.

Appendix 3
Map of Scotland Showing Locations of Pubs, Taverns and Hotels in Appendices 1 and 2 and in the List of Illustrations

Key to locations:

1. The Bluebell Inn, 10 High Street, Annan, Dumfriesshire DG12 6AG
2. The Globe Inn, 56 High Street, Dumfries DG1 2JA
3. Poosie Nansie's Inn, 21 Loudoun Street, Mauchline, Ayrshire KA5 5BA
4. The Crook Inn, Tweedsmuir, Scottish Borders ML12 6QN
5. Glasgow – Horseshoe Bar, G2 5AE; Lauriston Bar, G5 9HU; Lismore Bar, G11 6UN
6. The Four Marys, 65–67 High Street, Linlithgow, West Lothian EH49 7ED
7. The Hawes Inn, 7 Newhalls Road, South Queensferry, West Lothian EH30 9TA
8. Edinburgh – Bennet's Bar, EH3 9LG; The Blue Blazer, EH3 9DX; Guildford Arms, EH2 2AA; (Grosvenor) Maybury Casino, EH12 8NE; Oxford Bar, EH2 4JB; Sheep Heid Inn, Duddingston EH15 3QA
9. Prestoungrange Gothenburg Tavern, 227 High Street, Prestonpans, East Lothian EH32 9BE
10. The Golden Lion Hotel, 8–10 King Street, Stirling FK8 1DQ
11. The Salutation Hotel, 30–34 South Street, Perth PH2 8PH
12. Dundee – Phoenix Bar, DD1 4DH; Speedwell Bar, DD2 1AS; The Shand Bar (formerly the Jimmy Shand), Dickson Avenue, Menzieshill DD2 4HJ
13. Moulin Hotel, Moulin, Pitlochry, Perthshire PH16 5EH
14. Prince of Wales, 7–11 St Nicholas Lane, Aberdeen AB10 1HF
15. Stein Inn, Waternish, Skye IV55 8GA
16. Plough Inn, Rosemarkie, Inverness-shire IV10 8UF
17. The Old Inn, Gairloch, Wester Ross IV21 2BD
18. The Old Ship Inn, 1 North Ness, Hoy, Orkney KW16 (no longer an inn)

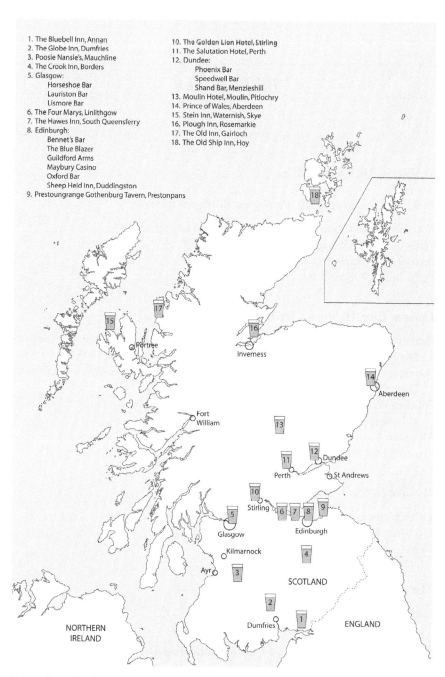

1. The Bluebell Inn, Annan
2. The Globe Inn, Dumfries
3. Poosie Nansie's, Mauchline
4. The Crook Inn, Borders
5. Glasgow:
   Horseshoe Bar
   Lauriston Bar
   Lismore Bar
6. The Four Marys, Linlithgow
7. The Hawes Inn, South Queensferry
8. Edinburgh:
   Bennet's Bar
   The Blue Blazer
   Guildford Arms
   Maybury Casino
   Oxford Bar
   Sheep Heid Inn, Duddingston
9. Prestoungrange Gothenburg Tavern, Prestonpans

10. The Golden Lion Hotel, Stirling
11. The Salutation Hotel, Perth
12. Dundee:
    Phoenix Bar
    Speedwell Bar
    Shand Bar, Menzieshill
13. Moulin Hotel, Moulin, Pitlochry
14. Prince of Wales, Aberdeen
15. Stein Inn, Waternish, Skye
16. Plough Inn, Rosemarkie
17. The Old Inn, Gairloch
18. The Old Ship Inn, Hoy

Map of Scotland showing location of pubs, taverns and hotels in Appendices 1 and 2 and in List of Illustrations.

Bibliography

MANUSCRIPT SOURCES

A. K. Bell Library, Perth, Perth and Kinross Archives

Account of the Commissioners for the Bridge of Perth, 1766
Perth Burgh Licensing Court
Perth Burgh Magistrates Court
Perth Burgh Police Commissioners

Dundee City Archives, City Square, Dundee

Draft Typescript History of Dundee Wine, Spirit and Beer Protection Association, 1863–1907 (*c*.1950)
Dundee, Lochee and Broughty Ferry Licensed Grocers' Association, Minute Books, 1877–1975
Dundee Wine, Spirit and Beer Trade Protection Association, Minute Books, 8 volumes, 1888–1966 and Letter Book, 1950–59
Maltmen Incorporation of Dundee, 1653–1871
Plans of Dundee Public Houses, 1903–1923

Dundee City Libraries

Lamb Collection
Licensing Court Records
Register of Inebriates, 1905

Mrs Judith Cooke, Dundee

Pae Manuscripts

Glasgow University Archives (Scottish Brewing Archive)

Campaign for Real Ale (CAMRA)
Glasgow District Licensed Trade Defence Association, Minute Books, 1899–1933

Glasgow District Licensed Trade Defence Association, Directors' Minutes, 1928–1933
Tennent Caledonian Breweries' Archives

Mitchell Library, Glasgow

Dollan Mss, Unpublished Autobiography of Sir Patrick Dollan, 'From the miners' row to the Lord Provost's room'
Glasgow Chamber of Commerce Papers
Glasgow Dean of Guild, Public House Plans, 1885–96
Sederunt Books of Alexander Baird, James Craig Jr, George Eunson Trust, J. Bryce Loudon, Patrick McAllister, Daniel Mackay, Lilias Smith

National Records of Scotland, Edinburgh

Breadalbane Estate Papers
Campbell of Jura Papers
Commissary Courts of Dundee, Edinburgh, Glasgow
Court of Session Papers
Monopolies Commission, Report on supply of beer, 1969
Sheriff Courts of Ayrshire, Edinburgh, Glasgow, Hamilton and Paisley

INTERVIEWS WITH SCOTTISH LICENSEES

Interviews between September 2013 and September 2014 with Marshall Bain, Queen Charlotte Rooms, Leith; Jim Clancy, Lauriston Bar, Glasgow; Alistair Don, Doublet Bar, Glasgow; Willie Mutch, Windsor Bar, Dundee; Jonathan Stewart, Speedwell Bar, Dundee; Paul Waterson, Golden Lion, Stirling; Petra Wetzel, West, Glasgow and Colin Wilkinson, Secretary, Scottish Licensed Trade Association, Edinburgh.

PRINTED SOURCES

Books and Articles

Abrams, L. and Brown, C. G. (eds) (2010), *A History of Everyday Life in Twentieth-Century Scotland*, Edinburgh: Edinburgh University Press.
Abrams, L., Gordon, E., Simonton, D. and Yeo, E. J. (eds) (2006), *Gender in Scottish History since 1700*, Edinburgh: Edinburgh University Press.
Alexander, J. (1992), *Dundee Pubs, Past and Present*, Dundee: Urban Printers.
Alison, Sir A. (1883), *Some Account of My Life and Writings*, Edinburgh: Blackwood.
Anon. (*c*.1870?), *Doings of a Notorious Glasgow Shebeener, How he made his Drink, with numerous Drink Recipes*, Glasgow.

A HISTORY OF DRINKING

Anon. (1920), 'The Fenwick Improvement of Knowledge Society', *Scottish Historical Review*, Vol. 17, pp. 118–35.

Anon. (no date), *The Works and Correspondence of Robert Burns*, Glasgow: William Mckenzie.

Archibald, M. (2012), *A Sink of Atrocity. Crime in 19th Century Dundee*, Edinburgh: Black and White Publishing.

Arnot, H. (1779), *The History of Edinburgh*, Edinburgh: William Creech.

Barnard, A. (1887), *The Whisky Distilleries of the United Kingdom*, reprinted 1969, Newton Abbot: David and Charles.

Barnard, A. (1889–91), *Noted Breweries of Great Britain and Ireland*, 4 vols, London.

Barrie, D. (1890), *The City of Dundee Illustrated*, Dundee: Winter, Duncan and Co.

Bell, C. (ed.) (1999), *Scotland's Century. An Autobiography of the Nation*, Glasgow: HarperCollins.

Bell, G. (1849 and 1850), *Day and Night in the Wynds of Edinburgh and Blackfriars Wynd Analysed*, reprinted 1973, Wakefield: E P Publishing.

Bennett, M. (1992), *Scottish Customs from the Cradle to the Grave*, Edinburgh: Polygon.

Berg, M. (2007), *Luxury and Pleasure in Eighteenth-Century Britain*, Oxford: Oxford University Press.

Berry, S. and Whyte, H. (eds) (1987), *Glasgow Observed*, Edinburgh: John Donald.

Blaikie, A. (2010), 'Rituals, Transitions and Life Courses in an Era of Social Transformation', in Griffiths and Morton (eds), A *History of Everyday Life in Scotland, 1800 to 1900*, pp. 89–115.

Bonner, A. (trans.) (1960), *The Complete Works of François Villon*, New York: Bantam.

Borsay, P. (1991), *The English Urban Renaissance: Culture and Society in the Provincial Town, 1660–1770*, Oxford: Oxford University Press.

Bremner, D. (1869), *The Industries of Scotland. Their Rise, Progress and Present Condition*, reprinted 1969, Newton Abbot: David and Charles.

Brotchie, T. C. F. (1905) *The History of Govan*, Glasgow: John Cossar.

Brown, A. (1795 and 1797), *A History of Glasgow and of Paisley, Greenock and Port Glasgow*, 3 vols, Glasgow: John Paton.

Brown, C. G. (1996), 'Popular Culture and the Continuing Struggle for Rational Recreation', in Devine and Lee (eds), *Scotland in the Twentieth Century*, pp. 210–29.

Brown, C. G. (1998), 'Religion', in Cooke, et al. (eds), *Modern Scottish History, 1707 to the Present*, Vol. 1: *The Transformation of Scotland, 1707–1850*, pp. 63–85, and Vol. 2, *The Modernisation of Scotland, 1850 to the Present*, pp. 142–60.

Brown, C. G. (1999), 'Piety, Gender and War in Scotland in the 1910s', in Macdonald and McFarlane (eds), *Scotland and the Great War*, pp. 173–91.

Brown, C. G. (2010), 'Charting Everyday Experience', in Abrams and Brown (eds), *A History of Everyday Life in Scotland in the Twentieth Century*, pp. 19–47.

Brown, C. G. (2010), 'Spectacle, Restraint and the Sabbath Wars: The "Everyday" Scottish Sunday', in Abrams and Brown (eds), *A History of Everyday Life in Scotland in the Twentieth Century*, pp. 153–80.

Brown, W. (1980), *Early Days in a Dundee Mill, 1819–1823*, No. 20, Dundee: Abertay Historical Society.

Bruce-Gardyne, T. and Skinner, J. (2007), *Rebus's Favourite, The Deuchars Guide to Edinburgh Pubs,* London: Orion.

Burnett, J. (2000), *Riot, Revelry and Rout: Sport in Lowland Scotland before 1860*, East Linton: Tuckwell Press.

Burns, E. (2004), *Ale in Stirling. A Celebration*, Stirling: Monument Press.

Burt, E. (1998), *Letters from a Gentleman in the North of Scotland, 1754*, Edinburgh: Birlinn.

Cage, R. A. (ed.) (1987), *The Working Class in Glasgow, 1750–1914*, London: Croom Helm.

Cameron, D. K. (1997), *The Ballad and the Plough*, Edinburgh: Birlinn.

Cameron, E. A. (2010), *Impaled upon a Thistle: Scotland since 1880*, Edinburgh: Edinburgh University Press.

Campbell, A. B. (1979), *The Lanarkshire Miners. A Social History of their Trade Unions, 1775–1874*, Edinburgh: John Donald.

Campbell, D. (1910), *Reminiscences of an Octogenarian Highlander*, Inverness: Northern Counties Printing and Publishing Company.

Campbell, J. (1899), *Balmerino and its Abbey. A Parish History*, Edinburgh: William Blackwood.

Cant, B. (ed.) (1993), *Footsteps and Witnesses. Lesbian and Gay Lifestories from Scotland*, Edinburgh: Polygon Press.

Carlyle, A. (1860), *Autobiography. Memorials of the Men and Events of his Time*, Edinburgh: William Blackwood.

Carnie, W. (1902), *Reporting Reminiscences*, Aberdeen: Aberdeen University Press.

Carruthers, G. (1998), 'Culture', in Cooke et al. (eds), *Modern Scottish History*, Vol. 1: *The Transformation of Scotland, 1707–1850*, pp. 253–74.

Carter, J. J. and Pittock, H. (eds) (1987), *Aberdeen and the Enlightenment,* Aberdeen: Aberdeen University Press.

Chambers, R. (1856 edition), *Traditions of Edinburgh*, Edinburgh: W. & R. Chambers.

Chambers, R. (1861), *Domestic Annals of Scotland*, Vol. III, *From the Revolution to the Rebellion of 1745*, Edinburgh: W. & R. Chambers.

Clark, A. (1873), *Reminiscences of a Police Officer in the Granite City. Thirty Years Service*, Aberdeen: Lewis Smith.

Clark, A. (1995), *The Struggle for the Breeches: Gender and the Making of the British Working Class*, Berkeley, CA: University of California Press.

Clark, P. (1983), *The English Alehouse. A Social History, 1200–1830*, London: Longman.

Clark, P. (2000), *British Clubs and Societies, 1580–1800. The Origins of an Associational World*, Oxford: Oxford University Press.

Clark, P. (ed.) (2000), *Cambridge Urban History of Britain*, Vol. II, *1540–1840*, Cambridge: Cambridge University Press.

Clark, P. (ed.) (2009), *European Cities and Towns, 400–2000*, Oxford: Oxford University Press.

Cleland, J. (1820), *The Rise and Progress of the City of Glasgow*, Glasgow: James Brash.

Cobbett, W. (1984), *Tour in Scotland in the Autumn of the Year 1832*, Aberdeen: Aberdeen University Press.

Cockburn, H. (1856), *Memorials of his Times*, reprinted 1977, Edinburgh: James Thin.

Colley, L. (2002), *Captives. Britain, Empire and the World, 1600–1850*, London: Jonathan Cape.

Collins, T. and Vamplew, W. (2002), *Mud, Sweat and Beers. A Cultural History of Sport and Alcohol*, Oxford: Berg.

Cooke, A. J. (2003), *Stanley: From Arkwright Village to Commuter Suburb, 1784–2003*, Perth: Perth and Kinross Libraries.

Cooke, A. J. (2006), *From Popular Enlightenment to Lifelong Learning. A History of Adult Education in Scotland, 1707–2005*, Leicester: National Institute of Adult Continuing Education.

Cooke, A. J. (2009), 'The Scottish Cotton Masters, 1780–1914', *Textile History*, Vol. XL, No. 1, pp. 29–50.

Cooke, A. J. (2010), *The Rise and Fall of the Scottish Cotton Industry, 1778–1914*, Manchester: Manchester University Press.

Cooke, A. J. (2012), 'An Elite Revisited: Glasgow West India Merchants, 1783–1877,' *Journal of Scottish Historical Studies*, Vol. 32, No. 2, pp. 127–65.

Cooke, A. J., Donnachie, I., McSween, A. and Whatley C. A. (eds) (1998), *Modern Scottish History, 1707 to the Present*, 5 vols, East Linton: Tuckwell Press.

Cowling, D. (1997), *An Essay for Today. The Scottish New Towns, 1947 to 1997*, Edinburgh: Rutland Press.

Crampsey, B. (1987), *The Young Civilian. A Glasgow Wartime Boyhood*, Edinburgh: Mainstream.

Crawford, G. and Robertson, G. (1818), *A General Description of the Shire of Renfrew*, Paisley: J. Neilson.

Crawford, R. (2009), *The Bard. Robert Burns, a Biography*, London: Jonathan Cape.

Cunningham, K. (2012), *Business as Usual. The Miquel Way*, Durham: Memoir Club.

Daiches, D. (1969), *Scotch Whisky: its Past and Present*, London: André Deutsch.

Dallas, J. and McMaster, C. (eds) (1993), *The Beer Drinker's Companion*, Leith: Edinburgh Publishing Company Ltd.

de Vries, J. (1984), *European Urbanisation, 1500–1800*, Cambridge, MA: Harvard University Press.

de Vries, J. (2008), *The Industrious Revolution. Consumer Behavior and the Household Economy, 1650 to the Present*, Cambridge: Cambridge University Press.

Defoe, D. (1724–26), *A Tour through the Whole Island of Great Britain*, reprinted 1971, London: Penguin.

Dempsey, B. (1992?), *Thon Wey. Aspects of Scottish Lesbian and Gay Activism, 1968 to 1992*, Edinburgh: Outright (Scotland).

Dempsey, B (2006), 'By the Law of This and Every Well-Governed Realm: Investigating Accusations of Sodomy in Nineteenth-Century Scotland', *The Juridical Review*, Part 2, pp. 103–30.

Devine, T. M. (1999), *The Scottish Nation, 1700–2000*, London: Penguin.

Devine, T. M. (2000), 'Scotland', in Clark, P. (ed.), *The Cambridge Urban History of Britain*, Vol. II, *1540–1840*, Cambridge: Cambridge University Press, pp. 151–66.

Devine, T. M. and Finlay, R. J. (eds) (1996), *Scotland in the Twentieth Century*, Edinburgh: Edinburgh University Press.

Devine, T. M. and Jackson, G. (eds) (1995), *Glasgow*, Volume 1, *Beginnings to 1830*, Manchester: Manchester University Press.

Devine, T. M., Lee, C. H. and Peden G. (eds) (2005), *The Transformation of Scotland. The Economy since 1700*, Edinburgh: Edinburgh University Press.

Devine, T. M. and Mitchison, R. (eds) (1988), *People and Society in Scotland*, Vol. I, *1760–1830*, Edinburgh: John Donald.

Dickson, A. and Treble, J. H. (eds) (1992), *People and Society in Scotland*, Vol. III, *1914–1990*, Edinburgh: John Donald.

Dixon, J. H. (1886), *Gairloch and Guide to Loch Maree*, Edinburgh: Co-operative Printing Company.

Dodgshon, R. A. (2010), 'Everyday Structures, Rhythms and Spaces of the Scottish Countryside', in Foyster and Whatley (eds), *A History of Everyday Life in Scotland, 1600 to 1800*, pp. 27–50.

Donaldson, W. (1986), *Popular Literature in Victorian Scotland*, Aberdeen: Aberdeen University Press.

Donnachie, I. (1979), *A History of the Brewing Industry in Scotland*, Edinburgh: John Donald.

Donnachie, I. (1979), 'Drink and Society, 1750–1850: Some Aspects of the Scottish Experience, *Journal of the Scottish Labour History Society*, No. 13, pp. 5–22.

Donnachie, I. (1982), 'World War One and the Drink Question: State Control of the Drink Trade', *Journal of the Scottish Labour History Society*, No. 17, pp. 19–26.

Douglas, M. (ed.) (1987), *Constructive Drinking: Perspectives on Drink from Anthropology*, Cambridge: Cambridge University Press.

Dudleston, A. and Murray, L. (2004), *The Nicholson Committee Report on Liquor Licensing Law in Scotland: Analysis of Consultation Responses*, Edinburgh: Scottish Executive Social Research.

Dunbar, J. G. (ed.) (1997), *Sir William Burrell's Northern Tour, 1758*, East Linton: Tuckwell Press.

Duncan, G. J. C. (1848), *Memoir of Henry Duncan, Minister of Ruthwell*, Edinburgh: William Oliphant.

Duncan, Reverend H. (1821), *The Young South Country Weaver; or a Journey to Glasgow, A Tale for the Radicals*, Edinburgh: Waugh and Innes.

Duncan, R. (2005), *The Mine Workers*, Edinburgh: Birlinn.

Dunlop, J. (1844), *Artificial and Compulsory Drinking Usages of the United Kingdom*, 7th edition, London: Hodder and Stoughton.

Durie, A. (2003), *Scotland for the Holidays: Tourism in Scotland, 1780–1939*, East Linton: Tuckwell Press.

Durie, A. (2010), 'Movement, Transport and Tourism', in Griffiths and Morton (eds), *A History of Everyday Life in Scotland, 1800 to 1900*, pp. 147–69.

Durie, A. J. (ed.) (2012), *Travels in Scotland, 1788–1881*, Woodbridge: Boydell Press.

Earnshaw, S. (2000), *The Pub in Literature*, Manchester: Manchester University Press.

Fenton, A. (2007), 'The Food of the Scots', in *Scottish Life and Society. A Compendium of Scottish Ethnology*, Vol. 5, Edinburgh: John Donald, pp. 82–130.

Finlay, R. (2004), *Modern Scotland, 1914–2000*, London: Profile Books.

Finn, G. P. T. (1994), 'Football violence: a societal psychological perspective', in Giulianotti et al. (eds), *Football, Violence and Social Identity*, pp. 90–127.

Foster, A. (2005), *The Literary Traveller in Edinburgh*, Edinburgh: Mainstream.

Foucault, M. (1976), *The History of Sexuality*, Vol. I, New York: Random House.

Foyster, E. and Whatley, C. A. (eds) (2010), *A History of Everyday Life in Scotland, 1600–1800*, Edinburgh: Edinburgh University Press.

Fraser, W. H. (1976), 'The Glasgow Cotton Spinners, 1837', in Butt, J. and Ward, J. T. (eds), *Scottish Themes*, Edinburgh: Scottish Academic Press, pp. 80–97.

Fraser, W. H. (1990), 'Developments in Leisure', in Fraser, W. H. and Morris, R. J. (eds), *People and Society in Scotland*, Vol. II, *1830–1914*, Edinburgh: John Donald, pp. 236–64.

Fraser, W. H. (2000), *Scottish Popular Politics*, Edinburgh: Polygon.

Fraser, W. H. (2010), 'Necessities in the Nineteenth Century', in Griffiths and Morton (eds), *A History of Everyday Life in Scotland, 1800 to 1900*, pp. 60–80.

Fraser, W. H. and Lee, C. H. (eds) (2000), *Aberdeen, 1800–2000. A New History*, East Linton: Tuckwell Press.

Fraser, W. H. and Maver, I. (eds) (1996), *Glasgow*, Vol. II, *1830–1912*, Manchester: Manchester University Press.

Fraser, W. H. and Morris, R. J. (eds) (1990), *People and Society in Scotland*, Vol. II, *1830–1914*, Edinburgh: John Donald.

Freer, W. (1929), *My Life and Memories*, Glasgow: Civic Press.

Fry, M. (1998), 'Politics', in Cooke et al. (eds), *Modern Scottish History 1707 to the Present*, Vol. I, *The Transformation of Scotland, 1707–1850*, pp. 43–62.

Fyfe, J. G. (ed.) (1942), *Scottish Diaries and Memoirs, 1746–1843*, Stirling: Eaneas Mackay.

Galt, J. (1821), *Annals of the Parish*, 1919 edition, Edinburgh: T. N. Foulis.

Geikie, A. (1906), *Scottish Reminiscences*, Glasgow: James Maclehose.

Gibbon, L. G. (1933), *Cloud Howe* (1973 edition), London: Pan Books.

Gibson, A. and Smout, T. C. (1989), 'Scottish Food and Scottish History, 1500–1800', in Houston, R. A. and Whyte, I. D. (eds), *Scottish Society, 1500–1800*, Cambridge: Cambridge University Press, pp. 59–84.

Gibson, J. (1777), *A History of Glasgow*, Glasgow: Chapman and Duncan.

Gilfillan, Reverend G. (ed.) (no date), *The National Burns*, Glasgow: William McKenzie.

Giulianotti, R (1994), 'Taking Liberties: Hibs casuals and Scottish Law', in Giulianotti et al. (eds), *Football, Violence and Social Identity*, pp. 229–61.

Giulianotti, R., Bonney, N. and Hepworth, M. (eds) (1994), *Football, Violence and Social Identity*, London: Routledge.

Gordon, E. (1991), *Women and the Labour Movement in Scotland, 1850–1914*, Oxford: Clarendon Press.

Gorevan, J. (2002), *Glasgow Pubs and Publicans*, Stroud: Tempus.

Goring, R. (2008), *Scotland: The Autobiography*, London: Penguin.

Gourvish, T. R. and Wilson, R. G. (1994), *The British Brewing Industry, 1830–1980*, Cambridge: Cambridge University Press.

Grant, E. (1972), *Memoirs of a Highland Lady, 1797–1827*, London: John Murray.

Grant, I. F. (1977), *Highland Folk Ways*, London: Routledge and Kegan Paul.

Griffiths, T (2010), 'Work, Leisure and Time', in Griffiths and Morton (eds), *A History of Everyday Life in Scotland, 1800 to 1900*, pp. 170–95.

Griffiths, T. (2012), *The Cinema and Cinema-going in Scotland, 1896–c.1950*, Edinburgh: Edinburgh University Press.

Griffiths, T. and Morton, G. (eds) (2010), *A History of Everyday Life in Scotland, 1800 to 1900*, Edinburgh: Edinburgh University Press.

Gunn, N. (1941), *The Silver Darlings*, London: Faber and Faber.

Gunn, N. (1998), 'Gentlemen – The Tourist! The New Highland Toast' (1937), in Cooke et al. (eds), *Modern Scottish History, 1707 to the Present*, Vol. 5: *Major Documents*, pp. 295–8.

Gusfield, J. R. (1972), *Symbolic Crusade. Status Politics and the American Temperance Movement*, Urbana, Chicago, IL: University of Illinois Press.

Guthrie, T. (1877), *Autobiography of Thomas Guthrie, DD and Memoir*, London: Daldy, Isbiter.

Gutzke, D. (1989), *Protecting the Pub. Brewers and Publicans against Temperance*, Woodbridge: Boydell Press.

Habermas, J. (1992), *The Structural Transformation of the Public Sphere. An Inquiry into a Category of Bourgeois Society*, Cambridge, MA: MIT Press.

Haldane, A. R. B. (1971 edition), *The Drove Roads of Scotland*, Edinburgh: Edinburgh University Press.

Haldane, A. R. B. (1973 edition), *New Ways Through the Glens*, Newton Abbot: David and Charles.

Hamilton, J. (1880), *Poems, Essays and Sketches*, Glasgow: James Maclehose.

Hammond W. (1904), *Recollections of a Glasgow Handloom Weaver*, Glasgow: Citizens' Press.

Hanley, C. (1958), *Dancing in the Streets* (1983 edition), Edinburgh: Mainstream.

Harman, C. (2005), *Robert Louis Stevenson. A Biography*, London: Harper Collins.

Harris, B. and McKean, C. (2014), *The Scottish Town in the Age of Enlightenment, 1740–1820*, Edinburgh: Edinburgh University Press.

Harrison, B. (1973), 'Pubs', in H. J. Dyos and M. Wolff (eds), *The Victorian City. Images and Realities*, Vol. I, London: Routledge and Kegan Paul, pp. 161–90.

Harrison, B. (1994), *Drink and the Victorians, The Temperance Question in England, 1815–1872*, 2nd edition, Keele: Keele University Press.

Hartwich, V. (1980), *Ale an' A' Thing, Aspects of the Grocery and Licensed Trades in Dundee, 1800–1950*, Dundee: Dundee Museums and Art Galleries.

Harvie, C. (1998, 3rd edition), *No Gods and Precious Few Heroes*, Edinburgh: Edinburgh University Press.

Hassan G. and Warhurst, C. (2002), *Anatomy of the New Scotland. Power, Influence and Change*, Edinburgh; Mainstream.

Heron, P. (1975), *Scotland Delineated, 1799*, Edinburgh: Mercat Press.

Hillyard, Y. (2012), *Raising the Bar: An Introduction to Scotland's Historic Pubs*, Edinburgh: Historic Scotland.

Hogg, B. (1993), *The History of Scottish Rock and Pop*, Enfield: Guinness Publishing

Hogg, J. (1888), *A Tour in the Highlands in 1803*, Paisley: Alexander Gardner.

Hogg, J. (1972), *Memoirs of the Author's Life and Familiar Anecdotes of Sir Walter Scott*, Edinburgh: Scottish Academic Press.

Hook, A. and Sher, R. B. (eds) (1995), *The Glasgow Enlightenment*, East Linton: Tuckwell Press.

Hopkins, A. (1975), *The Aberdeen Pub Companion*, Aberdeen: Retro Publications.

House, J. (1958), 'Leisure Interests', in Cunnison J, and Gilfillan, J. B. S. (eds), *The Third Statistical Account of Scotland, Glasgow*, Glasgow: Collins, pp. 606–33.

Houston, R. A. (1994), *Social Change in the Age of Enlightenment: Edinburgh, 1660–1760*, Oxford: Clarendon Press.

Hume Brown, P. (ed.) (1881), *Early Travellers in Scotland*, reprinted 1973, Edinburgh: Mercat Press.

Irvine, P. (2011), *Scotland the Best*, London: HarperCollins.

Jackson, H. (2000), *Neil Gow's Inver*, Perth: Perth and Kinross Libraries.

Jarvie, G. and Burnett, J. (eds) (2000), *Sport, Scotland and the Scots*, East Linton: Tuckwell Press.

Jenkins, R. (1992), *A Life at the Centre*, London: Pan Books.

Jenkins, R. (1996), *Gladstone*, London: Macmillan.

Johnston, E. (1867), *Autobiography: Poems and Songs of Ellen Johnston, the 'Factory Girl'*, Glasgow: Maclehose.

Johnston, T. (1952), *Memories*, London: Collins.

Kay, J. and Vamplew, W. (2000), 'Horse-Racing', in Jarvie, G. and Burnett, J. (eds), *Sport, Scotland and the Scots*, pp. 159–73.

Kelman, J. (1985), *The Bus Conductor Hines*, London: J. M. Dent.

Kenefick, W. (1998), 'Demography', in Cooke et al. (eds), *Modern Scottish History*, Vol. 2, *1850 to the Present*, pp. 95–118.

Kenefick, W. (2000), *'Rebellious and Contrary'. The Glasgow Dockers, 1853–1932*, East Linton: Tuckwell Press.

Kenefick, W. and McIvor, A. (eds) (1996), *Roots of Red Clydeside, 1910–1914?*, Edinburgh: John Donald.

Kenna, R. (2001), *The Glasgow Pub Companion*, Glasgow: Neil Wilson Publishing.

Kenna, R. and Mooney, A. (1983), *People's Palaces. Victorian and Edwardian Pubs of Scotland*, Edinburgh: Paul Harris.

King, E. (1979), *Scotland Sober and Free. The Temperance Movement, 1829–1979*, Glasgow: Glasgow Museums and Art Galleries.

King, E. (1987), 'Popular Culture in Glasgow', in Cage, R. A. (ed.), *The Working Class in Glasgow, 1750–1914*, London: Croom Helm, pp. 142–87.

King-Clark (ed.) (1991), *The John Caldwell Letters from Canada, 1821–1837*, Paisley: PDC Copyprint.

Kinghorn, A. M. and Law, A. (eds) (1985), *Poems by Allan Ramsay and Robert Fergusson*, Edinburgh: Scottish Academic Press.

Kirkwood, D. (1935), *My Life of Revolt*, London: Harrap.

Knox, W. W. (ed.) (1984), *Scottish Labour Leaders, 1918–1938: A Biographical Dictionary*, Edinburgh: Mainstream.

Knox, W. W. (1990), 'The Political and Workplace Culture of the Scottish Working Class, 1832–1914', in Fraser and Morris (eds), *People and Society in Scotland*, Vol. 2, pp. 138–66.

Knox, W. W. (1999), *Industrial Nation. Work, Culture and Society in Scotland, 1800–Present*, Edinburgh: Edinburgh University Press.

Knox W. W. and McKinlay A. (2010), 'Crime, Protest and Policing in Nineteenth-Century Scotland', in Griffiths and Morton (eds), *A History of Everyday Life in Scotland, 1800 to 1900*, pp. 196–224.

Kohl, J. G. (1844), *Scotland*, London: Chapman and Hall.

Ladurie, E. Le R. (1980), *Montaillou. Cathars and Catholics in a French Village, 1294–1324*, London: Penguin.

Lambert, R. A. (1998), 'Leisure and Recreation', in Cooke et al. (eds), *Modern Scottish History*, Vol. 2: *The Modernisation of Scotland, 1850 to the Present*, pp. 257–76.

Lee, C. H. (1999), 'The Scottish Economy and the First World War', in MacDonald and McFarlane (eds), *Scotland and the Great War*, pp. 11–35.

Leneman, L. (1986), *Living in Atholl: A Social History of the Estates, 1685–1785*, Edinburgh: Edinburgh University Press.

Leonard, T. (1990), *Radical Renfrew. Poetry from the French Revolution to the First World War*, Edinburgh: Polygon.

Levi, P. (ed.) (1984), Johnson, S., *Journey to the Western Isles of Scotland* and Boswell, J., *The Journal of a Tour to the Hebrides*, London: Penguin.

Levine, H. (1987), 'Alcohol monopoly to protect the non-commercial sector of eighteenth-century Poland', in Douglas, M. (ed.), *Constructive Drinking*, pp. 250–69.

Lewis, Reverend G. (1834), *Scotland: A Half Educated Nation*, Glasgow: William Collins.

Lindsay, M. (ed.) (2001), *A Book of Scottish Verse*, London: Robert Hale.

Lockhart, D. G. (1983), 'Planned Village Development in Scotland and Ireland', in Devine, T. M. and Dickson, D. (eds), *Ireland and Scotland, 1600–1850; Parallels and Contrasts in Economic and Social Development*, Edinburgh: John Donald.

Lockhart, D. G. (2012), *Scottish Planned Villages*, Edinburgh: Scottish History Society.

Logan, W. (1843), *An Exposure, from personal observation, of Female Prostitution in London, Leeds and Rochdale and especially in the City of Glasgow*, Glasgow: G. Gallie and R. Fletchfield.

Logan, W. (1864), *The Moral Statistics of Glasgow*, Glasgow: Porteous and Hislop.

Lumsden, L. I. (1927), *Memories of Aberdeen a Hundred Years Ago*, Aberdeen: Bon Accord Press.

McAlpine, S. (c.1852?), *Glaiska Fair. Sum of its Humours an' Sum of its Horrors*, Glasgow: Scottish Temperance League.

McCaffrey, J. F. (ed.) (1976), *Glasgow 1858, Shadow's Midnight Scenes and Social Photographs*, Glasgow: Glasgow University Press.

McCracken-Flesher, C. (2012), *The Doctor Dissected: A Cultural Autopsy of the Burke and Hare Murders*, Oxford: Oxford University Press.

McCraw, I. (1994), *The Fairs of Dundee*, Dundee: Abertay Historical Society.

McCrone, D. (2001), *Understanding Scotland: The Sociology of a Nation* (2nd edition), London: Routledge.

MacDonald, C. M. M. (2009), *Whaur Extremes Meet. Scotland's Twentieth Century*, Edinburgh: John Donald.

MacDonald C. M. M. and McFarlane, E. W. (eds) (1999), *Scotland and the Great War*, East Linton: Tuckwell Press.

McGonagall, W. (1969), *Poetic Gems, More Poetic Gems and Last Poetic Gems*, Dundee: David Winter.

McGregor, K. and Tweedie, L. (2011), *Life Behind Bars. Confessions of a Pub Landlady*, Edinburgh: Fledgling Press.

McIlvanney, W. (1975), *Docherty*, Edinburgh: Mainstream.

McIlvanney, W. (1977), *Laidlaw*, London: Hodder and Stoughton.

McIlvanney, W. (1989), *Walking Wounded*, London: Hodder and Stoughton.

Macinnes, A. I. (1996), *Clanship, Commerce and the House of Stuart, 1603–1788*, East Linton: Tuckwell Press.

McIvor, A. (1998), 'Women and Gender Relations', in Cooke et al. (eds), *Modern Scottish History*, Vol. 2, *1850 to the Present*, pp. 161–87.

Mack, J. A. (1958), 'Crime', in Cunnison and Gilfillan (eds), *Third Statistical Account of Scotland, Glasgow*, pp. 634–73.

McKean, C. (1987), *The Scottish Thirties*, Edinburgh: Rutland Press.

McKean, C. (2009), 'What Kind of a Renaissance Town was Dundee?', in McKean, C., Harris, B. and Whatley, C. A. (eds), *Dundee, Renaissance to Enlightenment*, Dundee: Dundee University Press, pp. 1–32.

Mackinnon, M. and Oram, R. (2011), *The Scots. A Photohistory*, London: Thames & Hudson.

MacLachlan, C. (ed.) (2002), *Before Burns, Eighteenth-Century Scottish Poetry*, Edinburgh: Canongate Classics.

M'Laren, D. (1858), *The Rise and Progress of Whisky Drinking and the Working of the Public Houses (Scotland) Act*, Glasgow: Scottish Temperance League.

McLean, I. (1983), *The Legend of Red Clydeside*, Edinburgh: John Donald.

McMillan, J. (2002), 'The Scottish Performing Arts', in Hassan and Warhurst (eds), *Anatomy of the New Scotland*, pp. 208–16.

MacQueen, T. and W. (eds) (1972), *A Choice of Scottish Verse, 1470–1570*, London: Faber & Faber.

Mair, C. (1990), *Stirling, The Royal Burgh*, Edinburgh: John Donald.

Maloney, P. (2003), *Scotland and the Music Hall, 1850–1914*, Manchester: Manchester University Press.

Martin, M. (*c*.1695), *A Description of the Western Islands of Scotland* (reprinted 1994), Edinburgh: Birlinn.

Martin, P. (2006), *Cupar, The History of a Small Scottish Town*, Edinburgh: Birlinn.

Marwick, J. D. (1909), *The River Clyde and the Clyde Burghs*, Glasgow: James Maclehose.

Mathias, P. (1959), *The Brewing Industry in England, 1700–1830*, Cambridge: Cambridge University Press.

Maver, I. (1994), 'Glasgow Town Council in the Nineteenth Century', in Devine, T. M. (ed.), *Scottish Elites*, Edinburgh: John Donald.

Maver, I. (1996), 'The Catholic Community', in Devine and Finlay (eds), *Scotland in the 20th Century*, pp. 269–84.

Maver, I. (2000), 'Leisure and Social Change: The Twentieth Century', in Fraser, W. H. and Lee, C. H. (eds), *Aberdeen, 1800 to 2000. A New History*, East Linton: Tuckwell Press, pp. 422–47.

Maxwell, A. (1884), *The History of Old Dundee*, Dundee: William Kidd.

Maxwell, A. (1891), *Old Dundee*, Dundee: William Kidd.

Miller, C. (ed.) (1970), *Memoirs of a Modern Scotland*, London: Faber & Faber.

Miller, H. (1874), *My Schools and Schoolmasters*, Edinburgh: William Nimmo.

Minutes of the Board of Green Cloth, 1809–1820, Glasgow: James Maclehose.

Miskell, L., Whatley, C. A. and Harris, B. (eds) (2000), *Victorian Dundee. Image and Realities*, East Linton: Tuckwell Press.

Mitchell, M. J. (1998), *The Irish in the West of Scotland, 1797–1848*, Edinburgh: John Donald.

Morgan, N. and Trainor, R. (1995), 'The Dominant Classes', in Fraser, W. H. and Morris R. J. (eds), *People and Society in Scotland*, Vol. II, *1830–1914*, pp. 103–37.

Morris, R. J. (1990), 'Clubs, societies and associations', in Thompson, F. M. L. (ed.), *The Cambridge Social History of Britain, 1750–1850*, Vol. 3, *Social Agencies and Institutions*, Cambridge: Cambridge University Press, pp. 395–444.

Morris, R. J. (1998), 'Urbanisation', in Cooke, et al. (eds), *Modern Scottish History*, Vol. 2, *1850 to the Present*, pp. 119–41.

Morris, R. J. (1998), 'Death, Chambers Street and Edinburgh Corporation', in Cooke, et al. (eds), *Modern Scottish History*, Vol. 4, *Readings, 1850 to the Present*, pp. 139–46.

Morris, R. J. (2010), 'New Spaces for Scotland, 1800–1900', in Griffiths and Morton (eds), *A History of Everyday Life in Scotland, 1800 to 1900*, pp. 225–55.

Morris, R. J. (2013), 'White Horse Close: Philanthropy, Scottish Historical Imagination and the Rebuilding of Edinburgh in the later Nineteenth Century', *Journal of Scottish Historical Studies*, Vol. 33, No. 1, pp. 101–28.

Morton, G. (2010), 'Identity out of Place', in Griffiths and Morton (eds), *A History of Everyday Life in Scotland, 1800 to 1900*, pp. 256–87.

Morton, G. (2012), *Ourselves and others. Scotland, 1832–1914*, Edinburgh: Edinburgh University Press.

Moss, M. S. and Hume, J. R. (1981), *The Making of Scotch Whisky*, Edinburgh: James and James.

Mozley, A. V. (1977), *Thomas Annan, Photographs of the Old Streets and Closes of Glasgow, 1868–1877*, New York: Dover Publications.

Muir, E. (1935), *Scottish Journey* (1979 edition), Edinburgh: Mainstream.

Muir, J. H. (2001), *Glasgow in 1901*, Glasgow: White Cockade.

Muirhead, I. A. (1974), 'Churchmen and the Problem of Prostitution in Nineteenth-Century Scotland', *Scottish Church History Society Records*, Vol. XVIII, pp. 223–43.

Murdoch, A. and Sher, R. B. (1988), 'Literary and Learned Culture', in Devine and Mitchison (eds), *People and Society in Scotland*, Vol. I, *1760–1830*, pp. 127–42.

Murray, B. (1984), *The Old Firm. Sectarianism, Sport and Society in Scotland*, Edinburgh: John Donald.

Murray, N. (1978), *The Scottish Handloom Weavers, 1790–1850*, Edinburgh: John Donald.

Myles, J. (1850), *Rambles in Forfarshire*, Edinburgh: A. & C. Black.

Nenadic, S. (1988), 'The Rise of the Urban Middle Classes', in Devine and Mitchison (eds), *People and Society in Scotland*, Vol. I, *1760–1830*, pp. 109–26.

Nenadic, S. (1995), 'The Middle Ranks and Modernisation', in Devine, T. M. and Jackson, G. (eds), *Glasgow*, Vol. I, *Beginnings to 1830*, pp. 278–311.

Nenadic, S. (2010), 'Necessities: Food and Clothing in the long Eighteenth Century', in Foyster, E. and Whatley, C. A. (eds), *A History of Everyday Life in Scotland, 1600 to 1800*, pp. 137–63.

New Statistical Account of Scotland (1845), Vol. 1, *Edinburgh*; Vol. 2, *Linlithgow, Haddington, Berwick*; Vol. 3, *Roxburgh, Peebles, Selkirk*; Vol. 4, *Dumfries, Kirkcudbright, Wigton*; Vol. 5, *Ayrshire and Bute*; Vol. 6, *Lanark*; Vol. 7, *Renfrew and Argyll*; Vol. 8, *Dunbarton, Stirling, Clackmannan*; Vol. 9, *Fife and Kinross*; Vol. 10, *Perth*; Vol. 11, *Forfar and Kincardine*; Vol. 13, *Aberdeenshire*; Vol. 14, *Ross and Cromarty*, Edinburgh: William Blackwood.

Noble, A. (1985), 'Urbane Silence: Scottish Writing and the Nineteenth-Century City', in Gordon, G. (ed.), *Perspectives of the Scottish City*, Aberdeen: Aberdeen University Press, pp. 64–90.

Outhwaite, W. (2009), *Habermas. A Critical Introduction* (2nd edition), Cambridge: Polity Press.

Pae, D. (1858), *Lucy the Factory Girl; or the Secrets of the Tontine Close* (2001 edition), Hastings, Sensation Press.

Pae, D. (1865), *Mary Paterson; or the Fatal Error*, Dundee: John Leng.

Paterson, L., Bechhofer, F. and McCrone, D. (2004), *Living in Scotland: Social and Economic Change since 1980*, Edinburgh: Edinburgh University Press.

Payne, P. L. (1998), 'Industrialisation and Industrial Decline', in Cooke et al.

(eds), *Modern Scottish History, 1707 to the Present*, Vol. 2, *1850 to the Present*, pp. 73–94.

Pennant, T. (1769), *A Tour of Scotland in 1769* (reprinted 1979), Perth: Melven Press.

Pennant, T. (1772), *A Tour in Scotland and Voyage to the Hebrides* (reprinted 1998), Edinburgh: Birlinn.

Penny, G. (1836), *Traditions of Perth*, Perth: Morison.

Phillips, D. (ed.) (1980), *Chapters in the Life of a Dundee Factory Boy*, Dundee: David Winter.

Rankin I. (1987), *Knots and Crosses*, London: Orion.

Rankin, I. (1998), *The Hanging Garden*, London: Orion.

Rankin, I (2001), *Set in Darkness*, London: St Martin's.

Rankin, I (2001), *Resurrection Men*, London: Orion.

Reid, R. (Senex) (1884), *Glasgow Past and Present* (3 volumes), Glasgow: David Robertson.

Ritchie, D. R., Imrie, A. and Junor, J. R. (1966), 'The Traveller and the Inn', in Keir, D. (ed.), *The Third Statistical Account of Scotland, Edinburgh*, Glasgow: Collins, pp. 672–85.

Robertson, I. A. (1986), 'The Earl of Kinnoull's Bridge: the Construction of the Bridge of Tay at Perth, 1763–72', *Scottish Economic and Social History*, Vol. 6, pp. 18–32.

Robertson, J (1839), *The Book of Bon Accord. A Guide to the City of Aberdeen*, Aberdeen: Lewis Smith.

Rodger, R. (2001), *The Transformation of Edinburgh. Land, Property and Trust in the Nineteenth Century*, Cambridge: Cambridge University Press.

Rothschild, E. (2011), *The Inner Life of Empires*, Princeton, NJ: Princeton University Press

St Fond, Baron Faujas de (1907), *A Journey Through England and Scotland to the Hebrides in 1784* (2 volumes), Glasgow: Hugh Hopkins.

Salmond, J. B. (1934), *Wade in Scotland*, Edinburgh: Moray Press.

Saunders, L. J. (1950), *Scottish Democracy, 1815–1840. The Social and Intellectual Background*, Edinburgh: Oliver and Boyd.

Scarfe, N. (ed.) (2001), *To the Highlands in 1786. The Inquisitive Journal of a Young French Aristocrat*, Woodbridge: Boydell Press.

Schofield, C. and Kamm, A. (1984), *Lager Lovelies. The Story behind the Glamour*, Glasgow: Richard Drew.

Scott, W. (1886), *Guy Mannering or the Astrologer*, Edinburgh: Adam and Charles Black.

Searle, J. and Muir, C. (2012), *The Big Picture. Cinemas of Dundee*, Dundee: Dundee Civic Trust.

Settle, L. (2013), 'The Social Geography of Prostitution in Edinburgh, 1900–1939, *Journal of Scottish Historical Studies*, Vol. 33, No. 2, pp. 234–59.

Sher, R. B. (1985), *Church and University in the Scottish Enlightenment. The Moderate Literati of Edinburgh*, Edinburgh: Edinburgh University Press.

Sher, R. B. (1995), 'Commerce, religion and the enlightenment in eighteenth-century Glasgow', in Devine and Jackson (eds), *Glasgow*, Vol. I, *Beginnings to 1830*, pp. 312–59.

Sher, R. B. and Smitten J. R. (eds) (1990), *Scotland and America in the Age of Enlightenment*, Edinburgh: Edinburgh University Press.

Sherwell, A. (1903), *The Drink Peril in Scotland*, Edinburgh: Oliphant, Anderson and Ferrier.

Shields, T. (1975?), *Great Scottish Pubs, Edinburgh, Glasgow, Stirling and Surrounding Districts*, Alexandria: Famedram.

Simmons, M. (1981), *The Scottish Licensed Trade Association, 1880–1980, The Centenary History*, Edinburgh: John Donald.

Simonton, D. (2006), 'Work, Trade and Commerce', in Abrams, L., Gordon, E., Simonton, D. and Yeo, E. J. (eds), *Gender in Scottish History since 1700*, pp. 199–234.

Sinclair, Sir J. (ed.) (1791–1799), *The (Old) Statistical Account of Scotland* (reissued 1973–83), 20 volumes, Bradford: E P Publishing.

Slaughter, M. (ed.) (2007), *Scotland's True Heritage Pubs: Pub Interiors of Special Historic Interest*, St Albans: CAMRA.

Smith, A. (1986), *The Wealth of Nations, 1776*, Books I–III, London: Penguin.

Smith, G. D. (2001), *The Scottish Beer Bible*, Edinburgh: Mercat Press.

Smout, T. C. (1963), *Scottish Trade on the Eve of Union*, Edinburgh: Oliver & Boyd.

Smout, T. C. (1967), 'Lead Mining in Scotland, 1650–1850', in Payne, P. L. (ed.), *Studies in Scottish Business History*, London: Frank Cass, pp. 103–35.

Smout, T. C. (1969), *A History of the Scottish People, 1560–1830*, London: Collins.

Smout, T. C. (1970), 'The Landowner and the Planned Village in Scotland, 1730–1830', in Phillipson, N. and Mitchison, R. (eds), *Scotland in the Age of Improvement*, Edinburgh: Edinburgh University Press, pp. 73–106.

Smout, T. C. (1986), *A Century of the Scottish People, 1830–1950*, London: Collins.

Smout, T. C. and Wood, S. (1990), *Scottish Voices, 1745–1960*, London: Collins.

Southey, R. (1929), *Journal of a Tour in Scotland in 1819*, London: John Murray.

Stephenson, P. (2001), *Billy*, London: HarperCollins.

Stevenson, R. (1970), 'The Emergence of Scottish Music', in Miller (ed.), *Memoirs of a Modern Scotland*, pp. 189–97.

Stevenson, S. (1987), *Thomas Annan, 1829–1887*, Edinburgh: National Galleries of Scotland.

Stewart, A. (2000), *Where is She Tonight? Women, Street Prostitution and Homelessness in Glasgow*, Glasgow: 57 Drop-In Centre.

Stewart, D. (1825), *Sketches of the Character, Manners and Present State of the Highlands of Scotland* (2 volumes), Edinburgh: Archibald Constable.

Stewart, G. (1881), *Curiosities of Glasgow Citizenship*, Glasgow: James Maclehose.

Strang, J. (1864), *Glasgow and its Clubs*, Glasgow: John Tweed.

Stuart, M. W. (1952), *Old Edinburgh Taverns*, London: Robert Hale.

Taylor, J. M. (ed.) (1879), *Weavers' Society of Anderston*, Glasgow.

Thom, W. (1880), *Rhymes and Recollections of a Handloom Weaver*, Paisley: Alexander Gardner.

Thompson, E. P. (1968), *The Making of the English Working Class*, London: Penguin.

Thompson, E. P. (1993), *Customs in Common*, London: Penguin.

Tomalin, C. (2012), *Charles Dickens. A Life*, London: Penguin.

Topham, E. (2003), *Letters from Edinburgh in 1774 and 1775*, Edinburgh: West Port Books.

Tranter, N. (1998), 'Demography', in Cooke, et al. (eds), *Modern Scottish History*, Vol. I, *1707–1850*, pp. 108–29.

Walker, D. (2003), 'Inns, hotels and related buildings', in Stell, G., Shaw, J. and Storrier, S. (eds), *Scottish Life and Society*, Vol. 3, *Scotland's Buildings*, East Linton: Tuckwell Press, pp. 127–89.

Walker, W. M. (1979), *Juteopolis: Dundee and Its Textile Workers, 1885–1923*, Edinburgh: Scottish Academic Press.

Warden, A. (ed.) (1872), *Burgh Laws of Dundee*, London: Longman Green.

Welsh, I. (2004 edition), *Trainspotting*, London: Vintage.

Welsh, I. (2013 edition), *Porno*, London: Vintage.

Whatley, C. A. (1988), 'The Experience of Work', in Devine and Mitchison (eds), *People and Society in Scotland*, Vol. I, *1760–1830*, pp. 227–51.

Whatley, C. A. (ed.) (1996), *The Diary of John Sturrock, Millwright, Dundee, 1864–65*, East Linton: Tuckwell Press.

Whatley, C. A. (2000), *Scottish Society, 1707–1830: Beyond Jacobitism, Towards Industrialisation*, Manchester: Manchester University Press.

Whatley, C. A. (2000), 'Altering Images of the Industrial City: the case of James Myles, the "Factory Boy", and mid-Victorian Dundee', in Miskell, Whatley and Harris (eds), *Victorian Dundee*, pp. 70–95.

Whatley, C. A. (2010), 'Order and Disorder', in Foyster and Whatley (eds), *A History of Everyday Life in Scotland, 1600 to 1800*, pp. 191–216.

Whatley, C. A. (2010), 'Work, Time and Pastimes', in Foyster and Whatley (eds), *A History of Everyday Life in Scotland, 1600 to 1800*, pp. 273–303.

Whyte, I. D. (1994), *Scotland before the Industrial Revolution c.1050 to c.1750*, London: Longman.

Wilson, A. (1970), *The Chartist Movement in Scotland*, Manchester: Manchester University Press.

Wilson, G. B. (1940), *Alcohol and the Nation, 1800–1935*, London: Nicholson and Watson.

Withers, C. W. J. (1998), *Urban Highlanders: Highland–Lowland Migration and Urban Gaelic Culture*, East Linton: Tuckwell Press.

Withrington, D. J. (2001), 'Education', in Cooke, et al. (eds), *Modern Scottish History, 1707 to the Present*, Vol. 1, *The Transformation of Scotland, 1707–1850*, pp. 275–98.

Wordsworth, D. (1803), *Recollections of a Tour Made in Scotland* (reprinted 1874), Edinburgh: Edmonston and Douglas.

Wrightson, K. (1981), 'Alehouses, Order and Reformation in Rural England, 1590–1660', in Yeo, E. and Yeo, S. (eds), *Popular Culture and Class Conflict, 1590–1914. Explorations in the History of Labour and Leisure*, Brighton: Harvester Press, pp. 1–27.

Young, H. (2010), 'Being a Man: Everyday Masculinities', in Abrams and Brown (eds), *A History of Everyday Life in Twentieth-Century Scotland*, pp. 131–52.

NEWSPAPERS AND TRADE JOURNALS

Aberdeen Journal
Daily Record
Dundee Courier
Evening News
Evening Telegraph
Evening Times
Glasgow Herald
Glasgow Journal
Herald to the Trades Advocate and Co-operative Journal
The Independent
National Guardian and Licensed Trade Journal
North British Daily Mail
Perthshire Advertiser
Perthshire Courier
The Saturday Evening Commonwealth
The Scotsman
Scottish Licensed Trade News
Stirling Observer
The Sun
The Telegraph
Victualling Trades Review

PARLIAMENTARY PAPERS AND OFFICIAL REPORTS

Report of the Select Committee on the State of Children Employed in Manufactures, *Parliamentary Papers, 1816*, Vol. III.

Factory Inquiry Commission Reports, *Parliamentary Papers, 1833*, Vols XX and XXI and *1834*, Vol. XX.

Report of the Select Committee on Drunkenness, *Parliamentary Papers, 1834*, Vol. VIII.

Report on the State of the Irish Poor in Great Britain, 1835, *Parliamentary Papers, 1836*, Vol. XXXIV, Appendix G

Reports from the Assistant Handloom Weavers' Commission, South of Scotland and East of Scotland, *Parliamentary Papers*, 1838–39, reprinted 1970, Irish University Press, Shannon, Industrial Revolution, Textiles, Vol. IX.

Tremenheere's Report on the Mining Districts, *Parliamentary Papers, 1849*, Vol. XXII.

Report of the Departmental Committee on Scottish Licensing Law (The Clayson Report), 1973, HMSO, Edinburgh.

Review of Liquor Licensing Law in Scotland (The Nicholson Committee), 2003, Scottish Executive, Edinburgh.

Index

EU Authorised Representative:

Easy Access System Europe Mustamäe tee 50, 10621 Tallinn, Estonia

gpsr.requests@easproject.com

Printed and bound by CPI Group (UK) Ltd, Croydon, CR0 4YY

13/05/2025

01869400-0001